Studien zur Migrations- und Integrationspolitik

Reihe herausgegeben von
Uwe Hunger, Münster, Deutschland
Roswitha Pioch, Kiel, Deutschland
Ina Radtke, Potsdam, Deutschland
Stefan Rother, Freiburg, Deutschland

Migration ist eines der zentralen Globalisierungsphänomene des 21. Jahrhunderts. Entsprechend groß ist das Interesse an Fragen der politischen Regulierung und Gestaltung der weltweiten Migration, den Rechten von Migrantinnen und Migranten und der Integration von der lokalen bis zur globalen Ebene. Die Buchreihe ist interdisziplinär ausgerichtet und umfasst Monographien und Sammelwerke, die sich theoretisch und empirisch mit den Inhalten, Strukturen und Prozessen lokaler, regionaler, nationaler und internationaler Migrations- und Integrationspolitik befassen. Sie richtet sich an Wissenschaftlerinnen und Wissenschaftler, Studierende der Geistes-, Sozial-, Wirtschafts- und Rechtswissenschaften sowie an Praktikerinnen und Praktiker aus Medien, Politik und Bildung. Herausgeber der Reihe sind die Sprecherinnen und Sprecher des Arbeitskreises ‚Migrationspolitik' in der Deutschen Vereinigung für Politikwissenschaft (DVPW): PD Dr. Uwe Hunger, Universität Münster, Prof. Dr. Roswitha Pioch, Fachhochschule Kiel, Ina Radtke, Universität Potsdam und Dr. Stefan Rother, Universität Freiburg. Den wissenschaftlichen Beirat bilden die ehemaligen Sprecherinnen und Sprecher des Arbeitskreises: Prof. Dr. Sigrid Baringhorst, Universität Siegen, Prof. Dr. Thomas Faist, Universität Bielefeld, Prof. Dr. Karen Schönwälder, Max-Planck-Institut zur Erforschung multireligiöser und multiethnischer Gesellschaften, Göttingen, Apl. Prof. Dr. Axel Schulte i. R., Leibniz Universität Hannover, Prof. em. Dr. Dietrich Thränhardt, Universität Münster.

Weitere Bände in der Reihe http://www.springer.com/series/11808

Nils Witte

Negotiating the Boundaries of Belonging

The Intricacies of Naturalisation in Germany

Nils Witte
Karlsruhe, Deutschland

Dissertation, Bremen International Graduate School of Social Sciences, 2015

Studien zur Migrations- und Integrationspolitik
ISBN 978-3-658-19786-5   ISBN 978-3-658-19787-2   (eBook)
https://doi.org/10.1007/978-3-658-19787-2

Library of Congress Control Number: 2017955696

Springer VS
© Springer Fachmedien Wiesbaden GmbH 2018
This work is subject to copyright. All rights are reserved by the Publisher, whether the whole or part of the material is concerned, specifically the rights of translation, reprinting, reuse of illustrations, recitation, broadcasting, reproduction on microfilms or in any other physical way, and transmission or information storage and retrieval, electronic adaptation, computer software, or by similar or dissimilar methodology now known or hereafter developed.
The use of general descriptive names, registered names, trademarks, service marks, etc. in this publication does not imply, even in the absence of a specific statement, that such names are exempt from the relevant protective laws and regulations and therefore free for general use.
The publisher, the authors and the editors are safe to assume that the advice and information in this book are believed to be true and accurate at the date of publication. Neither the publisher nor the authors or the editors give a warranty, express or implied, with respect to the material contained herein or for any errors or omissions that may have been made. The publisher remains neutral with regard to jurisdictional claims in published maps and institutional affiliations.

Printed on acid-free paper

This Springer VS imprint is published by Springer Nature
The registered company is Springer Fachmedien Wiesbaden GmbH
The registered company address is: Abraham-Lincoln-Str. 46, 65189 Wiesbaden, Germany

Acknowledgements

Above all, I want to express my gratitude to those who participated in the survey and agreed to meet for personal interviews. Without their responses, this book would not exist. On the academic side, there are many friends and colleagues who supported and advised me during my dissertation. I am indebted above all others to my four supervisors Rainer Bauböck, Olaf Groh-Samberg, Michael Windzio, and Matthias Wingens. I thank them for their interest, for their trust in my skills to realise the project, and for their skilful guidance at all stages of the project. On the institutional side, I thank the Bremen International Graduate School of Social Sciences (BIGSSS) for the generous financial support of my research and for providing a place to learn, meet friends, discuss research, and play table soccer.

For early discussions of my research proposal, I am grateful to Colin Brown, Ridhi Kashyap, Ruud Koopmans, Margrit Schreier, Janina Söhn, participants of the BIGSSS colloquium, and participants of a joined doctoral Workshop by WZB, HU Berlin, Science-Po Paris, and UCLA hosted at the HU Berlin. During questionnaire development, I got helpful advice from Klaus Boehnke, Claudia Diehl, Don A. Dillman, Patrick Fick, Olaf Groh-Samberg, Hanno Kruse, Max Trommer, and Michael Windzio. Also, I am grateful for the cooperation of the Türkische Gemeinde Hamburg e.V. Among others Tülin Akkoç, Meryem Çelikkol, and Selçuk Demirtaş offered their generous help there. Also, Doris Kersten of Hamburg's Municipality supported my, alas, futile endeavours to cooperate with the Senate. I thank Robert Tschöpe from the Public Register Office for his cooperation. For the translation of the questionnaire to Turkish, I could count on the generous help of Enis Bicer, Leman Korkmaz, Serkan Kulaksız, Fatma Rebeggiani, and Sahizer Samuk. *Çok teşekkür edirim*! At the stage of survey implementation, it proved truly helpful to be backed by an institution and a community. I vicariously thank Hartmut Asendorf, Margret Gels, Helmut Brammer, and Regina Präfke from the administration for their help in dealing with practical issues of survey implementation. The packaging of questionnaires into envelopes meant two days of work for a team of volunteering colleagues and friends at BIGSSS. Thank you once again!

It was great to have the opportunity to design my own survey. However, the treat of analysing original survey data comes with many tricks. For comments on the analysis of survey results, I want to express my gratitude to Rainer Bauböck, Petyo Bonev, Christoph Burkhardt, Mariah Evans, Adrian Favell, Patrick Fick, Olaf Groh-Samberg, Dirk Halm, Jonathan Kelley, Steffen Mau, Alex Street,

Peter Titzmann, Maarten Vink, Michael Windzio, and participants of the BIGSSS colloquia. I also thank participants of conferences at University of Aarhus (GLOREA) and University of Münster (DVPW) for their comments. I am thankful to the European University Institute (EUI) for hosting me in early 2014 during my work on the analysis and to the DAAD for their financial support of my stay. I want to thank Rainer Bauböck for integration into his group of supervisees at the EUI and Anna Triandafyllidou for the opportunity to present my work in the colloquium of the Migration Working Group (MWG).

My supervisors have been indispensable in developing a sampling strategy for my interviews. I should like to thank Herwig Reiter and Matthias Wingens for their help in preparing the interviews and developing a guideline. Thanks to Suzan Kalyaci for her help with the interview transcriptions. Many friends and colleagues carefully read my interview analyses and made helpful comments. I thank Rainer Bauböck, Enis Bicer, Jan Dobbernack, Martin O. Heisler, Anna Hokema, Juliane Klein, Lucia Leopold, Ruth Mandel, Fran Meissner, Max Schaub, Matthias Sommer, Djordje Sredanovic, Anna Triandafyllidou, Matthias Wingens, and Christina Zuber. Also, thanks to participants of presentations at the MWG of the EUI, at Regent's University, London, 2014, at the annual meeting of the American Political Science Association 2014 in Washington DC, and at the doctoral colloquium of BIGSSS.

Some friends and colleagues that I have not mentioned yet, read parts of the dissertation. Nate Breznau, Hanno Kruse, Robin Morris, and Mauricio Reichenbachs, thank you for your careful reading and your thoughtful comments! Thanks to the editors of this series for their comments and to the lector Annette Villnow. Last but not least I want to express my gratitude to my parents for their trust and support. Thanks to my father who hinted me at Hamburg's naturalisation campaign and to my family, friends, and to Beth for being there and believing in me.

Contents

1. **Naturalisation in a Post-National World** 11
2. **Theorizing Legal and Symbolic Membership** 29
   - 1.1 The Concept of Symbolic Boundaries 29
   - 2.1 Individual Legal and Symbolic Membership 38
3. **Research Methods** 45
   - 3.1 A Mixed Methods Research Design 45
   - 3.2 Case Selection 47
   - 3.3 Comparative Framework 53
4. **Survey Results: Symbolic and Legal Membership** 57
   - 4.1 Scope and Expected Findings 57
   - 4.2 Data and Methods 62
   - 4.3 Results 67
   - 4.4 Summary and Discussion 90
5. **Qualitative Interviews: Stigmatization and Destigmatization** 95
   - 5.1 Aim and Scope 95
   - 5.2 Data Collection 96
   - 5.3 Negotiating Symbolic Boundaries 100
   - 5.4 Summary and Discussion 139
6. **General Discussion and Conclusion** 151
   - 6.1 Insights from Mixed Methods 151
   - 6.2 General Conclusion 159

Original Interview Passages 173
References 183
Appendix A. Tables and Figures 197
Appendix B. Survey Material 209

Tables and Figures

Tables

Table 2.1 Typology of Boundaries 35
Table 3.1 Population in (Western) Germany and Hamburg 2012 (%)................ 50
Table 3.2 Conditions of Naturalisation in Germany by Country of Origin[a] 55
Table 4.1 Population and Sample by Gender and Family Initial 63
Table 4.2 Operationalization of Independent Variables 65
Table 4.3 Sample characteristics – Continuous Variables 68
Table 4.4 Sample characteristics – Discrete Variables 69
Table 4.5 Symbolic Boundary Items 72
Table 4.6 Ordered Logistic Regression on Intention to Naturalise 76
Table 4.7 Predicted Probabilities of Selected Ideal Types 80
Table 4.8 Ordered Logistic Regression on Intention to Naturalise by Gender ... 83
Table 4.9 Predicted Probabilities of Selected Ideal Types by gender 85
Table 5.1 Interview Participants and Survey Results 98
Table 5.2 Particular Responses to Symbolic Exclusion 109
Table 5.3 Segmented Assimilation and General Response Strategies 147
Table 5.4 Intention to Naturalise and Dominant Motivation by General Response Strategy 148
Table 5.5 Sampling and General Response Types 149
Table 6.1 Operationalization of Particular Responses 157
Table 6.2 Central Mixed Methods Findings on Intended Naturalisation 166

Figures

Figure 1.1 Share of Foreign Population in Selected Countries (2012) 12
Figure 2.1 Heuristic Model of Boundary Making by Superior Group 30
Figure 5.1 Responses, Strategies, and Boundary Outcomes 141

1. Naturalisation in a Post-National World

This is a book about a substantial flaw of Western democracies. Migration flows after WWII have produced large foreign populations that have remained excluded from political membership for decades. That applies to the receiving countries of guest-workers like Austria (12%), Belgium (11%), Germany (9%), and Switzerland (23%) (see Figure 1.1). Only the Netherlands fare better with just 5% of their population unnaturalised. In the Nordic countries, that received considerable flows of refugees, shares of foreigners are intermediate. The same is true for former colonial countries and classic countries of immigration. Some countries grant franchise to immigrants from particular origins or in local elections. Still, the majority of alien residents remain strapped of basic political rights. Their endowment with citizenship would be a precondition for their political integration. Attempts for understanding non-naturalisation of immigrants have considered legal barriers to and individual motives for naturalisation of immigrants. An aspect that has been missing from the picture is the role of symbolic recognition of newcomers for their naturalisation. With the third generation of post-war migrants grown up and xenophobic sentiment on the rise in many countries of immigration, the question how boundary definitions impact the naturalisation of immigrants is more pressing than ever. How can we understand low naturalisation rates in spite of liberal access to citizenship? And how much are symbolic boundaries responsible for low naturalisation rates?

The experience of Turks in Germany yields relevant insights for other countries of immigration. Large ethnic minorities challenge exclusive conceptions of cultural membership in societies around the world. Renegotiations of cultural boundaries may be necessary to assure the political integration that is in these countries' very own interest because their societies will be more cohesive when all residents are enfranchised. The focus on Turks in Germany is instructive for two major reasons. First, they represent the largest group of alien residents in the country. In 2014, two percent (1.53 million) of the German population held Turkish citizenship and one third of them had been born in Germany (0.455 million). Far from being literal newcomers, nine in ten Turkish residents (1.4 million) had been living in Germany for ten years or more with an average of 27 years of residence. Next to the numerical relevance, the case of Turks is intriguing because costs and benefits of their naturalisation are balanced. Most of them fulfil the necessary preconditions for naturalisation, they enjoy similar rights as EU citizens with the exception of local franchise, and they often remain attached to Turkey entertaining plans of return. How do costs and benefits of naturalisation play out?

Figure 1.1 Proportion of Foreign Population in Selected Countries (2012)

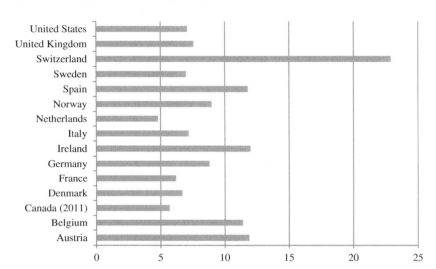

Sources: OECD ISCED97, OECD International Migration Database.

According to official statistics, Turkish non-naturalisation is widespread. In 2014, ten percent of the German population did not have German citizenship (8.15 million). What appears to be the consequence of exclusive citizenship is in fact often the result of migrants' unwillingness to naturalise. Their high average time of residence (18 years) suggests that many alien residents are entitled to naturalize and remain disenfranchised voluntarily. If many residents remain disenfranchised by choice, disentitlement for citizenship is not the only possible obstacle to political incorporation. How can we understand permanent residents' refusal to become full members of the political community, one they have been living in for many years?

Naturalisation rates are not equally low for all immigrant groups and reasons of stagnation vary by country of origin. First, irrespective of the country of emigration, some immigrants are not entitled to naturalise, the most common reason being insufficient time of residence. Second, immigrants from EU-countries enjoy a bunch of rights as EU citizens and that reduces the relative gains of naturalisation. Third, the reasons of migration often define the propensity of return. A plan to return to the country of emigration reduces the benefits of host country citizenship and increases benefits of the original one. These three factors point to the immigrant groups that are neglected in this book because explanations of their low naturalisation rates are rather trivial. Those who have arrived to Germany less than eight years ago are not entitled to naturalise; EU citizens gain little by acquiring citizenship of another EU country; and refugees (often from less developed countries) can be expected to cherish the security of German citizenship, while they renounce the original passport at low cost, if it is possible at all, and are therefore likely to naturalise once eligible (Vink, Prokic-Breuer, and Dronkers 2013; Wunderlich 2005). For Turkish residents, the intention to stay can be an issue, but generally the upsides and downsides of naturalisation are pretty balanced.

How can we understand *Turkish residents'* low naturalisation rates given liberalised access? The explanation of this seeming puzzle offered in this book is based on three assumptions. First, the legal shift from discretionary to optional citizenship for immigrants requires a shift in perspectives.[1] National comparisons have often focussed on citizenship regimes to explain cross-national variation in naturalisation outcomes whereas single-country studies account for group- and individual-characteristics to explain intra-national variations. It is the second perspective that rehabilitates immigrants as agents and is therefore adequate for understanding naturalisation where admission is optional. Therefore, I focus in this study on individual motives as opposed to legal structures. By no means should the legal context be ignored, but the effect of legal variation is not the focus of this book. Individual decisions depend on the preconditions for naturalisation that result from the particular citizenship constellation of sending and receiving country. Moreover, and this is the second assumption, naturalisation decisions are made against the background of rights granted to alien residents. The majority of Turkish residents enjoy encompassing rights that reduce the relative benefit of German citizenship. The secure legal status of permanent residence yields rights of free travel in most European countries and rights of family reunification. In addition, bilateral agreements ensure transferability of pension entitlements to Turkey. Third, I argue that naturalisation is best understood if we account for symbolic components of membership in addition to legal ones. I study how minority members perceive the boundaries of symbolic membership and which strategies they employ to negotiate them. In essence, I understand naturalisation of immigrants as individual decisions that are made in the

---

[1] The main difference is that optional admission implies an entitlement to membership whereas in discretionary admission there is none (terminology by Bauböck 1994b:71ff).

context of legal and symbolic accommodation. The conditions of their legal and symbolic accommodation define the attractiveness of citizenship acquisition.

What is this book's contribution to the growing research on the incorporation of immigrants in Western countries? Explanations of naturalisation have improved over the last years. While scholars have studied legal effects and individual motives separately in the past, more recent studies recognise the parallel impact of structural and individual characteristics (e.g. Street 2014; Vink, Prokic-Breuer, and Dronkers 2013). One divide that few studies have overcome is the one between quantitative and qualitative research methods. This study combines the strengths of both approaches. Qualitative studies yield encompassing overviews of potential motives for naturalisation (e.g. Prümm 2004; Wunderlich 2005). Informed by these studies' insights, I developed a questionnaire for the comprehensive assessment of motives for and against naturalisation. The resulting survey covers several motives that past quantitative studies were forced to ignore due to lack of information in general interest surveys. In addition, I offer a parsimonious theoretical model with a plain distinction of legal and symbolic motives that allows for an evaluation of these motives' relative significance. Recent quantitative studies have sometimes drawn on a distinction between legal and symbolic incentives, rights and identity, or love and money (Diehl and Blohm 2011, 2003; van Hook, Brown, and Bean 2006). These distinctions are helpful for organizing relevant elements of explanatory models. However, the operationalization of these concepts depends on the availability of respective items in secondary data sets where they are often scarce. Furthermore, standardized surveys are not appropriate to explore the dynamics of symbolic membership. As this study shows, these dynamics are at the roots of symbolic motives for and against naturalisation. These dynamics are explored analysing in-depth interviews that I conducted with a sub-set of survey participants. Interview analyses show three things: how symbolic exclusion is perceived; the myriad ways in which minority members respond to this exclusion; and systematic relationships between response patterns and naturalisation intentions. Through this, I contribute to the general understanding of naturalisation, I describe the symbolic dimension of exclusion of immigrants in Germany, and I provide the first systematic analysis of responses to stigmatization in the German context. Next, I argue why naturalisation matters in spite of claims to a post-national era. Then I give a short account of citizenship law in Germany since 1990 before I review the relevant literature.

National vs. post-national membership

Some scholars understand the spread of residence without citizenship as an expression of a supposed 'post-national' era (Jacobson 1996; Soysal 1994). In this view, international human rights regimes guarantee individual rights and render national citizenship obsolete. I agree with these scholars that human rights regimes have been more influential since the post-war period. But the sources of civil and social rights have been domestic, not international, as Joppke (2001, 339–66) shows exemplarily for EU citizens in the EU, and for alien residents in Germany and in the US. Even more relevant is the political dimension of citizenship (Marshall 1992). Of course, one may and I believe should ask how directly political rights should be yoked with citizenship. But as long as they are tied, and so far there are few exceptions, the post-national perspective is at risk of neglecting that the secure residence status of the denizen (Hammar 1990) leads to disenfranchisement. Precisely by offering a range of civil and social rights to alien residents, the status of denizen cements their exclusion from the political community. Liberal democracies produce this paradoxical situation through their tendency of granting rights based on mere personhood. By doing so, they reduce the attractiveness of citizenship and incidentally cause political exclusion unless they untie political rights from citizenship. Potential normative solutions to the problem of exclusion include granting political rights to permanent residents (Neuman 1991; Benhabib 2004; Rodríguez 2010; Owen 2010; Beckman 2006)[2] and reducing barriers to citizenship acquisition (Bauböck 1998; Calder, Cole, and Seglow 2010; Carens 2013; Walzer 1983). Member states of the EU practice the former when it comes to granting local franchise to citizens of other member states. However, they remain excluded in regional and federal elections although there is "no reason to assume that local decisions affect foreigners more than national ones" (Bauböck 1994a, 224). As for enfranchisement of aliens and EU citizens at the regional and national level, naturalisation remains the only gateway.[3] Most Western democracies have reduced the minimum time of residence, but have strengthened requests of cultural and economic assimilation (Joppke 2005; Joppke and Morawska 2003). Joppke (2007) sees a convergent trend towards repressive liberalism in Western Europe. A closer look, however, reveals the fortification of national models and particular responses to country-specific pressures (Goodman 2012; Goodman and Howard 2013). Germany reduced formal requirements on the one hand, but makes stronger demands on cultural

---

[2] The attempts to extend franchise to alien residents in Germany have been struck down by the Constitutional Court (see Benhabib 2004, 202; Joppke 1999; Neuman 1991).
[3] For an overview of the exceptions to non-citizen disenfranchisement in the EU see Arrighi et al. (2013, 51). For Germany see Pedroza (2013).

assimilation and civil conduct on the other. In light of the yoking of political rights and citizenship and continued contestation over German citizenship law, I strongly object to the post-national stance. Major shares of non-citizen populations should concern democracies because it "creates a problem for the legitimacy of political decision – even if this exclusion were a voluntary one" (Bauböck 1994b: 204).

German citizenship law, 1990-2014

This section provides some background information on the recent history of German citizenship law. Before 1990, legislation established naturalisation as the very end of successful assimilation and acceptance depended on the discretion of official personnel.[4] The citizenship law had been adapted from the German Reich. Its content was germane to hopeful reintegration with the separate Eastern Republic and incorporation of its returnees from former German regions in the East rather than for the incorporation of immigrants (Joppke 2001). A 1990 reform introduced 'naturalisation as a rule' (*Regeleinbürgerung*) after 15 years of legal and habitual residence for the first generation and after eight years for young persons (16-23 years). In 1993, 'naturalisation as a rule' was replaced by an entitlement to naturalise (*Anspruchseinbürgerung*). While dual citizenship remained banned as a principle the reform introduced new exceptions to the rule. In 2000, a modernized citizenship law (*Staatsangehörigkeitsgesetz, StAG*) replaced the old one. The new law is in many respects more liberal compared to its predecessor. The residence requirement was reduced to eight years for first generation immigrants and birth right citizenship was established for children of immigrants who would have their parents' citizenship in addition. Contrasting with the liberalizing innovations, it made a declaration of loyalty a precondition for naturalisation and the jus soli provision was relativized by a requirement to opt for one citizenship and renouncing the other one upon reaching the age of 23 (*Optionspflicht*).[5] The *StAG* also closed a loophole that had enabled third country nationals' re-application for citizenship in their countries of origin after naturalisation in Germany. Many Turkish immigrants had exploited this loophole. Smaller reforms followed (2004, 2007, 2009) that furthered dual citizenship toleration for EU and Swiss citizens. Furthermore, it introduced new require-

---

[4] This review of the legal development draws on Hailbronner and Farahat (2015) and Joppke (1999).

[5] The option duty has been softened by a 2014 reform, exempting children of immigrants born in Germany who either have eight years of residence before turning 21, or have attended a German school for at least six years. However, this last reform does not affect the observation period. Two empirical studies have evaluated these youngsters' predicament (Diehl and Fick 2012; Weinmann, Becher, and Babka von Gostomski 2012).

ments aiming at language assimilation, and a more stringent assessment of the criminal record. The combination of reducing formal requirements and raising civil and cultural ones results from the stakes of two major political parties with opposing interests. Although, on average, both parties have constituencies of similar size among immigrants (Wüst 2004), the conservative party seems to fear the alleged electoral preferences of Turks for the Social Democrats. That would also explain why the legal compromises of liberalization usually entail restrictions concerning dual citizenship, since Turkish residents' attachments to their citizenship is widely known. Overall, the tendency over the last decades has been a liberalization of access to citizenship combined with tightening of assimilatory requirements.

What are the external factors that brought about these changes of citizenship law? Instead of providing an exhaustive answer, I would like to highlight two crucial aspects. Part of the answer lies in the involuntary division of Germany after WWII. Western German citizenship law was directed towards the incorporation of those living in the Eastern Republic and other parts of the USSR. Joppke (2001) argues that politicians were afraid of touching citizenship law because it could have been read as interference with the Eastern brothers and sisters. This reservation dissipated once the two republics had been reunified. Still, political elites underlined the exclusive nature of the polity with their stance that Germany was 'not a country of immigration'. In this regard, former colonizing powers (e.g. France, Netherlands, UK) and settler countries (e.g. Australia, Brazil, Canada, US) had the historical advantage of being more familiar with diversity (Janoski 2010). After 1990, the presence of alien residents accelerated reforms. Germany had recruited 'guest workers' since the 1950s who were supposed to and often planned to return. However, eventually many decided to stay and were joined by their families later on. Those coming from EU countries enjoyed civil and social rights as EU citizens, and those from third countries benefited from bilateral agreements between their countries of origin and Germany, or with the EU respectively (Joppke 2001). Until 1990, few former guest workers had naturalised.[6] Immigrants from Romania, Poland, and other parts of the USSR accounted for the lion's share in naturalisations before 1990 and continued to do so until 2000. Persons from these countries included many resettlers (*Aussiedler*) that were conceived of, by German citizenship law, as German qua ethnic lineage. They were granted German citizenship upon formal request. While these recent arrivals - often unfamiliar with German language after generations abroad - became citizens without complication, guest workers' children and grandchildren were raised in Germany without prospect of naturali-

---

[6] Cumulative naturalisations in the five years between 1985 and 1989 amount to roughly 225.000 compared to 101.000 in 1990 alone (see www.eudo-citizenship.de).

sation. 'Return' migration of ethnic Germans and their prompt naturalisation skyrocketed after the end of the Cold War. This paradoxical situation of long-term resident exclusion and newly arrived re-settler inclusion pressured the government to change citizenship law (Kanstroom 1993). Consequentially, reforms in the 1990s brought incremental liberalizations of access to citizenship and the 2000 reform also ended citizenship upon request of re-settlers. In short, large scale immigration and permanent settlement combined with German reunification were central triggers for reforming German citizenship law.

The remainder of this chapter gives an overview of three relevant strands of literature. First, I report studies that yield explanations of immigrant naturalisation in Germany and elsewhere. Second, I summarize studies that deal with the negotiation of symbolic membership between Germans and newcomers. Third, I draw attention to the literature of responses to stigmatization as a complementary perspective to the second strand. Finally, I elaborate in how far these three literatures are relevant to this research project.

Naturalisation in Germany

Research on naturalisation behaviour of former guest workers in Germany has shown a decreasing importance of host country citizenship. This 'devaluation' was caused by the extension of civil and social rights for permanently resident aliens. Low naturalisation rates of immigrants from EU-countries can be partially explained in those terms. Even Germany's toleration of plural citizenship for EU citizens since 2007 has not dramatically increased naturalisations.[7] Like EU citizens, former guest workers from third countries gain little from naturalisation in terms of rights, because they enjoy a secure status of permanent residency.[8] Unlike EU citizens, they are required to renounce their former passport when naturalizing, which represents a major disincentive.[9] However, access to active and passive voting rights remains at stake. Additionally, non-EU citizens gain access to certain jobs in the public sector and special self-employed professions, and cross-border travel is facilitated. Obviously, these benefits are not necessarily relevant for individual migrants.

---

[7] In accordance with EU rules (Council of Europe 1993) legislation was changed in 1999 to allow for multiple citizenships of EU citizens. However, before 2007 this applied only in the case of reciprocity with a member state (Hailbronner and Farahat 2015).
[8] The permanent statuses are 'settlement permit' and 'EU long-term residence permit' (*AufenthG*, Part1, http://www.gesetze-im-internet.de/englisch_aufenthg/index.html; last access: 31.01.2017).
[9] Exceptions apply among others to states that do not release citizens from national allegiance (*StAG* §12; BMI 2009 Anwendungshinweise).

Studies providing explanations of naturalisation usually differentiate by country of origin. For the comparison of results, one has to take into account that some assess performed and some intended naturalisations, depending on what information the data provide. Surveys rather evaluate naturalisation intentions, whereas census data simply document changes in the legal status of citizenship. Part of the variation in findings is owed to the use of these two different dependent variables. However, there are also commonalities. German studies typically focus on the largest immigrant groups such as Greeks, Turks, Italians, and persons from former Yugoslavia. The focus on particular immigrant groups alleviates identification of factors that positively affect naturalisation proclivities irrespective of the dependent variable. That is the case for identification with the host country (Diehl 2002; Ersanilli and Koopmans 2010; Prümm 2004; Söhn 2008; Wunderlich 2005; Maehler 2012), political interest (Diehl and Blohm 2003, 2008, 2011; Kahanec and Tosun 2009; Hochman 2011; Prümm 2004; Söhn 2008; Wunderlich 2005), intention to stay (Diehl and Blohm 2011, 2008, 2003, Hochman 2011, Prümm 2004), and having (close) German friends (Constant, Gataullina, and Zimmermann 2007; Diehl and Blohm 2003; Söhn 2008; Wunderlich 2005; Hochman 2011). Furthermore, women are more likely to naturalise than men (Constant, Gataullina, and Zimmermann 2007; Diehl 2002; Diehl and Blohm 2008, 2011; Söhn 2008). Few studies find an effect of education which Gathmann and Keller (2014) interpret as a consequence of not accounting for non-linear effects and gender differences. They find noteworthy interaction effects for education. Among men, medium-skilled migrants are more likely to have naturalised than low-skilled or highly-skilled ones. Among women, highly-skilled are less likely to have naturalised than all other groups. Family related motives for naturalisation are most often explored in qualitative studies (Street 2014; Prümm 2004; Wunderlich 2005), but Street (2014) corroborates qualitative findings by making use of census data and showing that naturalisation decisions often involve the whole family. The host society's receptivity regarding naturalisations is rarely considered. Hochman (2011) finds a deterrent effect of perceived discrimination and Kahanec and Tosun (2009) find a negative effect of perceived and of actual negative attitudes towards foreigners. Finally, the non-acceptance of dual citizenship was shown to impede naturalisations both qualitatively (Prümm 2004) and quantitatively (Sauer 2013; Vink, Prokic-Breuer, and Dronkers 2013).

The aforementioned qualitative studies by Prümm (2004) and Wunderlich (2005) reveal a range of other issues that are potentially relevant in naturalisation decisions next to the reasons mentioned above. Some of the additional motives for naturalisation that their interviewees mention include imitation and response to pressure of family and peers, improved labour market opportunities, facilitation of travel including long-term stays abroad without loss of rights, avoidance of conscription, feeling of belonging, and the wish to get rid of a stigma related to the country of origin. Prümm (2004) further addresses motives for refusal. Persons who refuse to naturalise have no rights-oriented motives for naturalisation and are discouraged by the legal and symbolic loss connected with renunciation of the Turkish passport.

Naturalisation Elsewhere

Immigrants to Australia in the 1980s faced similar conditions of naturalisation as immigrants in Germany do today. As a consequence, naturalisation has been an issue in classic countries of immigration long before it drew the attention of European scholars (DeSipio 1987). Evans (1988) finds time of residence to be the strongest predictor of being naturalised in Australia. Also, immigrants from less developed countries and the Mediterranean are quicker than Northwestern Europeans in claiming Australian citizenship. She rules out socio-economic explanations for the decision to naturalise. Portes and Curtis' (1987) study of Mexicans in the US shows home ownership in the US, children in the US, and coming from a Mexican town as opposed to a rural area to be most predictive of naturalisation. From the 1990s on, scholars started to factor in more detailed source country effects. Yang (1994) accounts for sending country and receiving context factors next to individual characteristics. Based on 1980 US census data, he finds a negative association between naturalisation and GNP of the source country. Being a refugee, coming from a socialist country, and coming from a physically distant country are positively associated with naturalisation. Liang's (1994) analyses of the same data with a stronger theoretical foundation complements Yang's findings by showing how country differences become much smaller if individual characteristics are controlled for. The individual characteristics that are most predictive of naturalisation irrespective of the country of origin include occupational prestige, education, and naturalised family members. Other factors vary by country of origin.

Following the 1990s, scholars became more sensitive to sending country policies and receiving context conditions of naturalisation. Jones-Correa (2001a) draws attention to institutional frameworks and their relevance for naturalisation. Namely, he finds dual citizenship toleration by the sending country and electoral regulations of the receiving context to be decisive next to individual characteristics of immigrants. He analyses how Central- and South-American countries developed their nationality law with respect to dual citizenship (Jones-Correa 2001b). His comparison of naturalisation rates before and after reforms introducing dual citizenship toleration indicates a positive effect on naturalisation rates.

Since the US informally tolerates dual citizenship, it ultimately depends on the country of origin. Therefore, migrants from countries that do not tolerate dual citizenship in outgoing naturalisations find it more difficult to apply for citizenship in the US. This finding is supported by further qualitative (Brettell 2006) and quantitative research (Mazzolari 2009).[10]

Naturalisation in Comparative Perspective

Cross-national perspectives are another important development in the study of naturalisation. In response to the growing literature on citizenship regimes in the wake of Brubaker (1992), scholars aim at understanding the role of immigration and integration policies for explaining naturalisation. Bloemraad (2006) is concerned with explaining differential naturalisation rates of Canada and the US departing from similar figures in the 1950s. She argues that institutional framing of immigrants' legitimate political standing and the resulting support of self-mobilization explains the difference. Namely, states that conceive of immigrants as future citizens and support local providers of assistance make naturalisation more likely than states that frame immigrants as temporary guests or security threats without political say.

Street (2013) assesses the role of family in naturalisation decisions using qualitative and quantitative data. He does so for immigrants in the US and Austria (2013) and Germany (2014) respectively. Generally, immigrants include their family members' citizenship into their consideration of options. Persons with naturalised household members are more likely to have naturalised than those who have no naturalised household members. This effect is stronger in Austria than in the US (Street 2013). Street presents evidence that the absence of jus soli in Germany until 2000 provided an extra incentive for naturalisation of parents who wanted to endow their children with German citizenship. While this incentive still exists in Austria, it is missing in the US because children automatically become citizens by birth. Still, immigrants with children are more likely to be naturalised in the US, too (see also Liang 1994, Yang 1994). Since 2000, automatic naturalisation at birth has applied in Germany if certain conditions are met by the parents (see above). Consequently, Street (2014) attributes the fall in German naturalisations after 2000 to a combination of the ban of dual citizenship for third country nationals and the introduction of jus soli.

Dronkers and Vink (2012) evaluate the impact of citizenship policies on naturalisation rates in 15 European countries. They find a positive effect of permis-

---

[10] According to these studies, Mexico seems to be an exceptional case. It is the only country of origin were dual citizenship toleration does not have a clear positive effect on naturalisation in the US.

sive policies for naturalisation decisions of first-generation immigrants. Large part of the variation is explained, however, by other factors related to the country of origin and individual characteristics. For example, coming from less developed countries or having parents born in the destination country are positively related to being naturalised. In a related paper, Vink, Prokic-Breuer, and Dronkers (2013) assess the impact of sending and receiving country's citizenship policies and individual characteristics on naturalisation in 16 European countries. Their paper highlights the significance of human development in origin countries in understanding citizenship uptake. Liberal access is positively related to naturalisation, but only for persons from less developed countries.

Everyday Nationhood and Symbolic Boundaries

Anthropologists and sociologists usually focus on boundary making by the majority. Minorities' role in the negotiation of boundaries is considered less often. This section summarizes research in the German context. These studies seldom refer to the concept of symbolic boundaries but are nonetheless concerned with the phenomenon. Their methods include ethnographies, in-depth interviews, and quantitative research. In an ethnography, Miller-Idriss (2006) describes everyday understandings of citizenship of students at a vocational school (*Berufsschule*). Children of immigrants report symbolic exclusion at school. Their self-definition as Germans is questioned by other Germans for phenotypical reasons. Even naturalised persons are qualified as foreigners by some of the German classmates. However, the majority of students define being German by having German citizenship, being born in Germany, and speaking German fluently. Similarly, in his qualitative interviews with Germans and Turkish immigrants, Schneider (2001, 2002) finds birth in Germany, being of German descent, and fluency in German to be basic criteria for the recognition as German by other Germans. As in Miller-Idriss' study, dark skin, dark hair, and strange names indicate foreignness. Even legal membership does not suffice for discursive inclusion. Native interviewees identify German by not being foreign. The category of 'foreign' is often merged with the Turkish one and both bear negative connotations. This is exemplified by the disappointment of men after a woman they find attractive reveals herself as Turkish as opposed to Italian, French, or Brazilian (Schneider 2002: 16f.). Similarly, Mandel (2008) describes the active discursive exclusion of Turkish immigrants and their descendants from German mainstream definitions. According to her thick description of 'Turkish Challenges to Citizenship and Belonging', current understandings of belonging of German Turks in Berlin can be traced back to German legal traditions. Ehrkamp (2006) draws on qualitative interviews with Germans and Turkish migrants to describe boundary making on both sides. Being German and being Turkish are described as irreconcilable in public discourse and by interviewees alike. However, based on the same ethnography, Ehrkamp and Leitner (2003) argue that Turkish migrants' political practices question bright boundaries of citizenship by relating to both countries.

In one of the few quantitative studies on Germans' concept of belonging, (Mäs, Mühler, and Opp 2005) presented German citizens of the province Sachsen with vignette descriptions of persons and asked them to what extent each vignette qualified as German. Multivariate analyses of responses leave having German parents, being born in Germany, and being fluent in German as the strongest predictors of being qualified as German. The effect of not being born in Germany is negative but equally so for Turkey and France, the two countries used in vignette descriptions. A study by Kühnel and Leibold (2003, 154) assesses the popular relevance of potential criteria for naturalisation. German respondents deem the following qualities essential: economic autonomy, blank criminal record, speaking German, a long stay in Germany, adaptation to lifestyle, German descent, and being born in Germany. The only mentioned criterion respondents do not consider important for naturalisation is Christian denomination. Diehl and Tucci (2011) show that the folk-criteria for entitlement to German citizenship have shifted between 1996 and 2006 from descent-related ethnic criteria to civil and cultural ones such as language assimilation, adaptation to German life-style, economic autonomy, and a blank criminal record. They confirm that Christian religion is not considered a relevant membership criterion.

Bail (2008) compares symbolic boundaries against immigrants in 21 European countries based on 2003 ESS data. In European comparison, German symbolic boundary construction is in the middle field. Linguistic, cultural and educational boundaries are stronger, whereas religious, racial, and occupational boundaries are weaker than the average. Using ISS data from the same year, Hochschild and Lang (2011) explore the sense of belonging and the inclusion of others in ten highly developed, democratic countries. They find patriotism of Germans to be low and inclusion of others to be high. The identification with Germany of ethnic minority members is even lower and their inclusion of others is higher compared to Germans. Results for Germany are most similar to the ones for Sweden.

Amir-Moazami (2007, 2005) draws attention to the role of Islam for boundary construction. The headscarf of Muslim women has been an issue in public debates for a while, but increasingly so after 9/11. Amir-Moazami shows that besides being an object of debate, the headscarf may also help Muslim women to define their identity as distinct from the German one. Still, the construction of non-German identity (as Turkish, Muslim, or foreign) goes hand in hand with an appraisal of liberal values of German society and the inclination to live in Germany for good. What is peculiar about these women is their tendency to define themselves as foreigner (*Ausländer*), including those who are naturalised, as opposed to their French counterparts who describe themselves as French citizens. Amir-Moazami sees therein a confirmation for their transition from legal to symbolic foreigners.

This review has three relevant implications. First, symbolic membership in Germany is often but not always defined along ethnic lines. Second, many qualitative studies are pervaded by a notion of 'the Germans' as discriminators and 'the Turkish' as discriminated or excluded. In this way, the literature draws boundaries instead of merely describing them. And third, the literature tends to deprive immigrants of their agency by describing them as objects of exclusion. For once, members of the minority could make boundaries just as well as members of the majority. And second, the discriminated are not passive victims of exclusion, they may respond to perceived stigmatization. The strand that takes this element of agency into explicit account is addressed in the next section.

Responses to Stigmatization

A thriving literature has emerged that is complementary to the one on symbolic membership but broadens the perspective. It explores ethnic minorities' responses to racial discrimination and stigmatization, in other words, their strategies of destigmatization. This ground has been broken chiefly by Michèle Lamont who started by studying values of male working class in the US and France (2000) and extended this study to differing values between ethnic groups. Lamont, Morning, and Mooney (2002) identify five kinds of responses to racism of North African immigrants in France. Immigrants alternatively argue that (1) all people are equal, (2) their own cultures are similar to the French one, (3) racism is not aimed at them personally because they are 'good', (4) their nation or Islamic culture is superior to the French one, (5) or that racism is the racist's fault for he lacks experiences that would teach him otherwise. Notably, few interviewees refer to Enlightenment and French Republican values as mainstream institutional anti-racists would do. Instead, reference to Islam is dominant even among those who do not practice the religion.

Ethnic groups' responses to discrimination and stigmatization have been assessed in a range of other contexts including Brazil, Canada, Israel, and South Africa. The comparison indicates that individual strategies depend on the particular macro repertoires that are offered in each country (Lamont and Mizrachi 2012). For example, Crystal M. Fleming, Lamont, and Welburn (2012) find a whole different set of responses to stigmatization among Black workers in the

US compared to responses of North African immigrants in France (Lamont, Morning, and Mooney 2002). French immigrants refer to 'particular universalisms' to argue for general equality as a strategy to counter racism. In contrast, American Black workers more often rebut racism by confronting the perpetrator. Fleming et al. (2012) differentiate response strategies from the tools to implement them. The two dominant strategies are 'confronting' and 'deflecting' racism, the former being more frequent. The main tools to implement those strategies include sarcasm and getting used to it; and 'teaching the ignorant' about Black culture and 'managing the self' by conveying a positive image of oneself to others. Bickerstaff's (Bickerstaff 2012) study of first generation French Blacks shows responses to vary along the kind of relationship between perpetrator and victim (*personal vs. impersonal*) and along the social context (*public vs. private*). She mentions stigmatization in public, in job search, and by inquiring origins as examples of impersonal situations. Stigmatizations at work or school, in contrast, are categorized as personal situations. These situations constrain or enable particular responses depending on the social context. Generally, research on responses to stigmatization lately aims for systematization by cross-country and cross-group comparisons (e.g. Lamont et al. 2016).

In two book chapters, Lamont and her colleagues expand the analytical ground for studying the social conditionality of responses to exclusion (Lamont 2009; Lamont, Welburn, and Crystal Fleming 2013). Whereas my study is interested in the consequences for naturalisation intentions, she considers subordinate groups' destigmatization strategies' impact on mental and physical health (Lamont 2009). She argues that societal contexts enable contestations of the social ordering to different degrees. They do so through the provision of empowering cultural repertoires such as collective myths, imaginaries, and broadly accepted symbolic boundaries. If social contexts enable destigmatization strategies to different degrees, it is insufficient to consider coping strategies alone. Instead, she assumes better health outcomes for subordinate groups where cultural repertoires are available that support these groups' empowerment. Lamont et al. (2013) identify cultural repertoires that are salient in different country contexts. They argue that the neoliberal idea of individual accountability merges particularly well into the narrative of the American Dream. For once it is a chance to argue for equality among achievers, but at the same time, it is problematic for the lower classes that cannot live up to the ideal of economic success. Next to the individualist script, African Americans can draw on a history of racial discrimination, of a civil rights movement, and on a shared African American culture as sources for their destigmatization strategies. Different from that, Ethiopian Jews in Israel ground their responses on the Zionist narrative of equality of Jews and

Afro-Brazilians respond to stigmatization by referral to the national script of racial mixture (ibid.).

These three reviews demonstrate the quick development of a research field that has important implications for immigrant societies. Knowledge may not accumulate as quickly as political practitioners would need it, but, to speak with Merton, "[t]he urgency or immensity of a practical social problem does not ensure its immediate solution" (1968, 50). If we establish a "historical sense of proportion" (ibid.), social research has made quite some headway in developing an understanding of a relatively young social phenomenon (e.g. Anderson 1991; Tilly 1975; for the passport in particular, see Torpey 1998).

Implications for this Study

Each of these strands of research carries implications for this study. The boundaries of symbolic belonging are a central concern of my theoretical model. As the review of the first literature shows, however, naturalisation is best understood as a result of both symbolic and legal considerations. My hypotheses on legal motives for naturalisation are derived from these research findings. Although they can be roughly summarized under a rational choice logic, a selection of relevant motives was necessary and it was based on the literature. The relevance of legal motives implies that legal frameworks matter. In accordance, single-country studies and comparative studies alike have shown the importance of institutional contexts. In order to understand naturalisation, it is essential to consider the legal rules of the country of emigration, the country of immigration, and the constellation they build. This matter is addressed more extensively below along with the research design.

Some studies are informative for applying explanatory frameworks that are similar to mine. Comparable theoretical approaches can be found in the works of (Diehl and Blohm 2011, 2008; Hochman 2011; Kahanec and Tosun 2009). However, only studies by Diehl and Blohm (2011; 2008) and Hochman (2011) conceptualise naturalisation as ethnic boundary crossing. A limitation of these studies lies in their use of secondary data. These data impair elaborate operationalisations of the concept of symbolic boundaries. Instead, they rely on various indicators like social contacts with members of the mainstream (Diehl and Blohm 2011, 2008, Hochman 2011), perceived discrimination, in-group identification, and intention to stay in Germany (Hochman 2011). Kahanec and Tosun (2009) have richer data to account for the relationship of natives and newcomers. They include an index of perceived negative attitudes against foreigners, perception of religion as a complicating issue, and an objective measure of negative attitudes against foreigners by region. In addition to these quantitative operationalisations of symbolic boundaries, the reported qualitative studies are insightful for drawing attention to the idiosyncrasies of naturalisation decisions and the peculiarities of different generations and countries of origin. Overall, these studies provide a sound basis for the development of survey on naturalisation intentions and the formulation of hypotheses.

The review of the literature on symbolic boundaries qualifies the matter as relevant, especially in the case of Turkish residents in Germany. What is more, it yields ideas for the implementation of symbolic boundaries in the survey. Since operationalisations of symbolic boundaries have been unsatisfying in the past, it was imperative to aim for improvement here. Symbolic boundaries are based on questions of symbolic belonging and exclusion. Past research gives hints on boundaries' cultural content. For example, inner-German boundaries are often more pronounced towards Turks than against other groups and in particular against Muslims. This is relevant given that 90 per cent of Turks in Germany are Muslim (Haug, Müssig, and Stichs 2009, 68) and half of all Muslims in Germany are from Turkish origins (51%) according to official estimates (Stichs 2016, 29).

The literature on responses to stigmatization reminds us that symbolic boundaries are a bilateral project. Although the mainstream is normally in a better position to make boundaries towards other groups, those who are excluded are actors with resources to respond. Qualitative studies reveal that it is insufficient to consider symbolic boundary perception. Perceptions are not as consequential for action as are reactions to perceived exclusion. In that perspective, even migrants who perceive exclusion do not necessarily subject themselves to these definitions. First, they apply various strategies to deal with exclusion. And second, they make boundaries of their own by producing exclusive definitions of belonging. Hence, the literature on responses to stigmatization has implications for my theoretical model and provides valuable templates for my own interview analysis.

The specific research design of this study was motivated by the vast array of findings on naturalisation from qualitative and quantitative studies. The decision to collect original data was made against the backdrop of exhaustive analyses of GSOEP and Microcensus and the difficulty to measure relevant concepts with these data. Qualitative research provides rather systematic listings of potential motivations to naturalise, or to refuse, that inform further data collection. The aim is to explore how symbolic belonging influences or mediates naturalisation intentions and decisions. In order to enlighten this subject, it seemed plausible to combine the strengths of quantitative and qualitative methods starting with a general survey and following up with in-depth interviews.

Outline

This book seeks to answer two questions. How can we understand low naturalisation rates in spite of liberal access to citizenship? And how much are symbolic boundaries responsible for low naturalisation rates? Two methods of inquiry are applied: Statistical analyses of a standardized survey and qualitative analyses of in-depth interviews. The two parts are respectively tailored towards answering the first and second questions. In both cases, Turkish residents comprise the target population. In Chapter 2, I present the theoretical foundations of the empirical analyses. I introduce the concept of symbolic boundaries and discuss its implications on the macro- and the micro-level before I apply the model to the situation of Turkish residents in Germany. Finally, I conceptualise naturalisation intentions in terms of the Model of Frame Selection, a variant of rational choice theory that understands rationality as 'bounded'. Chapter 3 gives a description of the mixed methods research design and its rationale. Here, I also reflect on the difference between studying actual naturalisation and intended naturalisation before I elaborate on my case selection. Finally, I provide a comparative framework to position my study with respect to other migrant groups in other host countries. The two subsequent chapters present methods and analyses of the quantitative and the qualitative study respectively. Chapter 4 starts with the formulation of hypotheses that draw on the literature and are rooted in the theoretical model. Then, I present the method of data collection and provide basic information on the survey. Following uni- and multivariate analyses, I discuss limitations, summarize findings, and connect them to the literature. I show that naturalisation is best understood as resulting from legal and symbolic motives, the former being more of a decisive factor. Chapter 5 presents methods and analyses of 16 in-depth interviews. I introduce the concept of responses to stigmatization as a central analytical template for understanding boundary negotiations. The analysis of interviews provides insights into the content of symbolic boundaries, into particular responses to stigmatization at the level of action, and into general responses to stigmatization at the level of actors. I show what stigmatization is based on (e.g. headscarf, phenotype) and what responses it evokes (e.g. striking back, working hard, avoiding). Finally, I present implications of actors' response patterns for naturalisation intentions. These findings are discussed in light of the literatures on symbolic boundaries, responses to stigmatization, and the theory of segmented assimilation. In the final chapter, I discuss complementarities of qualitative and quantitative findings and make suggestions for future surveys. At the end, I summarize main findings and discuss how they contribute to understanding the (non)-naturalisation of immigrants and the symbolic boundary negotiations of immigrant minorities and societal mainstream.

2. Theorizing Legal and Symbolic Membership

There are two major research questions that this project aims to answer. The first one concerns naturalisation decisions of Turks in Germany. Here, the explanatory macro-variables include the legal framework and minority members' relation with the majority group. The legal framework is defined by rights granted to alien residents (*AufenthG, GG*), preconditions for naturalisation (*StAG, BMI 2009Anwendungshinweise*), and the citizenship constellation with the country of origin. I conceptualize these legal preconditions as legal boundaries. The relation with the majority group is theoretically defined by the symbolic boundaries that are negotiated between majority and minority. The next element of the explanation is to break down boundaries to individual perceptions. Here, the idea is to dissect how legal boundaries and symbolic boundaries are defining the situation of naturalisation choices and thus affect individual naturalisation intentions. The second research question refers to the negotiation of symbolic boundaries and the consequences of these boundaries for naturalisation decisions. Certain boundary definitions may be dominant in societal discourse, but individual perceptions do not necessarily conform to dominant definitions. Instead, they are expected to vary according to individual experiences and individual responses. Since boundary making is an exclusionary practice, I refer to the theoretical concept of 'responses to stigmatization' that I elaborate in Chapter 5. Next, I introduce the theoretical concept of symbolic boundaries starting broadly and moving to the case studied. Then, I elaborate on the implication of these macro-level variables for a micro-explanation based on the model of frame selection (MFS).

1.1 The Concept of Symbolic Boundaries

Positive vs. Negative Self-Definitions

According to Lamont and Molnár, "symbolic boundaries are conceptual distinctions made by social actors to categorize objects, people, practices, and even time and space" (2002, 168). Actors often make these boundaries implicitly by distinguishing themselves through taste, life-style, preferences, and values.

Bourdieu (1984) is the founding father of this literature interested in boundaries as self-oriented distinctions. However, that is not the only way to make boundaries. Sometimes actors draw boundaries in a way that is explicitly oriented towards the other and results in a negative self-definition. That kind of definition is negative in a dual sense: The other is defined by negative attributes and the self is defined by absence of those attributes. Scholarship on this aspect of boundary making stand in the tradition of research on stigmatization by Goffman (1963).[11] I would not claim that either of the two perspectives is superior. They simply draw attention to different aspects of symbolic boundaries and they are suited to study boundaries in different realms. Symbolic boundaries exist in far more constellations than in the one between natives and immigrants. Goffman (1963), for example, studied stigmatization of many groups such as handicapped people, felons, and homosexuals.

Figure 2.1 Heuristic Model of Boundary Making by Superior Group

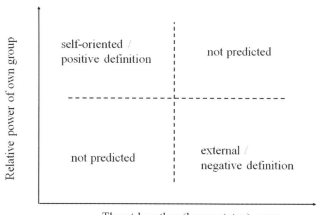

Figure by author.

Figure 2.1 presents a heuristic model for determining the kind of boundary making by the higher status group that is likely to prevail in a particular case. The two dimensions are 'relative power of the own group' and the 'threat by the lower status group'. If the threat is harmless, actors will tend to define bounda-

---

[11] "[...]; the stigmatization of those in certain racial, religious and ethnic groups has apparently functioned as a means of removing these minorities from various avenues of competition; [...]" (Goffman 1963, 165).

ries positively whereas more serious threats are likely to trigger negative definitions and stigmatization. However, the kind of boundary making is less predictable in mixed constellations of serious threats to a high status group, or weak threats to low status groups. Also, lower status-groups may represent various kinds of threats. Threats to socio-economic status and threats of interpretational sovereignty are most frequent. For example, homosexuals are not primarily a socio-economic menace to the Catholic Church, but their struggle for equal rights threatens the church's power to dominate the discourse on family and sexuality. Hence, in order to predict the kind of boundary making based on the heuristic model, further assumptions about the relative power of groups and the kind of threat posed by the lower status group are necessary. In the case of ethnic minorities, there are good reasons to assume lower relative power compared to the cultural mainstream.

Institutional Boundaries

I want to point out the relevance of institutions broadly defined, before I consider boundary definitions through social interactions. Institutions in this broad sense include structures and traditions that potentially support the regulation of boundaries. They are legitimate qua law or tradition. For example, the boundary between immigrants and natives is not merely defined socially. The ascription of different legal statuses to members of both groups supports the boundary institutionally because these statuses regulate access to resources. The gender boundary in an academic board of a liberal democratic country, however, is likely not to be polished through legal discrimination by gender but, if at all, by the historically established numerical male domination. Students of symbolic boundaries should therefore consider the interaction of social and institutional elements in boundary making and preservation. That is also, why I introduce institutional boundaries before symbolic ones. They often define power hierarchies between groups of actors Wimmer 2008b.

Kinds of Symbolic Boundaries

Scholars interested in symbolic boundaries between upper and middle class usually focus on different self-presentations and life-styles (e.g. Lamont 1992; Sachweh 2013; Weingartner 2013). Studies like this one, which are interested in symbolic boundaries between majorities and minorities, will often find that the cultivation of differences takes more explicit forms including stigmatization and physical violence (e.g. Wimmer 2002).[12] Elias and Scotson's (1965) seminal study of established and newcomers in an English suburban community illustrates that applications are by no means restricted to ethnic groups.[13] However, the stigma is visible and audible to different degrees depending on the kind of constellation. If stigmatization is the mode of boundary making, the dominating group defines itself negatively by pointing to absent characteristics. Visible features then increase the persistence of boundaries. In both boundary making modes, the more powerful group (normally the one with a higher social and/or economic status), is in a better position to define the nature of boundaries. That implies more permeability of symbolic boundaries towards the inferior group than the other way around. For example, the American Civil Rights movement included white members (Chappell 1996) while Black members in the opposite camp, for example the Ku Klux Klan, would hardly find recognition. In this example, phenotype is the main identifier of the higher status group. But even where boundary definitions are based on less visible identifiers, the higher status group normally defines itself by features that are hard to imitate by lower class members (e.g. dress, manners, taste etc.) the reason being that the higher group developed those distinctions precisely in order to set itself apart (Bourdieu 1984). At the same time, recognition in the group with higher status is often more desirable, e.g. for an immigrant to be recognised as full member of mainstream society, for a middle-class member to be recognised in the polo club, or for a female professor to be recognised as competent member of a male dominated academic board. If we accept these assumptions, then it should be more interesting to focus on the upward permeability of boundaries. Put differently, the question how dominant groups regulate membership is more interesting than how the respective inferior group polishes its upper boundary.[14] In any case, students of symbolic boundaries should have a hunch about what mode of boundary definition seems more likely in their case and is therefore more fruitful to examine.[15]

---

[12] Obviously, negative self-definitions may well mix with positive self-definitions.

[13] The stigmatization of Swabian newcomers in 2000s Berlin is an interesting case because they are ethnic German. In 2013 the president of the national parliament complained about their deficient willingness to assimilate in the capital (http://www.spiegel.de/international/germany/nazi-references-used-in-anti-swabian-berlin-gentrification-feud-a-900078.html; last access 27.01.2017).

[14] Obviously, the lower status group of one constellation is often the higher status group in another one.

[15] In his proposition of a multilevel-process theory of ethnic boundaries, Wimmer (2008b) considers actors' political alliances next to institutions and power hierarchies. That is sensitive for a general theory, but those alliances are not as relevant for the case studied here.

Implications of the Boundary Approach

Finally, I want to draw attention to the dynamic of group relations implied by the boundary approach. If Herder's heritage is a primordial understanding of ethnicity, as Wimmer (2009) claims, then Barth's (1969) heritage is the revolution of this static perspective on the social world in the realm of ethnicities. The main advantage of the boundary perspective over classic approaches to immigrant integration is the interactive and dynamic conception of intergroup relations (Brubaker 2009; Jenkins 1997, 2004; Nagel 1994; Ong 1996; Wimmer 2008a). Ethnic groups do not exist per se, but are defined as products of social interaction.[16] This has two important implications. First, both groups are involved in the construction of boundaries. Hence, a comprehensive analysis would explicitly address boundary making on both sides. But, as I have argued above, due to my interest in naturalisation intentions I account for one side only: boundary perceptions. Second, the dynamic perspective implies some autonomy of individuals to define themselves as members of one or the other group. In the words of Laitin (1998), "people are limited by, but they are not prisoners of, their genes, their physiognomies, and their histories in settling on their own identities" (ibid: 21). However, institutions and self-definitions of the groups they want to join impose additional constraints on their choices. A person of Turkish descent living in Germany then is not per se a Turk, but either German, or Turkish, or German-Turkish, or Hamburger, or none of all. In boundary perspective, individuals are structurally constrained but not determined in their affiliations. It is precisely these constraints that this study seeks to elucidate.

Although positive and negative self-definitions are not mutually exclusive, the literature shows negative self-definitions to be of particular relevance to the constellation under scrutiny here. Accordingly, the research design does not account for positive definitions of the majority group. I study the nature of the boundary between both groups by asking members of the lower status group of Turkish residents for the perceived permeability of that boundary. By asking for boundary perceptions, I can still account for the non-existence of boundaries, namely when minority members do not perceive exclusion. Also, by looking at their responses to exclusion, I can account for boundary making of migrants. The focus on boundary perception, however, is particularly suited for understanding how minority members are made subjects of boundaries involuntarily. This perspective has less to say about migrants' active partaking in boundary making, although in reality this could be the case, and it only indirectly assesses majority members' actual boundary making. However, while the focus on perceptions

---

[16] This also sets the perspective apart from social psychological identity theory that emphasizes self-definitions but ignores the external definition of groups.

misses part of the picture, it is in line with the broader research question of understanding the role of symbolic boundaries for migrants' naturalisation intentions. If intentions are based on *subjective* gains, then it is coherent to consider boundary *perceptions* instead of more 'objective' measures. To take full account of those boundaries, the analytical model includes their institutional support through the legal institution of citizenship. I conceptualise citizenship as a legal boundary that is closely connected to the making and unmaking of symbolic boundaries and argue that both kinds of boundaries should be considered synchronically. Next, I explain the general model of legal and symbolic boundaries, before the implications for the particular case of Turks in Germany are considered.

Table 2.1 illustrates nine hypothetical constellations that result from these two boundary dimensions. Boundaries are either bright, blurred, or shifted (Alba 2005; Zolberg and Woon 1999). They are bright where the location of individuals is discrete and unambiguous, forcing them to opt between remaining at one side and crossing. Legally, that is the case when naturalisation is conditional upon renunciation of the former citizenship. Boundaries are said to shift when "populations situated on the one side are now included on the other" (Alba 2005, 23). The legal implementation of a boundary shift is the unconditional endowment with citizenship as was the case for ethnic German re-settlers.[17] The third category of blurred boundaries applies when the location of a person on either side is ambiguous, for example when two nationalities are acquired by birth as is the case under the new German jus soli (see above). How are symbolic boundaries different from legal ones? While Alba's (2005) focus is on the institutionalization of boundaries, Zolberg and Woon (1999) do mention social and institutional elements of boundaries but do not explicitly differentiate between them. As pointed out above, this study is based on a conceptual separation of both elements. In the long run, legal and symbolic boundaries are likely to align. However, this process may sometimes take several generations. Symbolic blurring and shifting may precede legal dismantling of boundaries or the other way around. Therefore, it is sensitive to allow both kinds of boundaries to vary independently, especially in the context of rather recent immigration. For example, where a legal boundary is blurred because dual citizenship is accepted, a naturalised individual may still perceive her action as boundary crossing (B1 in Table 2.1). A possible reason would be peers questioning simultaneous attachment to two nationalities. Also, she might naturalise where the legal boundary is bright, because blurred symbolic boundaries resolve loyalty doubts (A2). What are the implications of this model for the case of Turks in Germany?

---

[17] See Dumbrava (2014) for a systematic assessment of legal boundary shifting based on ethno-cultural membership in European countries.

Table 2.1 Typology of Boundaries

		Legal boundary			respective definition of belonging
		bright	blurred	shifted	
Symbolic boundary	bright	A1	B1	C1	exclusive definition of belonging
	blurred	A2	B2	C2	hyphenated identities accepted
	shifted	A3	B3	C3	redefinition of identity for the new group as a whole
	respective legal rule	exclusive citizenship	dual citizenship	unconditional naturalisation	
	examples for Germany	Turkish citizens	Jus soli children	German repatriates from USSR	

Source: Own adaptation from Alba (2005), and Zolberg and Woon (1999).

For the empirical case considered, the model can be simplified. The legal boundary for the constellation is a bright one, because by default, dual citizenship is not tolerated. Namely, Turkish residents who want to naturalise in Germany are required to renounce their former passport.[18] Consequently, in this case, claiming citizenship corresponds to crossing the legal boundary between national groups. Whether symbolic boundaries that come with this bright legal boundary are perceived as bright (A1), blurred (A2), or shifted (A3) remains to be answered empirically. This question is relevant because the answer could explain different inclinations to naturalise. In order to assess symbolic boundary perception it should be made clear what is meant in each case. Bright symbolic boundaries make identities exclusive. For the case studied here, it means that individuals are considered either German or Turkish, not German-Turkish. In this case, symbolic membership is not an individual choice alone, but preconditions are defined by the current members who regulate access. If boundaries are bright, the regulation of membership tends to be rigid and therefore, bright boundaries are less permeable than the other types. Non-exclusive definitions of identities correspond to blurred boundaries. Where blurred boundaries prevail, hyphenated identities are legitimate. Whereas the distinction of blurred and bright boundaries is straightforward, blurred boundaries are more difficult to distinguish from shifted ones.

---

[18] There are exceptions to this rule (see BMI 2009 for the then relevant exceptions, more recently BMI 2015, but the model refers to the typical case. As pointed out above, the legal boundary may vary according to the country of origin and the country of birth.

The former are often the antecedent of the latter. Shifting of symbolic boundaries requires a fundamental redefinition of the new group. Three German journalists of non-German descent recently formulated a redefinition of German identity that fits the concept of boundary shifting: "We are part of this society. We are different. Hence difference in kind is part of this German society"[19] (Topçu, Pham, and Bota 2012, 13). In other words, shifted boundaries imply inclusive redefinitions of belonging that allow for greater diversity inside the new group.

In order to clarify the empirical implications of the theoretical concept, I want to illustrate the process of legal and symbolic boundary blurring and shifting towards ethnic minorities by considering the historical examples of Italians and Africans in the US, and of Polish miners in the German West. In these cases, social categories that originally defined distinct groups either became part of national self-definitions or simply disappeared. For example, Blacks are doubtlessly Americans today but the category of Black has not disappeared, whereas Italians have altogether lost their stigma of the darker whites (Guglielmo and Salerno 2003). Similarly, after decades of distinct national identity and ethnic political organization Polish workers in the Ruhrgebiet largely abandoned a distinct Polish identity starting after WWI (Lucassen 2005; McCook 2007). However, they are different from Turkish migrants in two crucial aspects. First, they do not deviate from the phenotypical norm. Second, they have the same (Catholic) religion as natives in that region. In the case of Turkish migrants, dismantling of both aspects as markers of difference is more likely than change of Turks' complexion and religion. So far Germans' phenotypical boundary definition has been steadfast, as if there was an unspoken norm that only fair people can be German, whereas traditionally ethnically heterogeneous countries like Brazil or the US have relaxed phenotypical norms over the course of time (Lamont and Bail 2005). Next to skin tone, Islam is perceived by Europeans as a threat to their only common cultural ground (Foner and Alba 2008; Zolberg and Woon 1999). That may explain why the accommodation of Muslims in a German identity seems particularly difficult (Amir-Moazami 2005). Alba (2006) argues that the example of Jewish assimilation in the US after WWII through institutional boundary blurring could be instructive for European countries when it comes to accommodation of Islam. Although this study cannot provide an answer, the historical examples support the notion that symbolic boundary transformations are a matter of time. However, the transformation processes can be accelerated by political and institutional incorporation.[20] The examples illustrate

---

[19] Translation by author. German original: „Wir sind Teil dieser Gesellschaft. Wir sind anders. Also gehört die Andersartigkeit zu dieser deutschen Gesellschaft."
[20] Notably, since Poles were citizens of Prussia, political incorporation preceded socio-cultural assimilation. However, according to McCook (2007) assimilation succeeded only after WWII when

that "we can assume no simple one-to-one relationship between ethnic units and cultural similarities and differences. The features that are taken into account are not the sum of 'objective' differences, but only those which the actors themselves regard as significant" (Barth 1969, 14). In line with the boundary concept, these time varying definitions of difference are understood as boundary blurring and shifting.

If boundary definitions evolve over time, how is the difference between symbolic Germans and persons of Turkish descent defined today? By default, crossing, blurring, and shifting are expected to occur in this sequence. The process may take several generations and there can be backlashes against accommodation of newcomers. Today, the boundary between persons of Turkish descent and German majority seems to be bright and sometimes blurred but rarely shifting.[21] While members of the majority group have not been interviewed for this study, findings of other researchers point to bright boundary definitions by the majority group in the German context. Also, political mobilization for legal enforcement of symbolic boundaries gives some impression of common boundary definitions. In 1999, the conservative party CDU collected five million signatures against the introduction of dual citizenship toleration. In this case, petitioners expressed their will to uphold the institutional support of a symbolic bright boundary (Holmes Cooper 2002).[22] This example illustrates the point that the separation of legal and symbolic boundaries is conceptual. In fact, rules of citizenship acquisition (legal boundaries) mirror at least to some extent the popular constructions of symbolic boundaries. According to Lamont (Lamont 1992, 71), subjective boundaries are a necessary but insufficient condition for the construction of objective boundaries. It remains to be seen how legal and symbolic boundaries against Turkish residents develop under the impression of new arrivals from countries that are not only more distant but often culturally more different from Germany than Turkey and certainly more different than most second generation Turks. This study gives a snapshot of the current state of affairs.

The causal connectedness of legal and symbolic boundaries has several implications for individual motives. As argued above, the institutional make-up

---

new arrivals from Southern Europe filled their place as lowest in the hierarchy. Also, only because Italians were officially defined as white they were eligible to naturalise before 1952 (Guglielmo and Salerno 2003).

[21] Members of the national football team and German politicians of Turkish descent may pave the way to future boundary shifting. Recently, demonstrations surfing the wave of German *Überfremdungsangst* and Islamophobia are countered even by conservative politicians. There is evidence for more inclusive and denationalizing definitions by the German elite compared to lower classes (Teney and Helbling 2014).

[22] According to a representative survey 52% of Western Germans and 59% of Eastern Germans opposed toleration of dual citizenship in 1996 (Wasmer and Koch 2003).

implies a bright legal boundary that is crossed upon naturalisation. Eventually, this transition is conducive to crossing the symbolic boundary as well. If that holds, immigrants who do not want to cross the symbolic boundary should be less inclined to naturalise unless they have rights-oriented motives to naturalise. In that case, they can be expected to devalue citizenship and conceive of it as a mere legal status without symbolic value, often depreciating citizenship as 'just a piece of paper'. If instead, they do want to cross the symbolic boundary, they are more likely to naturalise while recognizing the symbolic value of citizenship. Finally, sometimes migrants may devalue German citizenship because they do want to naturalise but find the procedure too expensive. The renunciation requirement in particular could be perceived as costly. In order to reduce cognitive dissonance (Festinger 1957) they may downgrade German citizenship, a mechanism that has been labelled the "sour grapes" phenomenon (Elster 1983).[23] In that case, it is virtually impossible to tell whether citizenship has become a sour grape, or if the person in question is actually uninterested in naturalisation. Still, it is important to keep in mind that expressions of disinterest may in fact be a reaction to the preconditions for naturalisation. In the next section, I elaborate micro-level implications of the macro-boundary concept more systematically.

2.1   Individual Legal and Symbolic Membership

It is assumed that individuals who consider naturalisation evaluate the costs and benefits of legal and symbolic aspects. This perspective is straightforward when it comes to the consequences of legal status and its change. I argue that legal boundaries affect migrants' perception of costs and benefits, for they define both preconditions for naturalisation and rights endowment of citizens and non-citizens. However, when it comes to symbolic membership, the language of costs and benefits is more debateable. Still, as I will argue, symbolic membership aspirations can be accommodated in a model of rational choice. From the perspective of the migrant, the crucial difference between symbolic membership and legal membership is its predictability. Legal membership is predictable while symbolic membership is not. German citizenship endows every citizen with the

---

[23] Topcu's (2007) story of a Turkish couple that applied for German citizenship may serve as an illustration. The woman's application was refuted on grounds of poor language skills. "She was rather happy, that she »failed« the exam. »I don't want to become German after all«, she says. In fact, she is »upset« that her husband renounced his Turkish passport" (ibid., 96; translation NW).

same rights.[24] Individuals may differ in how much they value the endowment with a particular right, e.g. franchise, but each migrant attains this right at the moment of naturalisation.[25] However, German citizenship does not endow every citizen with symbolic membership. Some feel accepted irrespective of citizenship, some will feel accepted once they naturalised, and some will not feel accepted although they are German citizens. For the naturalisation intention, the difference in *expectations* is more relevant than what *actually* happens after naturalisation. How can we understand that some migrants expect naturalisation to be conducive to symbolic membership and others do not expect this instrumentality? Before naturalisation, persons can but conjecture their future recognition upon citizenship acquisition. Their forecast draws on experience. Perceptions of recognition vary among non-citizens depending on how they are usually addressed; as German or as foreign. Also, they find examples of (un-)successful symbolic membership acquisition among their peers and family in different numbers. Along these lines, the assumption of an instrumentality of citizenship for symbolic membership should be more likely for persons who feel recognised and for persons who find many examples of naturalised symbolic members among their peers and family. In short, the attractive ness of legal membership increases with the distance between actual rights as a non-citizen and rights-aspiration through naturalisation. The appeal of symbolic membership decreases with the distance between actual and aspired recognition as a symbolic member. Accordingly, the strongest inclination results from symbolic recognition of non-citizens who are at stark legal disadvantage compared to citizens. The rationale behind the conceptual separation of macro-boundaries from their consequences for micro-perceptions is to provide a micro explanation of varying naturalisation intentions.

The relation of legal and symbolic membership is complicated through their factual amalgamation. While symbolic membership does not guarantee legal recognition, legal membership may in some situations support symbolic recognition. Obviously, naturalised persons are not likely to present their German ID in everyday interactions as a claim to symbolic membership. However, in official situations (e.g. border control, public office, voting) legal status may fulfil a social function next to the legal one. First, legal status defines the treatment that is foreseen for a certain legal category of persons (e.g. EU-passports in a different line than non-EU at border control). Second, it defines the situation socially

---

[24] My theoretical reflections focus on the particular constellation of Turks with eligibility for German citizenship. For a broader reflection on motives for naturalisation in various constellations of host and origin countries see Bauböck (1994b, 71).

[25] Of course, there are limitations to the exercise of certain rights, for example referring to age and mental accountability, but they equally apply to all citizens.

and frames social interactions with official personnel. This is the case because legal statuses are not only different in kind, but also different in the implicit or explicit valuations they receive. For example, border controls of third country nationals at EU borders are more thorough and time-consuming than controls of EU citizens. This becomes particularly apparent for family members with different legal statuses, for example, when those with EU citizenship have to wait for their Turkish parents behind the border. Both, the thorough control through border police and the social situation that makes the differentiation apparent to anyone queuing in one of the two lines, devalue Turkish citizenship as opposed to German citizenship in that particular situation.[26] Similar differentiations in public office can be imagined and are known from empirical studies (see Wunderlich 2005). Voting is another socially relevant expression of legal membership with implications for symbolic membership. While in everyday interactions citizenship is hardly visible, the practice of voting makes legal membership *visible* to others and it implies an *involvement* in society. That is how it becomes an expression of symbolic membership. The consequence of the intertwining for my theoretical model is a difficulty to define citizenship acquisition per se as *either* a motive for symbolic recognition *or* a motive to exercise rights (e.g. have a say in politics), when in fact it might be either or both at the same time. For the sake of conceptual clarity, I treat all legal aspects as rights-oriented motives. Nevertheless, it is important to keep in mind that in reality legal and symbolic membership are intertwined.

A Model of Frame Selection for Naturalisation

The intention to naturalise is theorized in terms of the Model of Frame Selection (MFS), assuming that actors maximize their subjectively expected utility (SEU). Sociologists usually do not go along with neoclassical versions of rational choice theory (RCT) (Boudon 2003; Kroneberg and Kalter 2012). Instead, sociologists have further developed RCT in order to account for behavioural patterns that escape a simple cost-benefit-logic like hiding Jews in the German 'Third Reich' (Kroneberg 2012) or participation in general elections (Kroneberg, Yaish, and Stocké 2010; Edlin, Gelman, and Kaplan 2007; Hechter and Kanazawa 1997).[27]

---

[26] At the Russian border the situation could be rather different. But for the case studied here the chosen example has more empirical relevance.

[27] Kroneberg (2012) understands this behaviour to result from the variation of individual prosocial orientations and situational incentives and opportunities. Edlin et al. (2007) point to social preferences to explain voting while Kroneberg et al. (2010) emphasize norms of civic duty. For an overview of successful RCT applications in fields that are often deemed inapt see Hechter and Kanazawa (1997).

Rationality of actors is described by these scholars as 'bounded' or 'variable'. One of the most promising adaptations of RCT is the Model of Frame Selection (MFS) (Esser 2009; 2002b, 2002a; Kroneberg 2005). It systematically accounts for the 'variable rationality' of social actors by differentiation of two modes of information processing that are activated unconsciously. One mode is automatic-spontaneous (as) and the other one reflective-calculating (rc). The first one refers to situations that are familiar and situations where subjective opportunities to reflect are scarce. Opportunities to reflect are defined by restrictions of time and cognition. The second mode refers to situations that allow for more extensive calculations of costs and benefits and situations where the alternative that can be activated automatically is not ideal. In that mode, rationality assumptions have more explanatory power than in situations of the first kind. Actors may unconsciously switch between these two modes of information processing at three stages of selection: Selection of an interpretational frame, selection of a behavioural script, and selection of an action. The first selection is analogous to the classic definition of the situation that shapes social behaviour and is to a certain extent guided by social norms. Frames are actors' mental representations of typical situations. The second selection refers to actions that are adapt to, or regularly expected in, such situations. Scripts are manuals that guide behaviour in defined situations. The third selection is the decision to either follow a known script or to deviate from the known. Although the MFS claims to be a general theory of action, I go along with the more flexible approach of the self-proclaimed school of 'analytical sociology' that is in favour of pragmatic use of behavioural mechanisms suited to the respective phenomenon (Hedström and Ylikoski 2010). And the MFS is a useful framework to structure the behavioural assumptions that explain naturalisation intentions.

As an intermediate step, it is important to consider differences between the intention to naturalise and actual naturalisation and their implications. Do motives that explain the intention also explain actual naturalisation? The short answer is: sometimes but not necessarily. However, this substantial question is interwoven with practical issues of data collection and that is why an exhaustive answer is given in the next chapter. For the moment, it may suffice to say that pragmatic reasons tipped the balance in favour of naturalisation intentions.

There is a range of simplifications of the MFS for the application to naturalisation intentions in this project. First, migrants have no time pressure to come up with a decision and the decision is consequential, which implies the reflecting-calculating mode of selection. Second, a common script is not likely to exist because individuals typically naturalise only once in their lifetime.[28] Hence, this

---

[28] Those who want to re-naturalise after 2000's unintended dispossession are a noteworthy exception are (see Ch.4). In their case, it is indeed possible, but not to be taken for granted, that they resort to

application does without the automatic-spontaneous mode and without script-selection. What remains to be defined then are frame-selection and action-selection. In accordance with the differentiation of legal and symbolic membership, I assume one of the following four frames to be selected: Naturalisation is framed as legal membership change, as symbolic membership change, as both legal and symbolic membership change, or as consequential neither for legal nor for symbolic membership. The MFS predicts a selection of the frame that promises the largest SEU. The same applies to the action-selection. Here, the model-adaptation remains simple since there are but two basic (mental) actions: Naturalisation intended vs. not intended.[29] The calculation of the SEU of a frame must account for legal and social costs and benefits. They are expected to choose a frame that is in line with the (mental) action. For example, a person who is interested in the legal benefits of German citizenship but is under high social pressure from peers not to betray Turkish loyalty by passport renunciation is likely to frame naturalisation as legal membership change. In such cases, citizenship is downgraded to 'just a piece of paper', a framing that secures legal benefits of the German passport and reduces social costs of renouncing the Turkish one.[30] I have pointed to the consequences of this interconnectedness of legal and symbolic motives above. The explicit hypotheses for subjectively expected legal and social costs and benefits are articulated and tested in Chapter 4.

Next to naturalisation intentions, the MFS has some implications for 'responses to stigmatization'. In this application, the MFS cannot be simplified as has been done in the case of naturalisation intentions. For once, each stigmatizing situation is different in nature and second, actors differ in their experiential background in the sense that some have had experiences with stigmatization in the past and others have not. For these reasons, none of the two information-processing modes is more likely per se. Also, the three selections of frame, script, and action are not pre-defined. However, regularities can be expected within individual actions. Experiences of stigmatization lead to social learning (Bandura 1977) and thereby make frames, scripts, and actions more easily available in repeated interactions. As a consequence, actors may attribute being treated unfriendly to their ethnicity and frame situations as racial stigmatization when the behaviour should more accurately be attributed to the situation.[31] Along the

---

their familiar script of action. Another hypothetical exception would be a script like 'I do everything to accommodate here'. However, the formalization always accounts for the typical case.

[29] My operationalization measures these two actions gradually as tendencies towards one or the other end.

[30] Kahneman and Tversky (1986) show how alternative wording of the same scenario leads to different decisions of those judging and dealing with the scenario.

[31] Social psychologists describe this tendency to underestimate external causes of social behaviour as the fundamental attribution error (for critical review see Sabini, Siepmann, and Stein 2001).

same lines, those who are successful in conciliatory responses may frame social behaviour as context-given even where it is indeed racially stigmatizing. Systematic analyses of responses to stigmatization are given in chapter 5 along with interpretations in terms of the Model of Frame Selection.

Although not the focus of this study, it would be worthwhile to analyse of naturalisation dynamics among friends or families as Street (2014, 2013) has done. In terms of the MFS, observation of peers and family helps individuals to reduce insecurity in calculations of SEU through naturalisation. Since symbolic membership after naturalisation is not predictable, 'vanguard naturalisers' are particularly helpful in reducing the insecurity about recognition upon naturalisation. Individuals can simply observe whether their naturalised peers are recognised as symbolic members or not. Further, naturalised peers reduce information costs since they can easily help with administrative procedures. In the realm of families, the law may encourage collective decision-making. Naturalisation of minor children with their parents reduces aggregate opportunity costs and, depending on the law, financial costs. In other words, naturalisation may become cheaper if several family members apply jointly. I do assess the impact of naturalised peers and family members, but I have insufficient information on the timing of naturalisations to address the aggregational dynamics adequately.

The hypotheses for multivariate analyses and the guiding questions for the interviews are introduced in chapters 4 and 5 respectively. The hypotheses are the specification of the MFS that I put forward in this chapter. I present them at the beginning of chapter 4 in order to be consistent throughout both empirical chapters. Similarly, guiding questions are introduced in chapter 5 since they emerged only once the multivariate analyses were finished. Following the epistemological logic of my qualitative research, I reflect responses to stigmatization in the light of the MFS once the analyses are finished. For these reasons, I open the quantitative empirical chapter with the formulation of hypotheses and oscillate between theoretical concepts and interview analyses in the qualitative empirical chapter. In this way, implications of the theoretical foundation for the quantitative and the qualitative part of this study are tailored to the analytical need of each application respectively and the presentation of the argument is aligned with the chronological order of the research project.

To sum up, legal and symbolic boundaries as structural preconditions of naturalisation intentions have to be analysed in different ways. Boundaries of the former kind refer to institutional conditions represented by the body of law that concerns naturalisation and alien resident rights. The measurement of symbolic boundaries is more difficult as these definitions refer to socially negotiated definitions of belonging. As argued above, the dominant group is in a stronger position to define the symbolic boundary. However, the definition is negotiated in ongoing interactions among members of the majority group and newcomers. A complete analysis of this 'informal nation membership' (Brubaker 2010, 65) and its symbolic boundaries would therefore encompass boundary definitions and perceptions on both sides: on the part of the majority group and on the part of the newcomers. This study focuses on the boundary perceptions of the newcomers and their descendants who have not naturalised. The role of boundaries for naturalisation intentions is assessed both quantitatively and qualitatively. Multivariate analyses focus on the relative relevance of boundary perception compared to legal aspirations for citizenship acquisition. The analyses of in-depth interviews aim for a demarcation of the varying boundary perceptions of immigrants. Interviews reveal how responses to stigmatization mediate the effect of symbolic exclusion on naturalisation intentions. Since minority members' naturalisation intentions are the point of departure of this study, their perceptions of and reactions to symbolic boundaries are crucial.

3. Research Methods

This chapter is structured as follows. First, I explain why a mixed methods design is appropriate for this project and I elaborate on the benefits of the particular design of a survey followed by semi-structured interviews (3.1). The second section explains the case selection and its implications (3.2). Here, I also discuss the implications of measuring intentions to naturalise vs. actual naturalisations. The final section of this chapter introduces basic dimensions of a comparative framework in order to relate the studied case of Turks in Germany to other citizenship constellations (3.3).

3.1 A Mixed Methods Research Design

This book is concerned with two explananda: The naturalisation of immigrants (E1) and symbolic boundaries (E2). The point of departure is a twofold research question: How can we explain low naturalisation rates in spite of eligibility for citizenship? And what is the role of symbolic boundaries in understanding naturalisation intentions of permanently resident aliens? In order to answer both questions, I first establish that naturalisation intentions are best understood as an outcome of manifold motives that are differentiated as referring to symbolic or legal boundaries respectively. Then I assess the explanatory value of symbolic boundaries for naturalisation intentions. In this way, I contribute to a theoretically developed and empirically grounded understanding of symbolic boundaries. Although the concept of 'ethnic boundaries' (Barth 1969) has seen a recent revival in the social sciences, no one has analysed the connection of legal and symbolic membership systematically. Still, there is a sufficient amount of theoretical formulations of the concept of symbolic boundaries to develop initial ideas for its operationalization in a questionnaire. Therefore, I decided for a 'sequential mixed methods design' (as defined by Teddlie and Tashakkori 2009) with a survey followed by semi-structured in-depth interviews. The survey aims at understanding naturalisation of immigrants more broadly (E1), while in-depth interviews are concerned with symbolic boundaries and how they are perceived and dealt with by minority members (E2).

Past research has established a rather sound understanding of naturalisation decisions and intentions (see Ch.1). It seemed fruitless to start the research project with explorative interviews as if these findings were inexistent. Instead, the groundwork was seen as a chance to invest resources in follow-up interviews instead. These interviews provided a chance to qualify survey results and clarify remaining uncertainties. At the same time, the sequence allowed for purposive sampling of relevant cases. Arguably, one could have started with qualitative interviews in order to better understand individual boundary perception as a basis for designing the questionnaire. It was not self-evident how to operationalise symbolic boundaries in the survey, but there were many hints in the literature. In addition, to start with qualitative interviews implied a risk of replicating former qualitative studies, since two recent and encompassing studies of naturalisations based on qualitative interviews (Prümm 2004, Wunderlich 2005) already had convergent findings. However, there are also pragmatic reasons for the restriction to follow-up interviews, i.e. limited resources. Fortunately, past research offered a sound basis for designing a survey and new interviews were not desperately needed. Follow-up interviews provided the chance to question and qualify results of quantitative analysis, and the chronology allowed for purposeful sampling of survey participants. Therefore, preference was given to follow-up interviews.

What were the concrete foundations of the survey and how was the survey combined with the semi-structured interviews? The survey questionnaire was developed based on two literatures. First, substantial research on naturalisation decisions and intentions identified relevant motives that promised to explain naturalisation intentions. However, past quantitative studies used to resort to secondary data, a limitation that I aimed to overcome by enriching the questionnaire with insights from qualitative studies (see Ch.1). As I have argued above, the legal conditions of naturalisation that result from particular country constellations are a crucial ingredient for understanding naturalisation intentions and decisions. Therefore, I focussed on studies that dealt with the same constellation as I do – Turkish residents in Germany. The second literature behind the questionnaire refers to the theoretical concept of symbolic boundaries as formulated by Alba (2005) and Zolberg and Woon (1999). These authors applied the concept in the realm of national membership. However, they based their ideas on macro-sociological observations and analyses of institutional traditions, whereas I am interested in individual perceptions. Individual boundary perceptions have been assessed only superficially in past quantitative works. The qualitative literature on symbolic boundaries and responses to stigmatization is more fruitful in this respect, but usually these works do not make the connection to naturalisation intentions that are relevant for this project. Still, both literatures provide sufficient material to design a survey that would establish a better connection between migrants' boundary perceptions and their naturalisation intentions. Semi-structured in-depth interviews followed one year after the survey. The aim was to qualify findings from the survey and enquire where the insight based on the survey remained unsatisfying. Finding minority members with adequate profiles was facilitated by purposeful recruitment of survey participants.

3.2 Case Selection

This section addresses the rationale behind and implications of my case selection. I study one immigrant group in a single receiving country and collect data in one city. To explain these design decisions and their implications, I provide some background information on the case of Turks in Germany and consider idiosyncrasies of the particular local context.

Turks are by far the largest group of immigrants in Germany. Research has repeatedly pointed to particular difficulties of that group in adapting to the educational system and to the labour market (Bender and Seifert 2003; Diehl and Schnell 2006; Kristen and Granato 2007; Kalter, Granato, and Kristen 2011; Kalter 2006; Kalter and Granato 2002; Worbs 2003; Euwals et al. 2007). Furthermore, they are shown to have less social contact with Germans than other immigrant groups (Haug 2003; Kalter, Granato, and Kristen 2011; Kalter 2006; Schacht, Kristen, and Tucci 2014) and children's friendships are less often paralleled by their parents' friendship (Windzio 2012). In addition, they have problems with German language more often than other immigrant groups (Diehl and Schnell 2006; Kalter 2006). Finally, comparatively low intermarriage rates (González-Ferrer 2006; Lucassen and Laarman 2009)[32] and lower identification as Germans than migrants from the EU and former Yugoslavia (Diehl and Schnell 2006) support the notion that Turks have so far accommodated less than other immigrant groups. These findings are supported by Steinbach's encompassing evaluation (2004, 149) showing that compared to Italian and Greek immigrants and Russian-German re-settlers, Turkish parents and their children have lower German skills, are more often in blue collar jobs, have German friends less often, choose ethnic names more often, and are less inclined to marry Germans. Interestingly, they do have higher educational aspirations than all other

---

[32] Intermarriage rates of Turks in Germany are not lower than in other European countries though (Lucasssen and Laarman 2009). In the male first generation rates are even slightly higher. Generally, Turks and Moroccans have much lower intermarriage rates compared to other immigrant groups in Europe. Still, Gonzalez-Ferrer (2006) shows that once the availability of co-ethnic partners is controlled for, Turks are more likely than other groups to marry German partners.

groups (Salikutluk 2016). Still, in the terminology of Esser's (2006, 23) multidimensional assimilation model, Turkish immigrants are the group that is least assimilated structurally, socially, and culturally. Further, there is some evidence for their weak identificatory, or, emotional assimilation. However, it should be kept in mind that Turks are least assimilated in relative terms, which says little about their absolute mainstream assimilation. Also, their assimilation says little about the way they are received by the host society. For a more comprehensive understanding of the situation of Turkish immigrants in Germany, I next consider their reception.

Turks receive particularly negative evaluations by Germans. Based on 1996 survey data (ALLBUS), Wasmer and Koch (2003) provide evidence that Germans are less inclined to grant equal rights to Turks than to Italians. Opposition to concrete rights for alien residents tends to be more pronounced among Eastern Germans and persons with little formal education. Relying on 1999 representative survey data Steinbach (2004, 144ff) confirms that Turks receive particularly negative evaluations from Germans, but also from other immigrant groups. Germans evaluate Europeans most positively, followed by ethnic German re-settlers. They have least affection for Africans, Turks, Vietnamese, and Russians. Using the aforementioned data from ALLBUS1996, Alba and Johnson (2003) show more than 40% of Germans to believe that foreigners produce a tight housing market, burden the social net, and disproportionately contribute to the crime rate. Agreement with such statements tends to be higher in Eastern Germany. They conclude that Germans are equally divided between positive, negative, and indifferent attitudes towards foreigners. If a third of Germans is hostile towards immigrants and two thirds are not, how do these attitudes become relevant? Results from several field experiments underline the practical relevance of the described negative evaluations. Kaas and Manger (2012) show Turkish names to reduce the likelihood of call-back upon a student internship application. This effect is more pronounced in small companies with fewer than 50 employees. Discrimination of Turks in the labour market is corroborated by a field experiment on applications to apprenticeship trainings (Jan Schneider, Yemane, and Weinmann 2014). Apprenticeship trainings are crucial entries into the job market for persons with lower than tertiary degrees. According to the study, persons with Turkish names need on average seven applications for an interview invitation where Germans need five. Discrimination is more pronounced in applications for car engineering and in companies with fewer than six employees. It is less pronounced in applications for office administrators and in medium and large companies. Next to the labour market, there is evidence for ethnic discrimination in housing and restaurant reservations (Klink and Wagner 1999). Ethnic discrimination is apparently moderated by remoteness and social status to the extent that discrimination is stronger in remote as opposed to face-to-face interactions, and it is stronger if the social status of the minority member is low. Although Klink and Wagner's (1999) study did not focus on Turkish migrants, results are relevant, for they point to the consequences of symbolic exclusion for everyday life.

Turkish immigrants in Germany are less assimilated than other immigrants and they receive the lowest evaluations by Germans. These are two sides of the same coin and there is some evidence for behavioural manifestations of low recognition, namely statistical discrimination of Turks in the labour market. Against this backdrop, it may be surprising that Turkish immigrants and their descendants have far higher naturalisation rates than immigrants from former Yugoslavia (Statistisches Bundesamt 2012), who have a similar status and enjoy similar rights. Turkish residents are an interesting case because they can live comfortably on a permanent residence status, have some practical advantages from naturalisation and get suffrage, but have to renounce their Turkish citizenship to apply for the German one. This generates in many cases a relatively stable equilibrium of advantages and disadvantages. For example, not having to apply for visas for traveling to the US can be an attractive pay-off for naturalisation, but is it attractive enough if the Turkish passport has to be renounced in return? What about those who want to confirm their emotional attachment to Germany through naturalisation but refuse to give up Turkish citizenship because they have a similar emotional attachment to Turkey? It is this predicament in combination with relatively encompassing rights for permanent residents that makes the Turkish population of Germany an interesting case.

What are the consequences of studying the Turkish population in a single German city? Do findings for the city of Hamburg translate to the rest of Germany? In order to make that transfer, Hamburg's institutional characteristics and socio-demographic distributions should be more or less similar to the federal average. As can be seen from Table 3.1, the relative size of the Turkish population in Hamburg is slightly bigger than the German average and above the average of Western German federal states. The exclusion of Eastern German states is reasonable, because the bulk of foreign population arrived before German reunification to the Western part of Germany. At the same time, cities tend to attract more migrants than rural areas for economic reasons. Being a city-state, Hamburg therefore has a relatively high share of non-German population. Overall, the share of Turks is not dramatically divergent from the national average, although the share of alien residents from all origins is considerably higher in Hamburg than elsewhere. The total population of Hamburg was 1.7 million in the year of the survey (2012) including 50,000 Turks and a total of 244,000 alien residents.

Table 3.1 Population in (Western) Germany and Hamburg 2012 (%)

	Germany			Hamburg			Western Germany*
	Total	Male	Female	Total	Male	Female	Total
Share of Turkish	2.0	2.1	1.8	2.9	3.2	2.6	2.3
Share of non-German	9.0	9.4	8.5	14.1	14.8	13.3	10.2

*Including Berlin. Own calculations. Sources: Statistisches Bundesamt (2012) and official estimation based on *Mikrozensus 2011*.

What about the institutional set-up in Hamburg? Are there relevant differences to other federal states? As a relatively small state, Hamburg has a single naturalisation authority. Although other states differ in this regard, centralization is an advantage because it implies a rather coherent implementation of administrative policies. Hamburg also sticks out as the federal state with the highest naturalisation rates in recent years (Gesemann and Roth 2014). However, in the case of naturalisation policies, immigrants face the same legal framework irrespective of the state. Comparing federal implementations of national citizenship law, Farahat (2013) finds states with high (Hamburg and Hessen) and low naturalisation rates (Bayern) to handle naturalisation requirements in similar ways in spite of their discretion. Still, diverging naturalisation rates between states could be a consequence of their general support of naturalisation. Hamburg has been one of the strongest promoters of naturalisation in recent years. The city has been running a campaign to encourage naturalisations. A prominent element of the campaign is a letter of invitation by the mayor sent to all aliens who fulfil the residence requirement, an approximate number of 137,000 persons. Since letters were sent in monthly margins of 4,000 pieces, it took almost three years until all migrants had been contacted.[33] Next to the letters, the ongoing initiative entails ceremonies of naturalisation in the town hall, a mentoring program for persons willing to naturalise ('*Einbürgerungslotsen*'), a PR campaign for identification featuring naturalised testimonials, and the introduction of naturalisation issues at school.[34] The rationale behind the choice of this specific context for the survey was to push salience of the naturalisation issue and thereby improve survey response. Obviously, the naturalisation campaign matters not only for its potential positive effect on the survey. What is more, the political campaign is a case of an elite project of boundary shifting. Bauböck (1998) proposes conceiving of liberal

---

[33] The campaign had been started under the conservative and green party coalition government even earlier in November 2010. The social democrats, in office since 2011, embraced the campaign by adding said letter of invitation.

[34] For further information on Hamburg's idiosyncrasies see Farahat (2013).

nation-states as cultural agents that shape the boundaries between national and minority cultures because the "reproduction of dominant national cultures thorough state legislation, institutions and policies implicitly defines other cultural groups as minorities or as foreign" (ibid, 43). The municipality fulfils a similar function at the local level. Its campaign titled 'Hamburg. My Port. Germany. My Home'[35] signals accommodation of diversity within the concept of German and Hamburg identity. The elite discourse and its political implementation represent invitations of alien residents to become members of the local and national polity. This boundary transformation is not necessarily mirrored in everyday communications and in experiences of minority members. Also, not all addressees of the mayor's letter may find the message credible and it may not even reach parts of the alien population. Still, if the campaign should have any effect on naturalisation proclivities, it should be a positive one. Therefore, the questionnaire contains questions concerning perceptions of Hamburg's naturalisation campaign.

Intention to Naturalise vs. Actual Naturalisation

This section discusses the implications of studying the intention to naturalise as opposed to actual naturalisation. Actors may intend to do something for long before they actually set out to do it, or, they may never realise their plan at all. That begs the question if motives that explain the intention also explain actual naturalisation? Since the answer given is rather pragmatic in nature, it given in this chapter on the research design. Motives for naturalisation *intentions* are an imprecise measure of motives for naturalisation, but they are the best that can be had. The differences result from the time-variance of opportunities, desires, and beliefs (Hedström 2005). *Opportunities* defined by the law can change in two ways. For one, the law can change independently of the actor and second, the opportunities may change depending on actors' development. For example, dual citizenship may be banned at one point in time but tolerated at the next (institutional change) and a migrant may not fulfil language criteria at one point in time but do so five years later (actor change). An actor's *desires* may change, for example, when she develops a preference to work in a profession restricted to nationals. In addition, the *beliefs* may change, for example at labour market entry, when the experience of discrimination against non-citizens leads to the expectation of labour market gains connected to naturalisation. If motives are time-variant, it is reasonable to ask, if there is no better way to measure naturalisation motives than by asking for intentions. The most obvious way would be to

---

[35] Translation by author. Orig.: "Hamburg. Mein Hafen – Deutschland. Mein Zuhause." (http://einbuergerung.hamburg.de/; last access: 27.01.2017)

ask naturalised persons why they naturalised. Practical problems of sampling these persons aside, their answers would still encounter similar problems as the procedure of asking before. Are the remembered motives really the same as the actual motives at the time of naturalisation? Next to the usual recollection problems of retrospective questions, respondents would be likely to factor in their actual experiences after naturalisation. For example, if expected labour market gains did not materialise, persons may simply cease to report these motives in order to reduce cognitive dissonance (Festinger 1957). Instead, they might argue that they always felt at home in the country of immigration and now affirmed their symbolic membership, although their initial motivation was predominantly pragmatic. A third measurement option is to use indicators of naturalisation and formulate bridge assumptions that connect these indirect measurements to naturalisation motives (cf. Kalter and Kroneberg 2014). This is regularly the 'choice' of studies that analyse secondary data. Obviously, combinations of the three measurements are theoretically possible especially where longitudinal data are available. They would allow for tracing and comparing prospective and retrospective motives. However, longitudinal data do not automatically solve the explanatory puzzle and they are not available for the phenomenon of interest. To sum up, all measurements of naturalisation motives have their drawbacks. This project favours direct over indirect measurement where possible. Indicators are a good choice whenever secondary data do not allow for direct measurements. The choice between prospective and retrospective measurement is based on two pragmatic considerations. First, public register data does not keep track record of former citizenship. Thus, onomastic phonebook sampling is the only way to reach naturalised citizens. Besides being more costly, this method identifies residents *and* citizens with Turkish names who naturalised at very different points in time under different legal conditions. Therefore, and this is the second reason, the perception of legal and symbolic boundaries would potentially refer to different legal and social contexts that individuals faced at the moment of naturalisation. For example, I might compare persons naturalised in 1980, when there was no legal entitlement to German citizenship, to persons naturalised in 2005 when there was one. Also, I would compare those who naturalised as minors with their parents to persons who made their own deliberate decision. In this section, I have described some of the implications of my measurement. Although the prospective measurement of naturalisation has some problems, it is the most feasible choice from a selection of suboptimal options.

3.3 Comparative Framework

Naturalisation under equal conditions makes immigrants' motives comparable. That is the main reason for the focus on one country of origin and one country of immigration. This section shows how this study relates to other sending-country-receiving-country-constellations. The comparative framework clarifies the significance of studying constellations of sending and receiving countries and it shows which constellations are comparable to Turks in Germany. Depending on the constellations that are compared, the defining dimensions of a comparative model will need to be adjusted. For the exemplary model visualised in Table 3.2, inspired by Marshall (1992), I picked three crucial dimensions that define the legal constellation of naturalisation in Germany: Dual citizenship toleration in incoming naturalisations by Germany (yes/no), dual citizenship toleration in outgoing naturalisations by the respective sending country (yes/no), and rights granted to alien residents in Germany (civil rights/ civil+social rights/ civil+social+political rights). Other aspects that are neglected here but are crucial in other cases include rights to family reunion, preconditions for naturalisation, rights of expatriates, and rights of former citizens to name a few. The comparative model presented here is merely an example that should be adapted to the study of particular constellations.

Table 3.2 illustrates how these three dimensions generate 15 potential outcomes of which nine have empirical representations for Germany as a receiving context.[36] The two dimensions relevant for 'dual citizenship toleration' follow from respective nationality laws. Dual citizenship toleration (DC) results in four out of nine existing sending-country-Germany constellations. The dimension of 'rights granted to aliens' is operationalised as follows: Civil rights are enjoyed by all residents, social rights refer to bilateral social security agreements (*Sozialversicherungsabkommen*), and political rights refer to enfranchisement. In the last category, only EU-countries are to be found and their citizens are enfranchised at local and EU-level only. This differentiation could easily be expanded further, especially for the dimension of 'rights granted to alien residents'. An even more complete typology would take into account rights granted by the country of origin: What rights do external citizens enjoy, and what rights do former citizens enjoy once they lost citizenship? For example, Turkish citizens can cast votes from abroad and former Turkish citizens retain many rights after release from Turkish citizenship. Scholars comparing immigrants from different origins should adapt their analytical framework to the sending and receiving

---

[36] If the sending country refuses to release citizens, Germany automatically accepts naturalisation under dual citizenship toleration (see BMI 2009).

contexts they study.[37] When the model for explaining naturalisation intentions is specified, I account for the most relevant rights related to the country of origin. If, for example, rights for family reunification are a relevant issue at stake in naturalisation of a particular group, it should be included in the comparative model. However, Turks in Germany do not depend on German citizenship for the right to family reunification. The typology shown in Table 3.2 may not be complete, but the three differentiations define crucial conditions that make naturalisation more or less attractive from the outset. For the case studied here, political rights are the main gain of naturalisation and renunciation of Turkish citizenship is the main loss. According to this typology, naturalisation in Germany is most attractive for immigrants from countries like Iran and least attractive for those from countries like Austria. Iranians earn social and political rights while they keep their former citizenship whereas Austrians lose their former citizenship and gain only few additional rights in Germany compared to their former status. The benefits are intermediate for all other types of countries including Turkey. This typology makes it also apparent, why the analysis of immigrants' naturalisation motives is misguiding if countries of origin are unaccounted for. However, even where different countries of origin have been accounted for, researchers have not paid enough attention to rules of naturalisation that relate to the country of origin. Although more recently some scholars have drawn attention to the "constellations of citizenship" between sending and receiving countries (Bauböck 2010, also Jones-Correa 2001a; Freeman and Ögelman 1998; Vink and Bauböck 2013), not enough efforts have been made to take this aspect into account in empirical studies (exceptions include Jones-Correa 2001b; Reichel and Perchinig 2015; Vink, Prokic-Breuer, and Dronkers 2013). This outline of a typology integrates the case of Turks in Germany into a comparative framework and shows how it relates to other sending-country-receiving-country-constellations. Migrants that can reasonably be compared to Turks come from countries that have social security agreements with Germany and cannot keep their original citizenship upon naturalisation, for example migrants from Bosnia, Chile, Kosovo, Macedonia, Montenegro, or the USA. Also, they could be compared to migrants from any origin country that withdraws their citizenship if they naturalise in another country, for example Germans who naturalise abroad.

---

[37] Resources for comparative studies are plentiful and recently expanding (e.g. Bauböck et al. 2006, Jeffers, Honohan, and Bauböck 2012 for CITLAW, Beine et al. 2016 for IMPALA, Helbling et al. 2016 for IMPIC, http://www.mipex.eu for MIPEX).

Table 3.2 Conditions of Naturalisation in Germany by Country of Origin[a]

rights granted to alien residents			dual citizenship toleration		
civil rights	civil rights + social rights	civil rights + social rights + political rights	citizenship release in *outgoing* naturalisations	dual citizenship toleration in *incoming* naturalisations	DC
Iran	Tunisia	-	renunciation difficult or impossible →	Yes	✓
-	-	Austria	No	Yes (EU)	✗
-	Switzerland	Italy	Yes	Yes (EU)	✓
Azerbaijan	Japan	-	No	No	✗
Russia[b]	Turkey	-	Yes	No	✗

[a]One example per cell; [b]Special rules apply to Russians with German ancestry; DC = dual citizenship allowed at naturalisation in Germany. Sources: German bilateral social security agreements (http://www.deutsche-rentenversicherung.de/Allgemein/de/Inhalt/2_Rente_Reha/01_rente/01_grundwissen/05_rente_und_ausland/01a_grundlagen/01_02_grundlagen_sozialversabkommen.html), Social Insurance Agreements between Switzerland and EU (http://www.bsv.admin.ch/themen/internationales/02094/index.html?lang=en), Japanese Nationality Law (http://www.moj.go.jp/ENGLISH/information/tnl-01.html), Azerbaijani law (http://www.multiplecitizenship.com/wscl/ws_AZERBAIJAN.html)[Last access to all: 31.01.2017]. Table by author.

4. Survey Results: Symbolic and Legal Membership

4.1 Scope and Expected Findings

The survey's purpose is to map the variety of motives for and against naturalisation. Past research gives many directions and informs the questionnaire. As a result, survey data allow for testing a wide range of hypotheses. Reasons for naturalisation and reasons to abstain are manifold and often intertwined. Multivariate analyses are therefore essential. The questionnaire was designed with the purpose of testing which motives are dominant for Turkish residents of Germany. In the remainder of this chapter I introduce the respective hypotheses referring to symbolic and legal membership, before I describe data and methods (4.2). Then I present findings (4.3), and summarize and conclude (4.4).

Symbolic Membership

Considerable rights have been granted to permanently resident Turkish citizens in Germany. At the same time, the Turkish state increasingly guarantees rights for its former citizens. Hence, the gains from acquisition of the new citizenship are rather small as are the losses caused by the renouncement of the old one. This is true at least for those indifferent about exercising their political rights and those who do not need it for professional reasons. Are political participation and labour market access then the only remaining stakes in naturalisation? Obviously, next to rights, citizenship involves feelings of belonging and sharing of a collective identity (Benhabib 1999). As Rogers Brubaker aptly put it, nation membership in a more informal sense "is not administered by specialised personnel but by ordinary people in the course of everyday life, using tacit understandings of who belongs and who does not, of us and them" (2010, 65). In order to account for this 'informal membership' (ibid.), I conceptualise citizenship as a legal boundary that is closely connected to the making and unmaking of symbolic boundaries (see Ch.3). Boundary perception is measured by feelings of accommodation and experienced discrimination. Accommodation is an indicator of symbolic membership while perceived group discrimination indicates exclusion. I have argued above that symbolic membership should make naturalisation more likely. Hence, I expect feelings of accommodation to make naturalisation more attractive and discrimination to make it less attractive. In terms of the MFS, symbolic recognition before naturalisation makes symbolic membership after naturalisation more predictable. Also, it reduces the costs of a potential loss of symbolic belonging in Turkey.

Hypothesis 1a: Turkish residents who feel at home in Germany are more inclined to naturalise.

Hypothesis 1b: Turkish residents who experience group discrimination are less inclined to naturalise.

Crossing a bright boundary is likely to involve considerable symbolic costs. The identity connected to the former citizenship will be at risk, if not lost, because there is no ambiguity in symbolic belonging. Where a symbolic boundary is perceived as bright, hyphenated identities are not permissible. Hence, renunciation of the Turkish passport may involve a perceived loss of the former cultural identity. That loss translates into costs in the SEU-model.

Hypothesis 2a: Turkish residents who perceive the Turkish passport to be expressive of a Turkish identity are less inclined to naturalise.

Besides symbolic costs, there might be symbolic benefits of attaining host country citizenship. The passport has a symbolic meaning that potentially supports recognition as a symbolic member. Research findings imply an exclusive definition of belonging to German society and corresponding perceptions of a bright boundary by Turkish immigrants (see Ch. 2). While it is unclear whether naturalisation is actually instrumental in achieving informal membership, the expectation of such an effect should be conducive to naturalisation intentions of persons willing to cross. The benefit of German citizenship is the affirmation of symbolic membership.

Hypothesis 2b: Turkish residents who perceive the German passport to be conducive to attaining a desired German identity are more inclined to naturalise.

So far, symbolic membership has been considered in terms of relations with the majority group. Further, family and friends may change symbolic boundary perceptions. First, role models can be expected to affect the decision to naturalise. The more peers who have naturalised, the more insecurity is reduced concerning the administrative procedure. And second, the consequences of naturalisation become more predictable. Individuals can observe in their social environment whether naturalisation has led to symbolic inclusion or not. Consequently, the effect of having German friends or family members can go either way. I test the hypothesis that, on average, reduction of transaction costs and imitation of role models cause a higher inclination to naturalise in migrants with naturalised family and peers.

Hypothesis 3a: Turkish residents with more naturalised family members are more inclined to naturalise.

Hypothesis 3b: Turkish residents with more naturalised friends are more inclined to naturalise.

Everything else equal, children of immigrants should feel a stronger connection to Germany than their parents. While raised in a Turkish parental home, they were socialised in a German social and cultural environment. This group consists of those who were born in Germany (second generation) and those who arrived during childhood or adolescence (1.5 generation). On average, these generations should have a stronger sense of belonging to Germany. Naturalisation is more likely to be an affirmation of their status and therefore is more likely to increase the benefit.

Hypothesis 4: Members of the 1.5 and second generation are more inclined to naturalise than 1st generation immigrants.

Legal Membership

There are few tangible benefits of naturalisation for most Turkish persons in Germany. Social and civil rights have been granted as part of bilateral agreements between Turkey and the European community, to attract the then so-called guest workers and calm unions who feared the competition of cheap labour.[38] The German Federal Constitutional Court promoted rights expansion by mandating the intransigent application of constitutional rights to all residents regardless of German citizenship (Joppke 2001). These rights encompass the generous application of social insurance rules through bilateral agreements between Germany and Turkey, and extensive rights of family reunification for permanent residents. Remaining legal benefits belong to three realms: (1) Political rights, (2) cross-border mobility, and (3) work. (1) Enfranchisement is a substantial consequence of naturalisation for both state and individual. (2) A range of benefits of naturalisation is related to cross-border mobility. Visa obligations are absent for many countries where they would be required based on the former citizenship and EU citizenship potentially improves diplomatic protection

---

[38] I refer to the 1963 Ankara Agreement and its protocols (http://www.abgs.gov.tr/index.php?p=113&l=2; last access 27.01.2017).

abroad.[39] Also, in some cases naturalisation may entail certain convenience vis-à-vis public administration. Residence permits need not be renewed, border controls might be less strict and time consuming, and leaving Germany for more than six months is possible without losing the right to re-enter, an asset for transnational migrants.[40] (3) Cross-border mobility at the same time improves job opportunities, because the German passport might facilitate work related travels. Besides, naturalisation provides access to jobs restricted to German or EU citizens to be found in the public sector and in independent personal services. Examples include dentists, medical doctors, pharmacists, lawyers and architects (Steinhardt 2012: 815). In addition, naturalisation might clear obstacles for borrowing from banks, a relevant issue in particular for self-employed persons. More broadly, naturalisation potentially fosters a trustful relationship between employer and employee, because it signals long-term commitment to the country of residence the pecuniary side of which economists have assessed as 'naturalisation premium'.

Although some of the motives considered may hold for other immigrant groups, based on the argument that specific citizenship constellations should be accounted for, I formulate hypotheses for Turkish residents. The hypotheses are at the same time the bridge assumptions for the MFS introduced in chapter 2. Hypothesis 5 means in terms of the MFS that migrants who expect utility from voting in Germany expect a higher utility from naturalisation. Hence, they are more likely to opt for the (mental) action 'intention to naturalise'. The same trivial logic applies to hypotheses six and seven.

Hypothesis 5: Turkish residents who want to have the right to vote in Germany are more inclined to naturalise.

Hypothesis 6: Turkish residents who expect job-related benefits from German citizenship are more inclined to naturalise.

Hypothesis 7: Turkish residents who expect travel-related benefits from German citizenship are more inclined to naturalise.

Naturalisation can be perceived as instrumentally disadvantageous. First, obligations towards the host country arise that might be considered undesirable. This holds in particular for conscription, an obligation that, besides its symbolic sig-

---

[39] In 2010 the German passport yielded 69 visa waivers as opposed to 35 for Turkish citizens (Mau et al. 2015). A private law firm offering expertise in citizenship ranks Germany at the top of the list indicating absence of visa restrictions along with Sweden, Finland, and the UK (https://www.henleyglobal.com/international-visa-restrictions/; last access 27.01.2017)

[40] See *AufenthG* §51, 1.

nificance, is time consuming as is its surrogate civil service.[41] Second, loss of the former citizenship may involve the loss of rights. Legislation has been changing over the years in this respect, but it indisputably involves the loss of political rights. Since 2014, Turkish expatriates can cast a vote abroad. The possibility of external voting is likely to increase the significance of the loss. However, the survey was conducted before the last provision enabling external voting became effective.[42] Still, the subjective utility of voting in Turkey may be just as high as the SEU of voting in Germany. If the subjective utility of voting is equal for both countries, individuals are likely to decide against naturalisation because the expected loss is weightier than the expected gain (Tversky and Kahneman 1986). In terms of SEU, costs of naturalisation increase for migrants who want to retain their right to vote in Turkey.

Hypothesis 8: Turkish residents who want to keep their franchise in Turkey are less inclined to naturalise.

Until 1995, more rights were dependent on the retention of Turkish citizenship. Release from Turkish citizenship involved the loss of considerable rights in the home country that affected heritage and house ownership. The 'pink card' (*pembe kart*), introduced in that year, granted citizenship-like rights to former Turkish citizens, hence eliminating these disincentives. However, it has not been claimed quite often (Çağlar 2004).[43] The pink card, renamed blue card in 2009, broadly guarantees the retention of rights for former citizens.[44] Renunciation of Turkish citizenship and dual citizenship were legally banned by Turkish law until 1981 (Kadirbeyoğlu 2007; Tiryakioğlu 2006). This is relevant because Germany requires Turks to renounce their citizenship if they want to naturalise. However, a considerable number reacquired Turkish citizenship during the 1990s responding to encouragement by Turkish authorities. Formally, this procedure did not conflict with German law ('*Inlandsklausel*') until the 1999 reform. An estimated number of 50,000 naturalised persons lost their German citizenship, following their reacquisition of Turkish citizenship, after the new law became effective.[45]

---

[41] If this obligation is a central disincentive, a rise in male naturalisations is conceivable after the abolition of conscription in Germany in early 2011. The last date of recruitment was January 1st 2011 (*WehrRÄndG 2011*, Section 7). Panel data including the years before and after reform would be necessary for an evaluation.
[42] See http://eudo-citizenship.eu/news/citizenship-news/1080-external-voting-to-be-implemented-for-the-first-time-in-turkey-s-forthcoming-presidential-elections; last access: 27.01.2017.
[43] Those rights relate to residence, property, work, etc. (Law 4112/1995). Çağlar's (2004, 279) rough estimates of pink card claims rest on inquiries at the Turkish consulate in Berlin.
[44] Law No. 5901/2009 Turkish Citizenship Law, Art. 28.
[45] There were investigations on the numbers by German federal administrations. The numbers mentioned, however, rest on estimates by Turkish officials (cf. Bundestag Drucksache 15/5006).

Apparently, Turkish immigrants are rather keen on keeping their original citizenship. This is surprising because the 1995 legislation endows former citizens with citizen like rights. While in theory there is little loss of genuine rights, Turkish emigrants may be unaware of the possibilities to retain rights or they may doubt legal implementation. Thus, an *expected* loss of rights, especially connected to inheritance and real estate ownership, is a possible disincentive for renouncing Turkish citizenship. In terms of SEU, interest in retention of these rights increases the costs of naturalisation.

Hypothesis 9: Turkish residents who want to keep rights to real estate property and inheritance in Turkey are less inclined to naturalise.

Finally, the cumulative benefits from a German passport are more meaningful, the more years of potential residency remain during which the migrant has to deal with the German labour market and authorities. Besides, there are further issues that are not addressed separately in the questionnaire such as accessibility of credit schemes or eligibility for scholarships that are reserved for German students. The cumulative benefits of Turkish citizenship become more meaningful towards the end of the career, when many first generation immigrants make plans for return to Turkey or transnational arrangements between both countries.[46] Time discounting of future benefits after retirement makes the Turkish passport less beneficial for young migrants.[47] In contrast, at the end of the career, return is not only more predictable but also closer leading to less time discounting of benefits.

Hypothesis 10: Younger Turkish residents are more inclined to naturalise than older ones.

4.2 Data and Methods

This section provides a general introduction to the survey Attitudes towards Citizenship and Naturalisation (ACN) 2012 and describes the operationalization of central variables. Data analysis and hypothesis testing with multivariate regression models is followed by robustness checks and a discussion of limitations of the survey. Findings are summarized and discussed in light of the literature on naturalisation intentions and decisions.

---

[46] Many first generation migrants have property in Turkey but offspring in Germany. Those migrants often opt for perpetual migration between both countries once retired.
[47] See Elster (2007, 111) on time discounting/myopia.

Survey Design

A random sample was drawn from the public register in the German city-state of Hamburg. Two thousand permanent residents were contacted by mail with an optional online response (November-December 2012). The population from which the sample was drawn was restricted to Turkish citizens between the age of 16 and 60.[48] The rationale behind age limitations at the top and at the bottom was to focus on persons for whom naturalisation is potentially a salient issue at the time of the survey. This selection intentionally disregards persons that were already naturalised. Therefore, results should be understood with respect to non-naturalised Turks.

Table 4.1 Population and Sample by Gender and Family Initial

		Male	Female	Total
A-F	population	8,070	6,726	14,796
	sample	500 (6.2)	500 (7.4)	1,000 (6.8)
G-Z	population	11,854	9,967	21,821
	sample	500 (4.2)	500 (5.0)	1,000 (4.6)
Total	population	19,924	16,693	36,617
	sample	1,000 (5.0)	1,000 (6.0)	2,000 (5.5)

Share of respective population in parentheses. Source: Public Register Hamburg, 2012.

Further sampling criteria include gender and initial letter of the family name (see Table 4.1). Half of the sampled family names start with a letter between A-F, the other half starts with G-Z. Male and female participants are represented equally. In total, 5.5% of the population were contacted, with women and family names in A-F being slightly overrepresented. There is no reason to expect systematic differences between persons by their family name. Hence, the overrepresentation of A-F names has no influence on results. Sampling according to the alphabet was supposed to assure variance in the reception of an invitation to naturalise by the mayor (see Ch.3). Contact was established via mail with directions for an optional online-questionnaire to improve coverage and reduce costs (Leeuw, Hox, and Dillman 2008). The envelop contained a University of Bremen key tag as an incentive, assurance of confidentiality and data protection, and free answer envelopes. The letter was followed by a reminder-postcard one week later as recommended by the Tailored Design Method (Dillman 2007; Leeuw, Dillman, and Hox 2008; Schnell 2012).[49] Contact letter, assertion of confidentiality and

---

[48] This excludes multiple citizens.
[49] Dillman recommends further reminders and repeated delivery of the questionnaire. However, limited resources required some deviations from the recommended procedure. Next to Dillman, I followed recommendations for survey design by De Leeuw et al. (2008) and Schnell (2012).

data protection, and paper, and online questionnaires were bilingual in Turkish and German.

The questionnaire was developed from a thick literature on naturalisation motives of immigrants, with special focus on Germany. It covers all aspects of naturalisation that have been identified as relevant by the literature (see Ch.1). Furthermore, it includes several items that aim at capturing the perception of symbolic boundaries. Finally, it covers basic socio-demographic information. The questionnaire contains 105 items on eight DIN-A4 pages. It was translated to Turkish with 'simple direct translation' and combined with elements of the 'committee approach' (Pan and La Puente 2005). In addition to the author of the study, four Turkish speakers were involved in the translation, two of whom are fluent in German. Repeated pre-tests were run at several points in time including before and after translation. Both, the online-mode and paper-pencil questionnaires were tested separately. Pre-test participants included survey experts, migration scholars, representatives from the German Turkish Society of Hamburg that assist aliens interested in naturalisation, and (German-) Turkish residents.

Variable Operationalization

Variable operationalization is a rather straightforward task in this study. Thanks to the direct measurement of motives (see Ch.3), most items translate into variables without transformation. The possibility of direct translations from items into motives is one of the major upsides of original data collection. The corresponding item for the dependent variable is *'Do you intend to apply for German citizenship?'* and has the answer options *'yes, definitely'*, *'yes, probably'*, *'rather not'*, and *'definitely not'*. Some additional variables are identical with single items. For example, perceived group discrimination was measured by the item *'How often did you have the impression that in Germany persons of Turkish origin are treated unjustly only because of their origin?'*. Again, there were four options to indicate whether and how often this was the case according to the respondent. Operationalization of the remaining variables is presented in Table 4.2. Further variables that translate directly from the respective single items include feeling at home in Germany, perceived group discrimination, identity-relevance of the German passport, share of German family members, share of close friends that naturalised, gender, age, and education. A second class of variables was constructed by factor analysis. That includes interest in political rights in Germany, expected job-related benefits, expected travel-related benefits, interest in citizenship-specific rights in Turkey, and identity-relevance of the Turkish passport. Details on the results of the factor analysis are reported in the appendix (Tab. A1). The example of labour market prospects illustrates the construction of index variables from factor analysis. The index variable of labour market benefits results from combination of four items: *'By naturalisation... (1) my income would improve, ... (2) my chances of finding a job would improve, ... (3) colleagues and chiefs would discriminate against me less frequently'*, and *(4) 'I want to have a job, where I need German citizenship (e.g. certain public sector jobs, or jobs that involve travel)'*. Each statement was judged by respondents on a 4-point Likert scale. Then a factor analysis was run over all items that referred to the latent variables. In this way, I assured that the indices are uncorrelated. A third class of variables was generated based on additional information: Income and generational status. Income was constructed from direct and categorical answers to deal with item nonresponse. Generational status is defined by respondents' country of birth, parents' country of birth, and age at arrival. I stick to the common definition of the second generation as those who were born in the host country to foreign-born parents. For 1.5 generation persons, there is no common definition. They are variously defined as having immigrated before the age of 12 (e.g. Portes and Zhou 1993 drawing on the US Census) or more vaguely as having grown up mostly in the country of immigration (e.g. Bean et al. 2012). Here, 1.5 generation is defined by being born abroad to non-German parents and having arrived to Germany before the age of 18. The first generation then contains all persons who arrived at the age of 18 or later and are otherwise equal to the 1.5 generation.

Table 4.2 Operationalization of Independent Variables

Variables	Items	
Legal aspects		
Political rights in Germany[i] (Factor variable)	10. By naturalisation, you get certain rights. Disregarding your intention to acquire German citizenship: How important do you consider the following rights?[a]	
	a.	Franchise in federal elections (the federal parliament elects the chancellor)
	b.	Franchise in local elections
	c.	Franchise in European elections
Genuine rights in Turkey[i] (Factor variable)	11. In case of a naturalisation in Germany, you normally loose Turkish citizenship meaning loss of rights in Turkey. How important do you consider the following rights?[a]	
	a.	Franchise in national elections
	b.	Right to inheritance and real estate

(Table continues on next page)

Table 4.2 Operationalization of Independent Variables (cont'd)

Symbolic aspects		
Expected travel options[a] (Factor variable)	17. Irrespective of your current citizenship. In how far do you agree with the following statements about benefits of German citizenship for travel?[b]	
	a.	German citizenship is beneficial for my travels inside EU
	b.	German citizenship is beneficial for my travels between Germany and Turkey
	c.	German citizenship is beneficial for my travels outside EU and Turkey, e.g. Americas, Asia, Australia
Turkish passport identity-relevant[a] (Factor variable)	21. The loss of Turkish citizenship is standard in the case of naturalisation. Irrespective of your intention to apply for German citizenship, and irrespective of the obligation to renounce the Turkish passport in your case: In how far do you agree with the following statements?[c]	
	a.	If I lose Turkish citizenship, I am no longer a Turk
	b.	My loss of Turkish citizenship, means loss of my Turkish identity
German passport identity-relevant	21. The loss of Turkish citizenship is standard in the case of naturalisation. Irrespective of your intention to apply for German citizenship, and irrespective of the obligation to renounce the Turkish passport in your case: In how far do you agree with the following statements?[c]	
	a.	By naturalisation, you acquire some German identity
Feel at home in Germany	23b. I feel at home in Germany[c]	
	14. The following is about your family and friends (Options: All, more than half, less than half, nobody)	
Share of German family members	a.	How many of your next family members (parents, siblings, offspring) possess German citizenship?
Share of close friends that naturalised	b.	How many of your close friends acquired citizenship by naturalisation?
Sociodemographics		
	37. What is your highest educational degree?	years
Education	a. No degree	0
	b. Primary school (till 5th grade)	5
	c. Primary school / *Volksschule* /*Hauptschule* or similar (till 8th /9th grade)	8
	d. *Realschule* or similar (till 10th grade)	10
	e. Gymnasium or similar (till 12th/13th grade)	13
	f. University / University of applied sciences / *Hochschule*	18

[a]Options: Very important, rather important, rather unimportant, not important at all. [b]Options: Fully applies, rather applies, does rather not apply, does not apply at all. [c]Options: Totally agree, rather agree, rather disagree, strongly disagree. Source: Questionnaire ACN 2012. See also Appendix B.

4.3 Results

The response rate of 12.5% is similar among male and female respondents (Table A2). The majority responded by mail while only 16% of respondents opted for the online-mode. The implications of the response rate for the interpretation of results are considered further below (Ch. 4.5).

Descriptive Statistics

Table 4.3 and Table 4.4 display descriptive statistics of relevant discrete and continuous variables respectively. Means, standard deviations, and information on imputed values per item are reported in Table 4.3. Values were imputed by regression, whenever $R^2>0.3$ in a linear regression model.[50] Where variables consist of several items, imputations are reported for all items. For example, the factor 'expected travel' consists of three items and these items have 6, 7, and 9 missing values respectively. Detailed information on the wording of items is given above. Additional information about the index variables resulting from factor analysis can be found in the appendix (Tab.A1). The means of all indices predicted from factor analysis are by definition 0 and the variance is 1 (see Table 4.3). Political rights, and property and inheritance rights in Turkey were combined to one factor because they are strongly correlated (r=0.55). This puts the respective hypotheses (H8+H9) to test in conjunction.

---

[50] Multiple imputations (e.g. Royston and White 2011) were impossible to calculate because of the amount of variables with missing values.

Table 4.3 Sample characteristics – Continuous Variables

Variable	Indicator(s)	Obs.	Mean	Std. Dev.	Imputed values*
Feel at home in Germany[i]	Single Item	249	3.23	0.81	28
Perceived group discrimination[i]	Single Item	249	2.63	0.77	46
Turkish passport identity-relevant[i]	2 Items - Factor variable	248	0	1	3/6
Political rights Germany[i]	3 Items - Factor variable	248	0	1	20/16/32
Expected job-related benefits[i]	4 Items - Factor variable	248	0	1	6/3/2/4
Expected travel-related benefits[i]	3 Items - Factor variable	248	0	1	6/7/9
Genuine rights Turkey[i]	2 Items - Factor variable	248	0	1	10/12
Age	Single Item	245	38.36	10.14	-
Log. Personal income[i, M]	Constructed from detailed and categorized income	249	6.82	1.47	70

Source: ACN 2012. Categories not reported since variables are continuous. The single item variables are continuous after imputation. *Column reports imputed values per item on each (factor) variable. [M]The median net income before imputation is 1290 Euro.

Table 4.4 reports frequencies for each possible answer. The dependent variable 'intention to naturalise' merits some attention. About half of the respondents intend to naturalise in the future, while half of them are reluctant. At the same time, annual naturalisation rates are below five percent of the eligible population. How can this apparent discrepancy be understood? Is it an effect of self-selection into the survey? Or is correlation between intended and performed naturalisation simply very low? Since the population's intentions to naturalise are unknown, the most promising way to rule out self-selection is to compare this finding to other studies with better response rates. In fact, some scholars present naturalisation intentions for immigrants from Turkey and former Yugoslavia similar to the ones obtained from ACN 2012 (Tab.A2). Although none of them reports results for Turks at regional level, naturalisation intentions reported by Kahanec and Tosun (2009) are similar for Turks at national level and for labour immigrants more generally at the regional level for Hamburg. Studies based on SOEP data yield lower naturalisation proclivities of Turks at the national level. This is confirmed by calculations based on the more recent IAB-SOEP-Migration Sample. At the same time, Turkish proclivities are higher for Turks than for other immigrant groups (Diehl and Blohm 2003). Apparently, the correlation of intended and performed citizenship acquisition is generally low. In line with that interpretation, 81% of respondents in ACN 2012 would naturalise 'rather' or 'definitely' if dual citizenship was tolerated. Since the regulation of dual citizenship is an ongoing debate in Germany, some migrants might postpone naturalisation hoping for legal change. There are two more reasons that may explain the difference. First, the temporal frame of reference of the annual rate exaggerates the gap between intentions and actual naturalisations.[51] And second, not all persons willing to naturalise are eligible.[52] Qualitative interviews provide some more insight concerning the gap between intended and performed naturalisations (see Ch. 5+6). Overall, the high share of persons willing to naturalise is not necessarily a sign of self-selection. Calculation of multivariate regression models would be little insightful if the dependent variable had no variance. First, both groups are of interest, those who are inclined to naturalise and those who are not. And second, technically, without variance on the dependent variable no effect of the independent variables could be found. Hence, the ayes *and* the nays should be represented in the sample - and they are.

Table 4.4 Sample characteristics – Discrete Variables

Variable	Indicator(s)	Obs.	Percent	Mean	SD	Imputed values
Intention to naturalise	Single Item	240	100.00			-
	4 - Definitely		20.8			
	3 - Rather yes		25.8			
	2 - Rather not		38.8			
	1 - Certainly not		14.6			
German passport identity-relevant	Single Item	244	100.00	2.40	1.08	-
	4 - Strongly agree		17.6			
	3 - Rather agree		32.8			
	2 - Rather disagree		21.3			
	1 - Strongly disagree		28.3			

(Table continues on next page)

---

[51] The cumulative naturalisation rate of Turks 1985-2012 with the 2012 population as a reference is 36% (own calculation based on Statistisches Bundesamt 2013; www.eudo-citizenship.eu). This is of course only a rough approximation of permanent residents' naturalisation because in- and out-migration is not taken into account. Calculations based on the IAB-SOEP-Migration Sample from 2013 yield a slightly lower rate of 33% (see Table A3).

[52] For example, 11% of respondents in ACN arrived in Germany less than eight years ago, 19% are not eligible if self-declared non-eligibility and self-reported poor or very poor German language skills are taken into account next to the residence requirement. Implications for the models are addressed along with robustness checks (Ch.4.4).

Table 4.4 Sample characteristics – Discrete Variables (cont'd)

Variable	Indicator(s)	Obs.	Percent	Mean	SD	Imputed values
Share of German family members	Single Item	244	100.00	2.31	0.90	-
	4 - All		10.3			
	3 - More than half		29.9			
	2 - Less than half		40.1			
	1 - Nobody		19.6			
Share of close friends that naturalised	Single Item	239	100.00	2.34	0.84	-
	4 - All		9.2			
	3 - More than half		30.5			
	2 - Less than half		45.6			
	1 - Nobody		14.6			
Gender female	Single Item	245		0.49	0.50	-
Education in years	Constructed from highest educational degree	246	100.00	10.45	4.70	-
	0 - No degree		5.3			
	5 - Primary School		12.2			
	8 - Hauptschule		21.1			
	10 - Realschule		23.6			
	13 - Gymnasium		20.3			
	18 - University		17.5			
Generation	Constructed from 'country of birth', 'year of birth', and 'year of arrival'	244	100.00	1.79	0.80	-
	1 - 1st (age at arr. >18)		44.7			
	2 - 1.5 (age at arr. 1-17)		31.6			
	3 - 2nd (age at arr. 0)		23.8			

Source: ACN 2012.

Excursion 1: Symbolic Boundaries

The impossibility to operationalise symbolic boundary perception from available datasets was a major reason for the collection of original survey data. Various were included with the aim of operationalizing the concept of boundaries. It draws attention to the fact that feelings of belonging to a country of immigration can only emerge if the cultural mainstream includes the newcomers and allows them to join their collective identity. I formulated items that would allow for understanding identity as the outcome of a two-way process. Table 4.5 presents selected items that give indications of symbolic boundary perception and their descriptive statistics. The items were assessed with regards to their predictive power in explaining variation in the dependent variable in multivariate analyses. The items that are most predictive of the intention to naturalise include 'perceived group discrimination' and 'feeling at home in Germany'. However, some of the remaining variables are insightful for the description of symbolic boundaries. The items on identification reveal that respondents are more often perceived as Turkish than they see themselves as Turkish. Two fifth of respondents tend towards hybrid (Turkish- or Kurdish-German) identities, but only 15 per cent are perceived as such by others in Germany. Among their friends, they are more often perceived the way they want to be seen. It is also noteworthy that few of the interviewees (4%) see themselves as Germans. On the one hand, this may seem obvious because they are not German legally. On the other hand, the majority of respondents grew up in Germany (55%). Hence, one might suspect more German or hybrid identities. Another item shows the difficulty of belonging in Germany by asking how easy it is to be counted in (*dazu gehören*). Very few people agree with the statement that it is easy (8%) but at the same time, few people disagree (7%). Instead, respondents are evenly divided around the middle. For the statement that only persons born in Germany are counted in, the disagreement is somewhat clearer. Sixty per cent of respondents disagree either slightly or fully. Still, half of respondents disagree either fully (8%) or partly (41%) with the statement that they entirely belong to Germany (*voll dazu gehören*). Discrimination may explain why people have the impression that they do not belong. Every time they are treated differently because of ascribed qualities, they are made others. Half of respondents who answered the question think that Turks are discriminated against 'often' or 'very often'. The prevalence of discrimination underscores the difficulty of counting oneself into the group of Germans. Overall, these are indications of a bright and hardly permeable boundary to German identity. At the same time, many Turkish residents feel connected to their country of origin and might not embrace a pure German identity. It rather seems that a blurred boundary would be more in line with Turkish residents' hyphenate self-identification.

Table 4.5 Symbolic Boundary Items

Item	Obs.	Disagree[a]	Rather disagree	Rather agree	Agree	Missing
If I give up Turkish citizenship, I am no longer a Turk.	246	48	27	12	12	1
Upon renouncement of my Turkish citizenship, I would also lose my Turkish identity.	243	51	29	10	8	2
Upon acquisition of German citizenship, you get some German identity.	244	28	21	32	17	2
I feel at home in Turkey.	216	6	29	23	29	13
I feel at home in Germany.	221	4	12	33	40	11
I feel at home in both countries.	240	7	20	34	35	4
The Turks who came to Germany changed the country.	243	3	11	49	35	2
As a person of Turkish descent it is easy to be counted in in Germany.	244	7	39	43	8	2
In Germany, you are counted in only if you are born here.	242	19	40	21	17	3
The Turkish residents in Germany have reason to be proud of Germany.	244	6	21	49	21	2
I belong in Germany.	245	8	41	26	23	2

	N	Range	Mean	SD		
How would you describe your feelings towards Germany on a temperature scale?	243	-5; 5	1.30	2.30		
How would you describe your feelings towards Turkey on a temperature scale?	244	-5; 5	1.98	2.30		

	N	Turkish[a]	German	Hyphen.	Other (e.g. Kurd)	Missing
I see myself as…	247	47	4	41	6	1
Other people in Germany perceive me as…	241	61	14	15	7	3
I wish people perceived me as…	237	43	8	36	8	5
My friends in Germany perceive me as…	244	53	11	29	5	2

(Table continues on next page)

Table 4.5 Symbolic boundary items (cont'd)

	N	Never[a]	Seldom	Often	Very often	Missing
How often did you have the impression, that persons of Turkish origin in Germany have been treated unfairly only because of their origin?	208	4	37	30	12	16
How often did you have the impression that you have been treated unfairly personally in Germany only because of your origin?	203	12	44	18	7	18

	N	Work[a]	Public Office	School/ University	Other	Missing
In which of the mentioned contexts have you ever had the impression of being treated unfairly?	123	47	54	35	45	2

[a]Figures are percentages; Source: Questionnaire ACN 2012. See also Appendix B.

Excursion 2: Dual Citizenship

This study assesses naturalisation intentions under specific legal conditions. One of the most debated elements of these legal conditions is the requirement to renounce the former citizenship upon naturalisation. If the government wanted to make naturalisation more attractive to non-EU immigrants, toleration of multiple citizenships would be the most effective move. Although not central to this project, this study's findings with respect to dual citizenship shall not be withheld. More than half of the respondents know that they have to renounce their Turkish passport upon naturalisation, only five percent can retain their passport (rest: 'Don't know' or missing). All but the five percent who can retain Turkish citizenship were asked how likely they were to naturalise if dual citizenship was tolerated. In that hypothetical situation 60 per cent of respondents would definitely naturalise and another 20 per cent would rather likely. Only 14 per cent of respondents would still be inclined to refrain. On average, respondents score one point higher on the response scale compared to the real situation where they have to renounce their former citizenship, e.g. those who would rather not naturalise under current law are rather inclined to naturalise under the hypothetical situation. This finding is in line with the notion of loss aversion and supports findings from other studies (for the US Jones-Correa 2001b, Mazzolari 2009, for Turks in Germany Sauer 2013; but weak effects in European countries, Vink et al. 2013).

Excursion 3: Naturalisation Campaign

There were some non-trivial reasons to choose Hamburg as the research site. The city Senate has been running a naturalisation campaign since late 2010 (see Ch. 3.3). This would help the study in two ways. First, collaboration with the municipality would increase support and attention. Second, the issue of naturalisation is likely to be more salient during a campaign. Although an official collaboration was not cherished by the government, the study received moral support from specific offices of the municipality and practical help from the Turkish Society Hamburg (TGH), a non-governmental migrant organization. Also, the public register office was cooperative in providing data and service. Whether the response rate would have been lower without the campaign cannot be known. In order to assess the potential, I included a couple of items to measure visibility and evaluation of the campaign. The respective items address the letter of invitation, posters of a PR campaign, and public service provision on the issue of naturalisation.

About 30 per cent of respondents had received the letter at the time of the survey and more than two thirds had not received it. However, 90 per cent of those who did not receive the letter lived in a household with somebody who did. In spite of well intentions of the letter, it does not seem to have any effect. The correlation between reception of the letter and intention to naturalise ($r=0.05$) is marginal. Similarly, inclusion of the respective dummy variable in multivariate analysis does not improve the regression models. The display of posters with testimonials and the slogan 'Hamburg. My Port. Germany. My Home' was another element of the campaign. One third had never seen any of those posters, another quarter of respondents had seen them 'barely', and only 12 per cent of respondents claim having seen them very often. Compared to letter reception, correlation between the awareness of the posters and the intention to naturalise is somewhat stronger but still rather weak ($r=0.1$). Those who evaluate the posters more positively are also more inclined to naturalise ($r=0.2$). Still, no claims about causality should be made for these items. Those who are more inclined to naturalise are more likely to be aware of and positively evaluate posters that support their attitude. Finally, I assessed respondents' familiarity with and usage of services around the issue of naturalisation. Around 40 per cent are familiar with each of the naturalisation services provided (i.e. mentoring program, TGH services, consultation via phone / personal consultation in public office) but only few persons actually used the services in the past. The most frequented service was personal consultation in public office, used by 11 per cent of respondents. Overall, it seems that the effect of the naturalisation campaign on naturalisation proclivities is moderate at best. However, the historical examples of boundary blurring and shifting presented in chapter 2 suggest that political shifting of symbolic boundaries should be expected to become effective in the long run and affect majority and minority alike. Indeed, Hamburg has seen a recent upward trend in naturalisation rates that sticks out in national comparison (Gesemann and Roth 2014).[53] Causality between the campaign and the rising rate should not be taken for granted. For once, different countries of origin could be affected to different degrees and other alternative explanations should be considered. For example, acceleration of administrative procedures could lead to provisional upsurge. Hence, a comprehensive evaluation of the campaign would cover a longer period making use of longitudinal data, compare various origin countries, and assess minority and majority perceptions and attitudes alike.

Multivariate Analyses

Results from multivariate analyses by and large confirm the expected effects on the intention to naturalise. The models point to prevalence of legal over symbolic incentives for naturalisation. Some effects are unexpected and deserve further consideration. Notably, I ran separate regression models by gender as discussed below. However, I start with calculation of models for the whole sample. Table 4.6 shows the results of five ordinal logistic regression models. In the first two models, symbolic aspects of membership are considered without socio-demographics (M1) and with socio-demographics (M2). Then, legal aspects of membership are considered without socio-demographics (M3) and with socio-demographics (M4) before the full model is presented (M5). Variables are structured in three blocks: Symbolic aspects, legal aspects, and socio-demographics. They appear in the same sequence as the hypotheses formulated above. Symbolic aspects include feeling at home in Germany (H1a), perceived discrimination against Turks in Germany (H1b), perceived identity relevance of the Turkish passport (H2a), perceived identity relevance of the German passport (H2b), share of naturalised family members (H3a), and share of naturalised friends (H3b). Legal aspects include interest in political rights in Germany (H5), expected job-related benefits (H6), expected travel-related benefits (H7), and interest in political, property, and inheritance rights in Turkey (H8+H9). Socio-demographic variables include dummies for gender and generational status (H5), age including a quadratic term to account for non-linearity (H10), logarithmic personal income, and education in years. Next, I describe the results. Due to the logic of logarithmic regressions I do not interpret the difference in effect sizes between the five models (see Mood 2010).

---

[53] In international comparison naturalisation rates of around 2% in the last years are not outrageous.

Table 4.6 Ordered Logistic Regression on Intention to Naturalise

	M1	M2	M3
Aspects of symbolic membership			
Feel at home in Germany[i]	0.949***	0.783***	
	(5.38)	(4.13)	
Perceived group discrimination[i]	-0.605***	-0.729***	
	(3.35)	(3.82)	
Turkish passport identity-relevant[i]	-0.074	-0.108	
	(0.56)	(0.77)	
German passport identity-relevant	0.160	0.186	
	(1.27)	(1.42)	
Share of German family members	-0.219	-0.224	
	(1.52)	(1.48)	
Share of close friends that naturalised	-0.049	-0.000	
	(0.31)	(0.00)	
Aspects of legal membership			
Interest in political rights Germany[i]			0.440***
			(3.29)
Expected job-related benefits[i]			0.303**
			(2.28)
Expected travel-related benefits[i]			0.326**
			(2.44)
Interest in genuine rights Turkey[i]			-0.879***
			(6.06)
Socio-demographics			
Gender female		-0.373	
		(1.39)	
Age		-0.156*	
		(1.69)	
Age squared		0.001	
		(1.23)	
Log. Personal income[i]		0.027	
		(0.30)	
Education in years		-0.001	
Generation 1 (omitted)		(0.03)	
Generation 1.5		0.437	
		(1.36)	
Generation 2		0.764*	
Cutpoints		(1.83)	
cut1	-0.826	-5.098**	-2.153***
	(0.92)	(2.57)	(10.04)
cut2	1.528*	-2.579	0.149
	(1.68)	(1.31)	(1.00)
cut3	2.844***	-1.122	1.599***
	(3.10)	(0.57)	(8.49)
N / Mc Fadden's Pseudo R^2	218 / 0.09	218 / 0.14	218 / 0.10
AIC / BIC (df)	541 / 572	529 / 583	529 / 553

(Table continues on next page)

Table 4.6 Ordered Logistic Regression on Intention to Naturalise (cont'd)

	M4	M5
Aspects of symbolic membership		
Feel at home in Germany[i]		0.695***
		(3.53)
Perceived group discrimination[i]		-0.614***
		(3.07)
Turkish passport identity-relevant[i]		-0.028
		(0.19)
German passport identity-relevant		0.024
		(0.17)
Share of German family members		-0.321**
		(2.00)
Share of close friends that naturalised		-0.046
		(0.26)
Aspects of legal membership		
Interest in political rights Germany[i]	0.629***	0.646***
	(4.36)	(4.21)
Expected job-related benefits[i]	0.325**	0.360**
	(2.28)	(2.43)
Expected travel-related benefits[i]	0.271**	0.235*
	(1.97)	(1.67)
Interest in genuine rights Turkey[i]	-0.819***	-0.665***
	(5.35)	(4.15)
Socio-demographics		
Gender female	0.180	0.002
	(0.66)	(0.01)
Age	-0.257***	-0.204**
	(2.75)	(2.11)
Age squared	0.003**	0.002*
	(2.47)	(1.75)
Log. Personal income[i]	0.020	0.066
	(0.21)	(0.69)
Education in years	-0.000	0.003
	(0.01)	(0.09)
Generation 1 (omitted)		
Generation 1.5	0.399	0.379
	(1.25)	(1.11)
Generation 2	1.109***	0.920**
	(2.77)	(2.04)
Cutpoints		
cut1	-7.028***	-6.387***
	(3.69)	(2.94)
cut2	-4.461**	-3.535
	(2.37)	(1.64)
cut3	-2.852	-1.821
	(1.53)	(0.85)
N / Mc Fadden's Pseudo R^2	218 / 0.16	218 / 0.21
AIC / BIC (df)	508 / 556	493 / 561

|z|-statistics in parentheses, [i]variable has imputed values; * $p < 0.10$, ** $p < 0.05$, *** $p < 0.01$; Source: ACN 2012, own calculations.

The first model partly confirms the expected effects for aspects of symbolic membership. Two variables capture the perception of symbolic boundaries: feeling at home in Germany and perceived discrimination of Turks. In line with the argument of symbolic boundaries, there is a positive effect of feeling at home and a negative effect of perceived group discrimination. Both effects are statistically significant. Model one also shows the expected effects of perceived relevance of passports for the respective identities on the intention to naturalise (H2a, H2b). There is a negative effect of perceiving the Turkish passport as relevant for a Turkish identity; and there is a positive effect of perceiving the German passport as relevant for a German identity. However, neither of these effects is statistically significant. So neither are persons who feel they would lose their Turkish identity by giving up their old passport less inclined to naturalise, nor are those who feel they would gain German identity by acquisition of the new passport more inclined to naturalise. The reference group is given by persons who consider these passports irrelevant for their identities, all else being equal. For the number of naturalised kin and friends (H3a, H3b), results are contrary to the hypothesised positive effect, though not significant. Hence, there is no support for the hypothesised imitation of peers. The addition of socio-demographic variables to the regression in M2 does not change the effects in major ways. Age has a negative effect (H10) and belonging to generation 1.5 or 2 has a positive effect (H4) on naturalisation intentions. Being female has a negative statistically insignificant effect.

The third model confirms expected effects for the legal aspects. Interest in political rights in Germany has a positive effect on the intention to naturalise (H5). The expectations of job- and travel-related benefits have positive effects (H6+H7). With relation to the country of origin, interest in political and property rights in Turkey has the expected negative effect (H8+H9). All effects are statistically significant. Effects of the legal aspects remain stable after the inclusion of socio-demographics in M4. Among the socio-demographic variables, the age terms and generational status are statistically significant. As hypothesised, persons that were born (second generation) or grew up (generation 1.5) in Germany are more inclined to naturalise than those who arrived as adults. However, the effect is significant only for the second generation (H5). Age has an independent negative effect (H10). So between two individuals born in Germany the younger one has a higher inclination to naturalise all else equal. The quadratic age-term means that the increase in the negative effect decreases with age. Income and being female both have positive effects on the intention to naturalise but neither is statistically significant. However, being female now has a negative statistically insignificant effect. This is an indication that symbolic and instrumental incentives are confounded with gender, an aspect that is discussed below. Education in years has no effect on the intention to naturalise according to M4.

Model five accounts for the whole model: Symbolic, legal, and socio-demographic variables. Findings for symbolic variables are similar to the ones reported in M1 and M2. The positive effect of accommodation and the negative effect of discrimination persist and are still highly significant ($p<0.01$). Also, the negative effect of having more naturalised family members persists, and is now significant ($p<0.1$). The effect of having naturalised friends is close to zero and still not significant. While identity relevance of the German passport was somewhat harder to refute based on M1 and M2, this becomes easier based on M5. The same is true for identity relevance of the Turkish passport. Both effects are now negligible. Findings for the aspects of legal membership are similar to those in M3 and M4. Effects are relatively stable for interest in genuine rights in both countries, and aspiration of job- and travel-related benefits, though the latter is less significant now ($p<0.1$). Among the socio-demographic variables, the negative main effect and the positive marginal effect of age are statistically significant. Further, there is still a positive effect of belonging to the second generation. The effect for gender has disappeared. All other effects are similar to the prior models and are not statistically significant.

Next, predicted probabilities of the intention to naturalise are calculated in order to make the results presented in Table 4.6 more accessible for interpretation (Long and Freese 2014). They demonstrate the relative significance of the central independent variables. Calculations are based on the final regression model in Table 4.6. The probability is predicted for each of the four outcomes of the dependent variable which makes interpretation more complex than for binary outcomes. The best way to judge each ideal type is to consider the column with the highest likelihood and its neighbouring cells in Table 4.7. For example, the first ideal type (1) has the highest likelihood to answer 'rather not' followed by 'rather yes'. Hence, on average respondents are rather not inclined to naturalise, but not entirely averse. Obviously, the average respondent is merely a hypothetical case with average characteristics such as hybrid gender, 38.3 years of age, and 10.4 years of schooling. Types (2) and (3) are designed as contrasting ideals. Type (2) perceives no barriers to symbolic membership and has no interest in rights in Turkey, but neither is he legally motivated. Type (3) in contrast faces significant barriers to symbolic membership but has strong legal motives. Among the two, (3) is more likely to be inclined to naturalise which is an indication that legal motivation is more relevant than symbolic accommodation for naturalisation intentions. Types (4) and (5) give a hunch how individuals deal with the predicament of opting for either passport if they are interested in political rights in both countries. Both have no other legal motivation than the one in political rights in Germany and citizenship-specific rights in Turkey and both feel at home. The only variation is in perceived discrimination, which is high for the former and low for the latter. The predicted probabilities illustrate that symbolic exclusion can have a considerable negative impact on naturalisation intentions even if legal incentives do exist. These ideal types are particularly relevant because they show how symbolic exclusion can frustrate migrants' aspiration of political membership. Finally, types (6)-(11) disentangle age effects and generational effects. In (6)-(8), the age is held constant at 20 and generation is varied between first, 1.5, and second. The likelihood to be inclined to naturalise is lowest in the first generation and highest in the second generation. In (9)-(11), the age is 60 and the generation is varied as in (6)-(8). Predicted probabilities suggest that age is more decisive than generational status. While the generational effect is still observable, all types of the 60 years condition are more likely to be averse to naturalisation. Overall, predicted probabilities of these ideal types show that migrants with average characteristics are rarely categorically opposed to naturalisation.

Table 4.7 Predicted Probabilities of Selected Ideal Types

Ideal type	--	-	+	++
(1) Mean outcome on all variables	0.068	**0.492**	0.316	0.124
(2) Low legal motivation, low rights interest Turkey, high feel at home, no perceived discrimination, all else mean outcomes	0.051	**0.433**	**0.355**	0.161
(3) High legal motivation, low rights interest Turkey, low feel at home, high perceived discrimination, all else mean outcomes	0.011	0.146	**0.351**	**0.493**
(4) High pol. interest in Germany and Turkey, other legal motivation low, high feel at home, high perceived discrimination, all else mean outcomes	0.271	**0.595**	0.107	0.027
(5) as (4) but low perceived discrimination	0.056	**0.449**	**0.345**	0.150
(6) 20 years old, first generation, all else mean outcomes	0.029	**0.309**	**0.401**	0.261
(7) as (6) but 1.5 generation	0.020	0.239	**0.401**	**0.340**
(8) as (6) but second generation	0.012	0.157	**0.361**	**0.469**
(9) 60 years old, first generation, all else mean outcomes	0.102	**0.561**	0.253	0.084
(10) as (9) but 1.5 generation	0.072	**0.502**	0.308	0.118
(11) as (9) but second generation	0.043	**0.397**	**0.374**	0.186

Calculations based on M5-regression model in Table 4.6. Response categories 'definitely not', 'rather not', 'rather yes', 'yes, definitely'. Response category with highest probability marked for better readability. Source: ACN 2012.

A comparison of M1 with M3 and of M2 with M4 gives us some idea of the significance of legal aspects, compared to symbolic aspects of membership. Measures of fit point to a little higher relevance of legal aspects for the intention to naturalise. Namely, AIC/BIC values are slightly lower (Table 4.6) in M1 and M2 compared to M3 and M4 respectively and adj.R^2 in linear regressions (Table A4) is higher. Put differently, information on the legal motives of citizenship acquisition allows for better predictions of the intention to naturalise than knowledge of symbolic motives. Among symbolic variables, there is strong support for Hypotheses 1a and 1b. Accommodation thus positively affects the intention to naturalise and experienced collective discrimination has the opposite effect. The confirmation of the generational effect (H4) underlines the relevance of a sense of belonging to Germany. The expected effects for identity-relevance of passports established in H2a and H2b cannot be confirmed in spite of some evidence for a positive effect of identity-relevance of the German passport in M1 and M2. Legal aspects seem to explain variance in M5 that is explained by identity relevance of the German passport in M1 and M2. Hypotheses 3a and 3b on following peers' example in crossing the boundary must be rejected according to all models. However, some rights-oriented motives like interest in political rights are of course intertwined with symbolic aspects of membership. Overall, the models lend support to Hypotheses 5-10. Legal aspects are strong explanatory factors for the intention to naturalise. Overall, AIC / BIC, Mc Fadden's R^2 (Table 4.6) and Adj.R^2 (Table A4) suggest a good fit of the theoretical model.[54] Next, I present the results of separate regressions by gender.

Separate regression by gender

Separate regression models are calculated for men and women because the change of direction in the gender effect between M2 and M4 is an indication that legal and symbolic motives vary by gender. Hence, separate models serve as a robustness check. Table 4.8 reports the results of separate regression models by gender. The models contain the same independent variables like the default models (Table 4.6). However, linear effects of gender are assumed in the first series of models. This assumption is dropped in separate regressions. Overall, results show the robustness of essential effects but they also reveal some variation of effects by gender. Effects of symbolic motives for naturalisation are similar for both genders. The main boundary indicators, feeling at home and perceived group discrimination, have the same effects as before for both genders. As in the benchmark models, the remaining symbolic effects are not significant.

---

[54] All measures of fit except BIC favour M5 over the smaller models. BIC favours M3 and M4 over all other models, because it punishes more strictly than the other measures of fit for the large number of parameters in M5 compared to M3 and M4 (Best and Wolf 2010, 843). Based on the other measures of fit I would still argue for M5 since it tests the full theoretical model.

Although not significant, the negative effect of identity relevance of the Turkish passport is stronger for women and the negative effect of the share of German family members is stronger for men. Legal aspects of membership persist, but not all effects are significant for both genders. The positive effect of expected job-related benefits is significant only for men. At the same time, the negative effect of interest in citizenship-specific rights in Turkey is only significant for women.

Remarkable differences for both genders are revealed concerning the effects of socio-demographic variables. Age and generation are shown to have gender specific effects. The negative age-effect including the positive quadratic term does only exist for women. For men the effects are very small. For generational effects, it is the other way around. There are strong positive effects of belonging to the 1.5 or second generation for men, but no statistically significant effects for women. Hence, men are more likely to naturalise if they were socialised in Germany, irrespective of age. Women are more likely to naturalise if they are younger, irrespective of the country of socialization.[55] To ease interpretation, I present predicted probabilities for selected ideal types.

---

[55] I checked whether age distributions are similar across generations for each gender to rule out statistical artefacts.

Table 4.8 Ordered Logistic Regression on Intention to Naturalise by Gender

	M2 male	M2 female
Aspects of symbolic membership		
Feel at home in Germany[i]	0.899***	0.867***
	(3.36)	(2.85)
Perceived group discrimination[i]	-0.774***	-0.779***
	(2.64)	(2.74)
Turkish passport identity-relevant[i]	-0.077	-0.349
	(0.39)	(1.58)
German passport identity-relevant	0.102	0.217
	(0.51)	(1.18)
Share of German family members	-0.309	-0.064
	(1.44)	(0.27)
Share of close friends that naturalised	0.056	0.045
	(0.22)	(0.19)
Aspects of legal membership		
Interest in political rights Germany[i]		
Expected job-related benefits[i]		
Expected travel-related benefits[i]		
Interest in genuine rights Turkey[i]		
Socio-demographics		
Age	-0.092	-0.161
	(0.55)	(1.28)
Age squared	0.000	0.002
	(0.12)	(1.11)
Log. Personal income[i]	-0.082	0.104
	(0.36)	(0.91)
Education in years	0.021	-0.028
	(0.48)	(0.64)
Generation 1 (omitted)		
Generation 1.5	0.993**	-0.088
	(2.06)	(0.18)
Generation 2	1.196*	0.393
	(1.77)	(0.68)
Cutpoints		
cut1	-4.450	-4.360
	(1.43)	(1.47)
cut2	-2.365	-1.161
	(0.76)	(0.39)
cut3	-1.053	0.601
	(0.34)	(0.20)
N / Pseudo R^2	108 / 0.18	110 / 0.13
AIC / BIC (df)	274 / 314	263 / 303

(Table continues on next page)

Table 4.8 Ord. Log. Regression on Intention to Naturalise by Gender (cont'd)

	M4 m	M4 f	M5 m	M5 f
Aspects of symbolic membership				
Feel at home in Germany[i]			0.787***	0.887***
			(2.69)	(2.78)
Perceived group discrimination[i]			-0.857***	-0.691**
			(2.59)	(2.35)
Turkish passport identity-relevant[i]			-0.193	-0.026
			(0.91)	(0.11)
German passport identity-relevant			0.094	-0.060
			(0.45)	(0.30)
Share of German family members			-0.411*	-0.188
			(1.83)	(0.77)
Share of close friends that nat.			-0.074	0.137
			(0.28)	(0.54)
Aspects of legal membership				
Interest in political rights Germany[i]	0.799***	0.640***	0.868***	0.685***
	(3.57)	(2.92)	(3.53)	(2.85)
Expected job-related benefits[i]	0.348*	0.272	0.567**	0.230
	(1.67)	(1.32)	(2.46)	(1.06)
Expected travel-related benefits[i]	0.490**	0.113	0.334	0.153
	(2.30)	(0.58)	(1.49)	(0.77)
Interest in genuine rights Turkey[i]	-0.560***	-1.066***	-0.260	-1.055***
	(2.61)	(4.45)	(1.11)	(4.14)
Socio-demographics				
Age	-0.111	-0.320**	0.005	-0.331**
	(0.69)	(2.46)	(0.03)	(2.40)
Age squared	0.001	0.004**	-0.001	0.004**
	(0.36)	(2.35)	(0.45)	(2.24)
Log. Personal income[i]	-0.110	0.065	-0.040	0.075
	(0.49)	(0.58)	(0.19)	(0.61)
Education in years	0.028	-0.016	0.049	-0.030
	(0.65)	(0.36)	(1.07)	(0.63)
Generation 1 (omitted)				
Generation 1.5	1.014**	0.203	1.457***	-0.102
	(2.06)	(0.42)	(2.61)	(0.20)
Generation 2	1.614***	0.860	1.618**	0.289
	(2.66)	(1.50)	(2.23)	(0.45)
Cutpoints				
cut1	-4.856	-8.598***	-3.150	-8.907***
	(1.61)	(3.20)	(0.96)	(2.66)
cut2	-2.677	-5.476**	-0.686	-5.247
	(0.89)	(2.09)	(0.21)	(1.59)
cut3	-1.258	-3.501	0.850	-3.102
	(0.42)	(1.36)	(0.26)	(0.95)
N / Pseudo R^2	108 / 0.20	110 / 0.16	108 / 0.26	110 / 0.23
AIC / BIC (df)	263 / 298	251 / 286	258 / 309	245 / 296

|z|-statistics in parentheses, [i]variable has imputed values; * $p < 0.10$, ** $p < 0.05$, *** $p < 0.01$; Source: ACN 2012, own calculations.

Table 4.9 Predicted Probabilities of Selected Ideal Types by gender

Ideal type	--	-	+	++
(1a) Mean outcome on all variables (male)	0.093	**0.454**	0.302	0.151
(1b) Mean outcome on all variables (female)	0.035	**0.549**	0.339	0.077
(5a) High pol. interest in Germany and Turkey, other legal motivation low, high feel at home, low perceived discrimination, all else mean outcomes (male)	0.037	0.276	**0.366**	**0.321**
(5b) As (5a) (female)	0.021	**0.432**	**0.423**	0.124
(6a) 20 years old, first generation, all else mean outcomes (male)	0.073	**0.408**	0.331	0.188
(6b) as (6a) (female)	0.009	0.244	**0.490**	0.258
(7a) as (6a) but 1.5 generation (male)	0.015	0.140	0.305	**0.539**
(7b) as (6b) but 1.5 generation (female)	0.006	0.195	**0.482**	0.317
(8a) as (6a) but second generation (male)	0.018	0.159	0.323	**0.499**
(8b) as (6b) but second generation (female)	0.010	0.262	**0.489**	0.239
(9a) 60 years old, first generation, all else mean outcomes (male)	**0.594**	0.351	0.043	0.012
(9b) 60 years old, first generation, all else mean outcomes (female)	0.018	0.393	**0.446**	0.144
(10a) as (9a) but 1.5 generation (male)	0.225	**0.548**	0.168	0.059
(10b) as (9b) but 1.5 generation (female)	0.013	0.330	**0.474**	0.183
(11a) as (9a) but second generation (male)	0.254	**0.546**	0.149	0.051
(11b) as (9b) but second generation (female)	0.019	**0.416**	**0.433**	0.132

Calculations based on M5-regression model in Table 4.6. Response categories 'definitely not', 'rather not', 'rather yes', 'yes, definitely'. Response categories with highest probability marked for better readability. Source: ACN 2012.

Table 4.9 shows predicted probabilities of the regression (M5m/f in) by gender to clarify the effects.[56] Overall, the predicted probabilities of intending to naturalise are similar for both genders (1a/b). Systematic variation of certain characteristics reveals the gender-specificity of some effects but the differences are moderate. Persons with strong political interest in both countries, otherwise low legal motivation, strong feeling at home, and low perceived discrimination are somewhat more likely to intend to naturalise if they are male (5a/b). Against the background of results shown in Table 4.8 the stronger negative effect of rights interest in Turkey for women may explain the gender difference. Next, I calculate predicted probabilities with systematic variation of age and gender to disentangle both effects. I start with a 20 year old person with otherwise mean characteristics and vary the generational status (6a/b-8a/b). A first generation migrant is more likely to be inclined to naturalise if she is female, whereas members of 1.5 and 2nd generation are more inclined if they are male. Next, the same procedure is repeated for a 60 year old person with otherwise mean characteristics. Here, irrespective of generational status, women are more inclined to naturalise, but the

---

[56] The numbers for the types are equal to those in Table 4.7 to facilitate comparison.

difference is most pronounced in the first generation. Hence, between a young person (20 years) and an old person (60 years) the younger is more likely to be willing to naturalise if it is a man, whereas for the older person the likelihood is higher if it is a she. This holds for all generational statuses except the first. Migrants of the first generation at both ages and with otherwise average characteristics are generally more inclined if they are female. It is important to note that the negative age effect for women is counterbalanced by the quadratic age-term, resulting in a turning point at age 42.3. At that age, women are least likely to be willing to naturalise compared to other ages.

Robustness Checks

Several robustness checks were performed on the models reported in Table 4.6. A first set of checks assesses robustness to the addition of further variables. It could be argued that several other variables not included in the models are relevant explanatory variables. Language skills and the residence status define eligibility for naturalisation and might therefore systematically affect the intention to naturalise. The addition of language skills to M5 does not change results. Results are neither changed if a dummy-variable for a limited vs. unlimited residence status is included although there is a positive non-significant effect of having a limited status on naturalisation intentions.[57] Finally, the eligibility to naturalise was controlled for in a more encompassing way as follows. All persons who declared not to be eligible, arrived less than eight years ago, or reported 'poor' or 'very poor' German skills were excluded. The application of the models on this subset of cases causes only minor changes in the results while reducing the sample size to N=175. It therefore seems reasonable to keep the cases in the sample. Further, I consider the possibility of a model misspecification. The results presented above rely crucially on the parametric assumptions of the logistic model. As an alternative specification, I consider a linear model. Table A4 shows the results to remain unchanged with respect to sign and significance. The results of a logistic regression with relaxed proportional odds assumption (gologit) are shown in table A5.[58] Here, five out of 18 variables have non-proportional odds. The affected variables include identity relevance of the Turkish passport, share of close friends who naturalised, education, and gender. The variation of gamma coefficients supports the calculation of separate regressions by gender. Although

---

[57] 16% of respondents have a limited residence status.
[58] Gologit models relax the assumption of proportional odds of the four outcomes of the dependent variable (R. Williams 2006).

the gologit model improves on the precision of coefficients, I stick to the proportional odds model for reasons of parsimony.

A second set of robustness checks deals with potential interaction effects. I include interaction terms of socio-demographic and explanatory variables into the benchmark model (M5) to test for subgroup-specific effects. Results for separate regression models by gender are reported above. Therefore, gender effects are not systematically reassessed here. I systematically test interaction effects of independent variables with education, age, and generational status. Indeed, the addition of interaction terms reveals non-linear effects of some independent variables. Net-effects that have a different sign for different sub-groups and result from significant partial effects are most worrisome. However, I also report instances of noteworthy sub-group specific differences. These sub-group specific effects are revealed by introducing dummy-variables for educational degrees, age, and generational status respectively. As for education, the introduction of interaction effects yields no clear indication of non-linear effects. The inclusion of interaction terms with age supports findings from separate regressions by gender (see Table A6 in appendix). The interaction term of age and female is positive and reveals a negative main effect for women (M5b). The age effect remains stable as in the default models. The interpretation is that the negative effect of age is less pronounced for women.[59] Another noteworthy interaction with age is found for the share of naturalised friends (M5a). The main effect is now positive but the interaction term is negative as is the effect of age. Thus, there is in fact a positive effect of having naturalised friends that is weaker for older migrants. The calculation of predicted probabilities for persons with different shares of naturalised friends and with different age (20 vs. 60) reveals a much stronger intention to naturalise of those who have friends if they are 20 compared to those who are 60 years old.[60] The introduction of an interaction term for feeling at home in Germany and age yields a negative main effect (M5c). Owed to a positive interaction term, the net-effect is positive for old people. Young individuals are even less likely to be willing to naturalise if they feel at home. As for interactions with generational status, two findings stick out (M5d). The main effect of feeling at home in Germany is positive, but smaller for the second generation once the interaction term is taken into account. The positive main effect of the second generation means that they are overall more inclined to naturalise,

---

[59] A comparison of predicted probabilities for the four outcomes of the dependent variable based on M5c gives more insight. Variation of age (20 vs. 60) and gender (all other variables are held constant at mean values) indicates that gender is more decisive than age. Men have a higher propensity to intend to naturalise at both ages (at age 20 Pr (DV='Yes, definitely')= 0.8).

[60] The predicted probability for a strong inclination to naturalise is 0.6 at age 20 and only 0.03 at age 60 for persons with the majority of their friends naturalised, everything else equal (calculated based on M5b).

but for other reasons than feeling at home. The interaction effect and the generational main effect are only significant for the second generation. All other interactions are not sufficiently robust to question the results of the standard models reported in Table 4.6.

Accounting for the sample size, the default models are as parsimonious as possible. Treating education as a continuous variable measured in years may be imprecise because some educational interaction-effects are actually non-linear but it seems justified because the inclusion of education-dummies does not change the reported results in major ways. Overall, results are robust to several tests. However, the tests also suggest that some effects vary by age and by generational status. The share of naturalised friends, which was assumed to have no effect based on the default models, has a positive effect that diminishes with age. Similarly, no effect was assumed for gender based on the default models but interaction with age reveals a negative effect for women that diminishes with age. For feeling at home, the effect is even reversed compared to the default models, but the negative effect diminishes with age until it becomes positive. The interaction effect of feeling at home with generational status corroborates this finding. While feeling at home generally has a positive effect, it is smaller for the second generation than for first and 1.5 generation. If interaction terms for generation and age are introduced in a single model, the interaction of feeling at home with age prevails (M5f in Tab.A6). Hence, feeling at home has a slightly negative effect on naturalisation intentions of young individuals, but is increasingly positive for naturalisation intentions of older individuals.[61]

Limitations

Despite efforts to enhance response as recommended by the literature (Edwards et al. 2002; Porst 2001), the response rate is just 12.5%. Shrinking response rates recent decades have been recognised as a general problem in surveys (Leeuw and Heer 2002) and for ethnic minorities in particular (Deding, Fridberg, and Jakobsen 2008; Feskens et al. 2006). The good news is that the entire population is ethnic minority; therefore biased response by origin is not a concern. Generally, non-representative selection of participants into the survey should be considered irrespective of the response rate. As Groves justly points out, "higher response rates do not necessarily reduce nonresponse bias for any survey or any given estimate" (Groves 2006, 663) and as Hellevik (2015) convincingly shows by using different survey data covering identical questions, low nonresponse rates

---

[61] According to M5f the turning point is at 26 years of age. Since the youngest sampled individual is 16 years old, the net effects for younger persons are not as strongly negative as it may seem.

may still lead to accurate results. In this section, I consider selectivity with respect to a number of characteristics, starting with gender and age. A paired t-test for equal means does not reject the null-hypothesis that both genders are represented equally (p>0.79). The distribution of age in the sample resembles a normal distribution. A comparison of realised and original sample reveals little difference between the two and a QQ-plot reveals no difference between age distributions of original and realised sample (Fig.A1).

Apart from age and gender, the distribution of respondent characteristics in the original sample and in the population is unknown. Following Groves and Peytcheva's (2008) recommendations, I consider characteristics that may cause systematic selection into survey participation. As shown above, persons inclined to naturalise and persons refusing to naturalise are equally likely to have answered the questionnaire. Further factors that are likely to affect addressees' inclination to respond include general interest in the question of naturalisation, literacy, affinity to social surveys, political interest and the desire to voice needs. While distributions of these characteristics in population and sample are unknown, there are reference points from other studies for actual distributions of German skills (Table A7), political interest (Table A8), and education (Table A9). The distribution of the respective variables points to an overrepresentation of educated, literate, and politically interested persons, in short, the top-groups. German skills, political interest, and educational degrees of the sample are above the population average. Hence, descriptive statistics should be interpreted carefully. Along the same lines, general interest in the issue of naturalisation is likely to cause an oversampling of two groups: Those with a strong inclination to naturalise and those who are unwilling and want to communicate their reasons. Oversampling of these groups should increase variation on the dependent variable.

What are the implications of these misrepresentations? Higher educated persons could differ systematically from those with lower or no formal education. For example, they might expect benefits for their job from naturalisation more often, because citizenship tends to be more relevant for white-collar jobs than for blue-collar jobs, as they are typically associated with higher rather than lower education. Multivariate analysis is a remedy to this simple kind of misrepresentation as long as the respective variables can be controlled for and as long as all groups are represented in the survey. A problem arises if the strength of effects of independent variables on naturalisation intentions is different for over- and underrepresented groups. Estimates of multivariate analyses are biased if there is an interaction effect between belonging to a misrepresented group (e.g. education) and one of the explanatory variables (e.g. expected travel-benefits), i.e. if an interest in travel-benefits increases naturalisation intentions of Gymnasium graduates but not of persons without formal education. This has been accounted for and no significant effect variation by educational degree has been identified (see above). Finally, as in any statistical analysis, unobserved variables that influence the naturalisation decision could bias results. For example, if dual citizenship is tolerated in some cases, this might change those persons' naturalisation intentions from the outset.[62] As a bottom line, the selectivity of the sample causes biased descriptive statistics but is less problematic for multivariate analysis.

4.4   Summary and Discussion

The empirical findings support the majority of the hypotheses. According to the measures of fit, the theoretical model does a good job in predicting naturalisation intentions. I summarize and discuss findings first for symbolic motives and then for legal ones.

Two of the symbolic motives for naturalisation are supported by the models. Individuals who feel at home in Germany are more inclined to naturalise and those who perceive discrimination of Turks as a group are less inclined. However, the introduction of interaction terms for feeling at home with age reveals that the positive effect is holds only for older, but not for younger persons. Further, I hypothesised that group identities are connected to the passports. However, there is no evidence that identity-relevance of passports affects naturalisation intentions. Individuals who perceive the Turkish passport to be expressive of a Turkish identity are not less inclined to naturalise and those who perceive the German passport to be conducive to attaining a German identity are not more inclined to naturalise. The hypothesised effects of having naturalised peers are neither supported by the models. Instead, having naturalised family members decreases the inclination to naturalise and having naturalised friends has no effect. Finally, I hypothesised that individuals who have been socialised in Germany are more inclined to naturalise. Indeed, there is some evidence that the second generation is on average more inclined to naturalise than the first generation. However, for those who were born abroad but arrived in Germany during childhood or adolescence – the 1.5 generation – effects are not significant. Hence, the hypothesised positive effect of a German socialization is only partly supported.

The perception of bright symbolic boundaries weakens the willingness to naturalise. The positive effect of accommodation in Germany (feeling at home

---

[62] That would also thwart the typology of Table 3.2. Thirteen survey participants stated in the respective item that they may have both citizenships but the response is uncorrelated with naturalisation intentions (r = -0.04) and their exclusion from regression does not change results presented in Table 5.7.

and generational status) and the negative effect of perceived group discrimination underline the empirical significance of immigrants' relation to the majority group for naturalisation. Following the concept of symbolic boundaries, these factors are understood as indicators of immigrants' perception of legal rules and of their relation to the majority group. The effect of feeling at home, an indicator for belonging, on naturalisation intentions is positive. The higher inclination to naturalise among generation 1.5 and second generation was interpreted as resulting from a stronger emotional attachment to Germany. However, models that account for interactions indicate that younger generations' higher inclination to naturalise does not result from their stronger feeling at home. Feeling at home positively affects naturalisation intentions of older individuals. Reasons for the stronger tendency of young individuals to naturalise remain to be explored.

It should be mentioned that the indicator of feeling at home overlaps with two alternative indicators used in other studies. One is the identification with the host country (Diehl 2002; Ersanilli and Koopmans 2010; Söhn 2008); the other one is the intention to stay (Diehl and Blohm 2011; 2008). Both of these indicators measure a similar concept as feeling at home. The problem with host country identification is that it is often presented as irreconcilable with ethnic identification in the German public debate. The second alternative of 'intention to stay' is a more neutral concept but incentives concerning naturalisation are ambiguous. On the one hand, rights connected to Turkish citizenship are more relevant for persons wiling to return. On the other hand, those who return would benefit from the unconditional right to re-enter Germany as German citizens. Another issue with the intention to stay arises from potential ethnic boundaries. The willingness to return to Turkey is not necessarily an a priori plan. It can be a consequence of feeling excluded rather than a reason for reduced investment in social and cultural host country capital. For these reasons, the concept of feeling at home is preferred over plans to return and host country identification.

The negative effect of having naturalised family members contradicts earlier findings. As with age, the selection procedure was offered as an explanation for this unexpected result. Street (2013) reports the phenomenon of family strategies for the case of Austria and United States; individual family members may deliberately decide to refrain at a moment when the rest of the family naturalises. The diversification of citizenship statuses within the family is a potential motive. This may explain why single older family members refrain. The negative effect of naturalised family members for male Turks in separate regression models indicate that mothers rather than fathers naturalise with their offspring. The introduction of jus soli in 2000 has eliminated an incentive of naturalisation for parents, namely, naturalisation with the aim of endowing under-aged offspring with host country citizenship (Street 2014).

Legal motives in particular have the expected effects on the intention to naturalise, all else equal. Namely, individuals who appreciate participation in elections are more inclined to naturalise. The same holds for those who expect job-related or travel-related benefits from naturalisation. An interest in rights that are connected to Turkish citizenship has the opposite effect. Those who value their political rights in Turkey and the right to heritage and property in Turkey are less inclined to naturalise. The main models further support the hypothesis that the cumulative legal benefits of rights connected to the German citizenship are higher for younger persons, while legal benefits connected to Turkish citizenship are more relevant for older persons. However, robustness checks indicate a reverse effect for female minority members. Female individuals are more inclined to naturalise when they are older.

The interest in voting and in property rights is closely connected to the intention to naturalise. While the positive effect of political interest in Germany confirms former findings, the negative effect of interest in citizenship-specific rights in Turkey has not been assessed before. I have argued above that based on Prospect Theory (Tversky and Kahneman 1986), we should expect a negative net-effect even if the gains of German citizenship were evaluated as highly as the benefits of the Turkish one. This finding shows that the attachment to the Turkish passport is rooted in concrete legal interests rather than affection. The absence of effects for identity-relevance of both passports supports that interpretation. Next to enfranchisement, there are further rights-oriented motives that increase inclinations to naturalise. The expectation of job- and travel-related benefits increase inclinations of all groups. While researchers already explored the positive economic effects of naturalisation, the expectation of a citizenship premium by immigrants and its effect on their naturalisation intention was assessed in this study for the first time.

Overall, younger individuals are more inclined to naturalise than older migrants, which was interpreted as a cumulative effect of legal benefits over the expected time of residence in Germany. If regression models are run separately by gender, it turns out that the negative age effect holds only for women, whereas generational status is predictive of male naturalisation intentions. As an alternative to separate models, I included an interaction effect for gender and age in the benchmark model. In that model the main effects of female gender and age are negative, whereas the interaction effect is positive. Hence, women are overall less inclined to naturalise compared to men but the negative age effect is weaker for them. Diehl and Blohm (2011, 2008), for example, use two datasets and also find negative age effects on the intention to naturalise, but positive age effects on actual naturalisations. This suggests self-selection into the respective populations. Persons who are less likely to naturalise remain part of the non-naturalised population while getting older. Older persons in a sample of un-naturalised are on average less likely to be willing to naturalise as a mere result of the sampling procedure. In a sample of naturalised persons, it would be the other way around since, once naturalised, they remain so and get older.

Measures of fit indicate that legal motives explain a larger share in the variation of naturalisation intentions than symbolic motives. Still, findings suggest that improved accommodation and reduced collective discrimination of aliens would increase naturalisation rates. That would need a joined effort of politics and society; a complementary blurring of legal and symbolic boundaries. Even where political reforms aim at blurring and shifting legal boundaries, transformations of symbolic boundaries occur only once these legal changes are reflected in everyday communications between immigrants and members of the cultural mainstream. The next chapter explores the nature of these communications. How do majority group and immigrants relate to each other? More precisely, how do immigrants perceive this relation and what are the consequences for their interaction with German mainstream society?

5. Qualitative Interviews: Stigmatization and Destigmatization

5.1 Aim and Scope

Social scientists rarely have the chance to talk to participants of surveys. It is a major asset of this research project that survey participants could be contacted for in-depth follow-up interviews. However, qualitative interviews are also necessary because of the impossibility to illuminate the subject of symbolic membership merely through standardized questionnaires. The in-depth interviews' purpose is to tackle three sets of questions. First, the interviews trace the processes of individual boundary perceptions from its roots to its consequences. They explore the empirical substance of the boundary concept. Thus, they yield answers to the question how individuals come to perceive symbolic exclusion or inclusion. Second, they provide insight into how individuals deal with experienced exclusion. What strategies do they develop to deal with it and what are these strategies' implications? And third, the analysis of interviews aims at disentangling the meaning of legal and symbolic aspects of membership for naturalisation.

The chapter starts with a description of the process of data collection including sampling, interview method, and the role of the interviewer (5.1). After presenting the method of analysis, the results of this analysis are structured in four blocks. I address minority members' boundary perception first. Do they feel excluded and why? Next, I address their particular responses to exclusion at the level of action. Since actors differ in their combination of particular responses, I third describe their general response strategies at the level of actors. Finally, I address the implications of these strategies for respondents' constructions of meanings of citizenship (5.2). In the discussion, I show how my findings relate to research on symbolic boundaries and to research on responses to stigmatization. Further, I relate my findings to alternative theoretical concepts. In the final section, I discuss responses' implications for naturalisation (5.3).

5.2 Data Collection

Sampling

The idea was to sample interview participants purposefully from the survey. Obviously, expression of will to participate in eventual follow-up interviews was voluntary. More than one hundred survey respondents (44%) provided contact information and agreed to participate in personal interviews. Categories for the sampling procedure have been developed based on results from multivariate analysis. For the purpose of sampling interview participants, predictors of naturalisation intentions have been condensed to two dimensions: Perceived permeability of symbolic boundary (blurred or shifted vs. bright) and rights-oriented motivation to naturalise (weak vs. strong). The first dimension combines information of two variables: feeling at home and perceived discrimination of Turks. The second one combines information on political interest in Germany, labour-related benefits, travel-related benefits, and rights interest in Turkey. Four ideal types of motivational structures of immigrants result and more vague motivational structures are excluded. Hence, respondents with neither strong nor weak motivation, or neither strong nor weak boundary perception, were not contacted. This strategy is known as "sampling according to schedule" (*Qualitative Stichprobenpläne*) or "selective sampling" (Kelle and Kluge 2010, 50). Thanks to the survey, there is rich information on potential interviewees beforehand. The typology serves to organize cases and develop some guiding questions. However, gathering evidence for or against this typology is not the aim of the interviews. The central goal is to add new information that was impossible to obtain based on the survey.

Since resources for in-depth interviews were limited, and not all types could be interviewed, it was an obvious strategy to select those types that allow for the least clear predictions of the intention to naturalise. A person perceiving the symbolic boundary as blurred or shifted and having strong instrumental incentives to naturalise is likely to have a strong inclination to naturalise (1). In the opposite case of a perceived bright symbolic boundary and weak rights-oriented motives, naturalisation is very unlikely (2). The remaining types are the most indeterminate ones. An immigrant who perceives the symbolic boundary as blurred or shifted and has a weak or no rights-oriented motivation: will she naturalise (3)? And what is likely to happen in the opposite case of a perceived bright boundary and strong instrumental motives (4)? Is the rights-oriented motivation a sufficient condition for naturalisation and the symbolic boundary of minor importance? Then naturalisation is rather likely in (4). Or is the perception of the symbolic boundary as weak a necessary condition, irrespective of existing legal motives? Even if legal motives do matter less, they may still be a necessary condition for naturalisation. Since answers seem to be rather straightforward for types (1) and (2), and not very clear for (3) and (4), the two latter types are more interesting for in-depth interviews.

Interview Method

The interviews followed the approach of the Problem-Centred Interview (PCI) (Witzel and Reiter 2012). They were conducted in late 2013 and mid 2014 in German with 15 participants from ACN 2012 who had consented to the follow-up. Witzel and Reiter (2012) characterize the PCI as an approach that takes the middle course between standardized non-reactive interviewing and narrative non-intervening interviewing. The main idea is to involve the interviewee into a process of active understanding. The first question is very open and ideally provokes a long opening account by the respondent. The guideline may contain several areas of interest, but in the course of the interview, the interviewer addresses only topics mentioned by the interviewee sticking to the sequence in which they are mentioned. The opening question in this study refers to the nexus of immigration and integration but in a rather open way: "How was it when you first came to Germany?" The beginning was varied slightly for those born in Germany. The first question for these people would be how it was to grow up in a different country than their parents. Whether respondents mentioned them or not, I addressed three additional areas of interest: experienced discrimination, feelings of accommodation, and citizenship.[63] Each of them aimed at provoking longer narrations. Besides, interviewees had answered the survey questionnaire one year earlier and therefore they may have remembered a broader range of topics potentially relevant to me. In addition, they knew from the contact letter for interview recruitment that my main interest was in citizenship acquisition. So while I did not ask them to relate to specific motives, I did introduce the three mentioned areas of interest. The issue of citizenship was introduced towards the end, in order to have them recount their experiences first, before having them reflect on the more abstract question of citizenship acquisition the consequences of which refer to a hypothetical future. Besides, the question of naturalisation tends to inspire reference to the political discourse that is further removed from respondents' personal experiences.

---

[63] The respective questions are "Have you ever had the impression of being treated differently?", "How do you feel in this country?", "Have you ever thought about German citizenship?".

The choice of the PCI is adequate for the broader research design of this study. The issues involved in naturalisation decisions are well researched and the research question is rather delineated. I launched the study with a survey instead of qualitative interviews for this reason. Considering the prior knowledge, it was pointless to conduct fully open narrative interviews. Fully structured interviews would also not improve our insight from the standardized survey. The PCI is a compromise between these two. It allows for a rather clear demarcation of the thematic field, while leaving space for respondents' interpretations and constructions of meaning. In order to deepen insights from the survey, it was reasonable to introduce the two thematic fields mentioned in addition to the opening question and the issue of citizenship. Table 5.1 presents an overview of interview participants including pseudonyms and some basic characteristics.

Table 5.1 Interview Participants and Survey Results

ID	pseudonym	symbolic boundary	instrumental motivation	type	age	generation
1	Yakup Karadeniz	strong	strong	4	60	1.5
2	Emre Güner	strong	strong	4	39	1
3	Ümit Okay	strong	strong	4	39	1
4	Ali Bilgic	strong	strong	4	59	1.5
5	Recep Dogan	strong	strong	4	27	1
6	Hatice Yilmaz	strong	strong	4	40	2
7	Zelife Arslan	strong	strong	4	40	1.5
8	Tayfun Akgün	strong	strong	4	39	1.5
9	Serkan Demiroglu	strong	strong	4	30	2
10	Hüseyin Topcu	weak	weak	3	35	1
11	Enes Demir	weak	weak	3	48	1.5
12	Murat Öztürk	weak	weak	3	43	1.5
13	Ibrahim Kaya	weak	weak	3	49	1.5
14	Zuhal Özcan	weak	weak	3	40	1
15	Lale Yildirim	weak	weak	3	51	1.5
16	Erkan Yildirim	Partner interview		-	50	1

Symbolic boundary, instrumental motivation, and type are based on the survey. Source: ACN 2012. Some but not all interviewees adapted the orthography of their names. In pseudonyms the orthography is adapted.

Selectivity and Role of the Interviewer[64]

This section discusses the selectivity of the sample and the role of the interviewer regarding respondents' self-presentation. The interviews are concerned with

---

[64] To emphasize neutrality I use the third person in this section although author and interviewer are identical.

the relation of Turkish residents and mainstream. At the same time the interviewee and interviewer are representatives the respective groups. The interviewer was an educated young white male with phenotypical features that are considered common in Germany and rare in Turkey. In addition, he was not fluent in Turkish and it was obvious after the letter and phone call that the language of the interviews would be German. These characteristics may have discouraged participation of potential interviewees at several stages of the sampling procedure. The selectivity of the survey is quickly reviewed here, since it conditions the sample for qualitative interviews. At the stage of the survey, bilingual letters and questionnaires aimed at minimizing drop out due to language. The relatively high percentage of Turkish questionnaires (41%) is indicative of a successful strategy. However, irrespective of language, some person may distance themselves from German society. Such persons are less likely to have participated than those who are interested in a friendly relationship with German society. Among those who participated in the survey, not all agreed to participate in the interview. This means another hurdle resulting in systematic drop out. However, there are indications that interview volunteers are not systematically different from those who refrained. Among volunteers, 40% filled out the Turkish questionnaire (survey 41%) and 41% were female (survey 48%). Also, the socio-economic status of volunteers was similar to that of survey participants.[65] At the stage of sampling for qualitative interviews, there were two further hurdles. The intentional two sub-groups was part of the sampling strategy. Members of these sub-groups differ systematically from the ones that were interviewed. The second hurdle was the unintentional exclusion of persons who were not fluent enough for fixing a date for the interview. As a consequence, the interviewed ones are more likely to be fluent in German, are confident enough to meet a member of mainstream society, and are unafraid to encounter a young male. Consequentially, females, persons with poor German skills, and persons with low self-confidence were less likely to be interviewed. Indeed, there were more male than female interviewees and, as shown below, many of them have strong self-confidence. Two potential interviews failed because of language problems on the telephone. In one of these cases, the telephone was handed to the male partner who rejected the interview of his wife. In the other case, the respondent seemed willing but communication was too difficult. In both cases, the potential interviewees were female. Still, compared to common procedures like convenience- or snowball-sampling the strategy of following-up on the survey may have the advantage of generating

---

[65] The mean income of interview volunteers is 1336 Euros and the mean income of survey participants is 1301 Euros, the standard variation being slightly higher for volunteers (1248) compared to survey participants (1070). The distribution of educational degrees is similar in both populations.

some initial trust and commitment to reaching persons who are usually more difficult to reach for qualitative interviews.

For those who were actually interviewed, a second set of questions concerning selectivity emerges. What are the possible consequences of the interviewer's characteristics for the way interviewees presented themselves? What was their motivation to meet the interviewer? The reasons for voluntary participation are similar to the reasons for survey participation. First of all, being interviewed means getting attention. Getting attention can be interesting for various motives that are not mutually exclusive: using the interviewer as a multiplier for political interest, gathering information about the naturalisation procedure, giving an example of a good citizen, and getting recognition or consolation from someone with relatively high social status. All of these motivations can be found among the persons that were interviewed. Some of them are not necessarily disadvantageous. The interviewer focussed participants' attention to interview issues and offered addressing issues of participants' choice at the end of the interview. Further, in some interviewees there were partners present, who interfered with their own agendas. Here, the interviewer aimed to get informed consent for interviewing both partners. In summary, questions of selectivity seem more problematic than participants' personal agendas during the interviews. However, selectivity is an even greater problem in alternative sampling procedures.

5.3 Negotiating Symbolic Boundaries

This section is structured as follows. Interview analysis follows after a short clarification of the method of analysis. The analysis starts with an interpretation of boundaries between Turkish residents and majority group. Then I identify particular responses to exclusion at the level of action. At the actor-level, the combinations of and the relevance given to particular responses result in general response types. I reflect particular and general response strategies in the light of the MFS. Finally, I present immigrants' construction of meaning of citizenship in order to understand the interplay of symbolic and legal aspects in naturalisation intentions. I conclude with a summary and discussion of main findings (5.3).

Method of Analysis

In order to analyse the interviews in a systematic way, interviews were transcribed, and then organized following a twofold strategy of "subsumptive" and "abductive" coding using a coding software (Kelle and Kluge 2010, 61; also 'heuristic coding' Kelle 2006, 448). Subsumptive coding starts with some basic categories that are refined and changed in the process of coding by comparison among cases. Abductive codes are developed from the interview material. The aim is to find categories that abstract from individual cases while remaining sufficiently neat to be informative. Initial categories were given by the interview issues: discrimination, accommodation, and motives for and against naturalisation.[66] These initial ideas derived from theory and empirical findings and guided the analysis of interviews. The development of new codes drew on suggestions by Saldaña's (2013) coding manual. Glaser and Strauss (1967) criticize the use of 'formal theory' as predetermined and undermining the strength of qualitative analysis. In order to uphold the strength of openness, the guiding theoretical concepts are treated as 'sensitizing' rather than defined and testable (cf. Kelle and Kluge 2010, 28ff). Symbolic boundary and its corollary of symbolic exclusion, for example, were such sensitizing concepts. However, former conceptualizations of symbolic boundaries are rather vague and not founded in individual practices. They refer to dominant conceptions, general discourses, and institutions such as citizenship, religion, ethnicity, and language. Others have addressed responses to stigmatization. However, those researchers tend to neglect the institutional support of symbolic boundaries. My interviews did not address symbolic exclusion explicitly. The aim was to understand how individuals relate to their country of residence and what considerations they make while reflecting on citizenship acquisition. Some mentioned exclusion, and implicitly 'boundaries', as consequential for their naturalisation intentions, while others did not. Immigrants' perceptions of boundaries define symbolic membership and whether there are consequences for naturalisation. Therefore, codes are introduced only for boundary aspects mentioned by respondents. Similarly, there are no prior assumptions about individual motives related to legal membership. Some motives may even be unknown from the literature. In that sense, the interview analysis provided here is inductive, open to new findings and new interpretations by respondents.

The development of particular and general responses to exclusion follows Kelle and Kluge's (2010; Kluge 2000) approach of empirically guided construction of types. They propose a four step procedure for the development of "empirically grounded types". The process starts with an identification of relevant dimensions. Second, cases are grouped according to their similarity to arrive at internally homogeneous categories. The third step is an analysis of meaningful

---

[66] The example of the initial code 'racial discrimination' may illustrate the flexibility of the coding scheme. It ended up as a sub-category to 'evaluation of Germans / Germany' and has further sub-categories of its own that specify the source or place of discrimination (e.g. 'at work', 'at school', 'police / public office' etc.).

relationships between cases. The purpose is to identify common attributes that make for the definition of types. Finally, the resulting types are described in detail by means of their attributes and by meaningful relationships with other types. This is an iterative procedure that is repeated until a coherent typology results. The consistency of the categories is questioned at each stage of the process. The final step is implemented once types have passed systematic tests of the preceding steps.

Perceived Boundaries Between

A majority of respondents perceives symbolic boundaries between immigrants and the majority group as bright. However, they have different reasons for doing so and different ways to deal with it. Interviewees' experience of boundaries can be roughly differentiated into two thematic fields: ethnicity and religion. The separation of the two domains is an induction from the interviews that is ideal typical and does not translate back to the empirical level in all cases.[67] It remains a heuristic categorization to present the things of boundaries in a more structured way. Since the author's translations of interview passages are by no means infallible, original quotations are attached as endnotes.

Ethnicity – Turkish Otherness

The ethnic component of symbolic boundary construction pools four markers mentioned in the interviews: language, phenotype, name, and habits. Several interviewees believe naturalisation would not change their standing with respect to the majority group because of their ethnicity. In their experience, having an accent, dark skin, black hair, or a Turkish name inhibits their recognition as German fellow citizens. In other words, the visibility and audibility of their ethnic difference provide for a negative self-definition of the stronger group. These characteristics are instrumental towards defining a bright symbolic boundary. However, many experiences of exclusion do not refer to specific difference. Labels like 'Turk' and 'foreigner' have a life of their own and the attribution of these labels is not necessarily related to individual properties and legal givens. Often, interviewees use these labels as self-evident ascriptions or self-descriptions. For example, the notion of being a foreigner in both countries, although based on experience, is reported like a familiar cliché. Serkan Demi-

---

[67]Both of them fit Goffman's category of phylogenetic stigma that comprise race, nation, and religion (1963).

roglu, second generation Turkish resident and day labourer, succinctly points out this boundary issue.

I'm pretty well Germanized, if you want to use that term, right? I've got more of the German mentality and hear a lot, you're no Turk no more and whatnot. Pretty common. When you are in Turkey as a Turk, you're a German. When you're here, you're always foreigner. (Serkan Demiroglu)[i]

Of course, persons of Turkish descent are not only made 'others'. The social category of 'Turk' is also devalued. In the view of some, 'Turk' and 'foreigner' are synonyms for a social category that is a nuisance to Germany at best and sometimes even a threat.

Well, if you refer to foreigners, you automatically refer to Turks. If something's wrong in the German state – and it's against foreigners – then it's mostly against Turks. Turks are the – there is a word for that – scapegoats. No matter which nationalities fuck up somehow, well, they're the Turks. That's sort of sad, because there are enough Turks who have been here long enough and established themselves and are perhaps self-employed, or they do a decent job, but still they are all lumped together. (Ibrahim Kaya)[ii]

The citizenship issue makes this boundary more salient because the possibility of naturalisation raises a crucial question for old and new Germans alike: what does it take to be German? Is legal membership a sufficient condition for symbolic membership? In the view of many interviewees, it is not. Tayfun Akgün made the experiment. He claimed to be naturalised in order to test whether his colleagues would treat him differently, but he was still referred to as "*der Ausländer*".[68] Others simply assume that it would make no change because cultural belonging is defined in ethnic terms.

Because the person won't change. That is, if I had German citizenship now, to my colleagues, I would still be the Ibrahim. I sure have the German ID but I am still the Turk, or the *Kanake* [derogatory for Turks; NW] as some colleagues say – for fun of course – and that I will remain. I will remain that a hundred percent. (Ibrahim Kaya)[iii]

In the remainder of this section, I contrast the boundary perceptions of Yakup Karadeniz (ID1) and Ali Bilgic (ID4). The comparison is meaningful because they immigrated under similar circumstances, but diverge in their experiences with the host country. They both immigrated in the framework of their apprenticeship, to learn their profession in a German hotel. Yakup Karadeniz married in Turkey, worked 40 years in German gastronomy, and invested his earnings in small business in Germany and real estate in Turkey. More recently, he sold his German business and has been working as a taxi driver ever since. Ali Bilgic left

---

[68] The term *Ausländer* (foreigner) is the legal category for non-Germans. The popular use is somewhat different and often includes Germans with non-German ancestors. In those cases, the official term used in German media and public sources is 'persons with migration background'. However, in non-official contexts *Ausländer* is still common. Also, some interviewees used the term as a neutral self-description. Further, the term is common in xenophobic contexts.

the hotel business, became a bodybuilder, and worked in various gyms. Finally, he established his own gym that went bankrupt five years ago. Today he carries a huge debt, lives on social security and small jobs suffering precarious working conditions in the gym business. Yakup Karadeniz' professional life has been rather successful but he is frustrated with German society. Experiences of racial discrimination mix with other experiences of rejection: His children face problems in the labour market because of their ethnicity and religion, he reports personal experiences of ethnic discrimination with police officers or other public officials, and finally, the 'NSU affair' augmented his mistrust.[69] These experiences feed a general uneasiness.

> German society doesn't perceive foreigners the way they are as human beings. Instead, they focus on the passport, if you have citizenship. That's very annoying. That is why I don't want to become German, because - to what end? I can work, I earn my money, I pay taxes and I have been in Germany for 42 years. For 42 years! And I cannot vote. Why not? (Yakup Karadeniz)[iv]

This discomfort keeps him from naturalisation in spite of his interest in franchise. He fulfils all necessarily criteria for an entitlement to German citizenship. He could naturalise, if voting rights were his main priority. But subjectively, he would lose one club membership without full recognition in the other one. In other words, bright boundary perception seems to impede his naturalisation although it is unclear to what extent that mirrors a personal ethnic conception of belonging.

> I won't change citizenship because of that. Why? I'll always remain Turk. My identity card holds my name. I am Yakup Karadeniz, hence, I remain Yakup Karadeniz. No matter if the ID cards says ‚German'. How can I be German? I have a different name. (Yakup Karadeniz)[v]

Although Ali Bilgic's professional life was less successful than Yakup Karadeniz's, he is more optimistic about the relation to the majority group. Interestingly, he mentions his phenotype as a reason for the absence of recognition problems. He does perceive an ethnic boundary, but does not feel excluded by it because people ascribe to him a non-Turkish ethnic identity.

> Well, as I said, I never really had any problems in Hamburg I'd say, because I always looked fair. I will show you some pictures later. People always thought I was Italian or Greek, I wouldn't know the difference between Greeks and Turks, they look alike.[vi] (Ali Bilgic)

For him, it is possible to perceive a boundary without subjecting himself to it. Different boundaries seem to apply to different immigrant groups. Ali Bilgic perceives a bright boundary towards Turks, but the one that applies to him and

---

[69] The NSU-affair refers to a series of xenophobic murders committed by a small group of neo-Nazis (National Socialist Underground) during the 1990s and 2000s uncovered in 2011. It gained wide media attention for racially biased police work and the still unclarified involvement of liaison officers.

other "Italians or Greeks" is blurred. He copes with exclusion in a pragmatic way. Ali Bilgic reports an experience of racial discrimination on the job market that might have led other immigrants to perceive a bright boundary. When he applied for a job he was refused on the telephone on racial grounds, but succeeded when he introduced himself personally the following day.

He was a very nice guy. Had I not had the courage to go there, I would have lost the job. Really, we got along fantastically, I did a decent job. He was decent, too. I brought up the issue later, "you told me, you wanted a German trainer". I don't even remember what he said. "Let's not talk about it anymore", or, "forget it". (Ali Bilgic)

Interviewer: He felt uncomfortable, hmm.

Yes. And it wasn't important. Also, it didn't hurt me. I can't say that. He didn't know me after all. And later he paid me more, or, he was generous. [vii](Ali Bilgic)

Ali Bilgic expresses understanding for his later boss's initial racial prejudice and frames the episode as a personal success. As the other interviews show, this is only one of several responses to exclusion. The issue of responses will be addressed more extensively below.

Religion – Muslim Otherness

Several interviewees mention discrimination on religious grounds as harmful to their relation to the majority group. In total, four respondents explicitly identified themselves as Muslims, in another four cases, it was mentioned in passing (includes the partner-interview), in three cases, respondents mentioned their wives' or children's religiosity, and in one case, the children showed me handicrafts they made in the mosque. That leaves three respondents who did not hint to their religiosity in any way. This section contrasts Hatice Yilmaz (ID6) with Tayfun Akgün (ID8) and with Enes Demir (ID11) for their opposing experience with religious discrimination. All three of them are faithful Muslims, but they experienced different reactions to their religion.

Hatice Yilmaz reports more experiences of racist discrimination and mobbing than most other interviewees do. She says to have lived a wonderful childhood in Germany. Incidences of discrimination started when she entered the labour market. In most cases, she reports personal experiences and she has a general feeling of exclusion, as in the case of Yakup Karadeniz. In her experience, being Muslim and being foreign are intertwined. Dissimilarity from Germans is generally understood as a deficit, no matter if the difference is ethnic or religious. However, among the outsiders she feels particularly rejected. She attributes that to her headscarf in combination with her confidence and achievement.

> Since I am covered, since I am Turkish, and since, well, I have to say it strikes me that Turkish women, or especially Muslim women, those who are covered – those who are open [without veil; NW], they are well received and so on – but if you are covered and you made it somehow, it always strikes me, it's not well received, they don't want that.[viii] (Hatice Yilmaz)

Several male interviewees also report the experience of discrimination against their covered female family members. They relate to discrimination on the street and on the labour market. For example, Yakup Karadeniz' daughter was dismissed twice from her job as a hairdresser after she started wearing a headscarf. One of the other respondents, who purportedly has "no problems", Ibrahim Kaya, notices discrimination against his wife when she drives the car compared to his cousin who wears no headscarf. Most of these experiences are made in the context of driving a car or while shopping. Once interviewees describe these experiences in detail, it sometimes becomes unclear, whether attribution of unfriendly treatment to the headscarf is reasonable. Obviously, it is generally difficult to distinguish racial discrimination from social behaviour that is not directed against the 'other'. However, in a context where racial discrimination is latent this problem of attribution is aggravated. I elaborate on this issue further below when I discuss findings in the light of the MFS. Hatice Yilmaz's experiences of religious discrimination are intertwined with ethnic discrimination. During the interview, she repeatedly refers to a 'we' that she contrasts with 'the Germans'. On probe, she specifies the 'we'-category as including those who are branded as Turkish or foreigner (*Ausländer*). As many others, she suggests that naturalisation does not necessarily imply recognition as a German.

> If you are not like a German, with respect to faith, with respect to going-out, and this and that, then you are labelled as Turk, foreigner, that's that. And we always means: We, who are labelled as foreigner, no matter if you have German citizenship or not.[ix] (Hatice Yilmaz)

As the following passage shows, Hatice Yilmaz does not cope as easily with the experience of exclusion as Ali Bilgic. Her experiences of discrimination have been more frequent than Ali Bilgic's and she has found no optimistic interpretation. For example, she reports immediate police intervention when she had a serious argument with her husband and describes her mixed feelings about that. On the one hand, she was happy about the quick reaction; on the other hand, she wonders why they are not similarly serious when Germans misbehave. The issue of responding to stigmatization will be discussed at more length below.

> For me this country is not our country but it is not different either, at least I don't perceive it differently. On the contrary, I would eventually behave differently in my country, because I would simply feel at home. Here I am more careful, more respect of course. That is even stronger for me then. Because, we may live here, we may do everything just as everybody else. That is why I appreciate this country. But unfortunately I have to say, they don't appreciate that in us. And that's what makes you sad […] It's really, if you understand everything, then everything hurts you, when they talk to

you, when they swear at you, when you are discriminated against, then you don't feel really comfortable here I have to say.[x] (Hatice Yilmaz)

Similar to Hatice Yilmaz, Tayfun Akgün is frustrated with a lack of recognition for his efforts to do what is asked from immigrants. Namely, he has been trying to build bridges between Germans and Turkish immigrants since his childhood and he had no extensive periods of unemployment. Still, he often feels rejected and excluded because people insist on labelling him 'foreigner' and 'Turk'.

The Germans, Germany recognises me only as long as I work. If I am unemployed and a welfare case, then I am negative. If I work, then I am positive and you get that from the media time and again. Another foreigner family that's living on social welfare [...] But you notice in society, even when you're positive, you belong to that group. You're foreigner.[xi] (Tayfun Akgün)

He experiences religious discrimination at work stemming from his employer and colleagues. While Hatice Yilmaz was mobbed by her neighbours to make her leave her apartment, Tayfun Akgün was mobbed by colleagues in order to justify his dismissal. He was fired after accusations of anti-Semitism. Although he got back his job after seven month of trials, he still faces his colleagues' (everyday) racism.

Well, one thing, again and again, it's disgusting but he [a colleague; NW] keeps repeating that, we're done with the Jews but you're next on the list. Things like that he says often. And I'm telling it people, supervisors too, persons who have a better position, whom I trust, I tell them. [imitating their response] Oh, who cares, let him talk.[xii] (Tayfun Akgün)

In this case, the reference is not explicitly Islam but an unspecific "you" designating the other. However, in the context of another religion, Islam is somehow implied. In some instances, however, discrimination evidently goes against Muslim religion. One of the more harmless examples includes the refusal of colleagues to arrange space for halal meat on the company's barbecue. Discrimination that is more consequential comes from his employer. The company refuses to accept breaks for prayer, although breaks for smokers are officially accepted; and it refuses to allow for balancing overtime by finishing earlier Fridays to enable participation in Friday prayer, although other employees can easily leave earlier for non-religious purposes.

So I asked whether I could clock out for prayer, thus, not at the expense of the firm. Clock out, have my five or ten minutes of gymnastics and get mental stability, then continue work. They said, no, that's private and that's impossible. [...] Well, feel free to do something else, but praying we don't accept.[xiii] (Tayfun Akgün)

Tayfun Akgün's resilience against discriminatory behaviour and racist jokes translates also to realms other than his work. Although he is frustrated with those experiences, he accepts them as a fate and keeps 'teaching the ignorant' (see below). Asked if he considered leaving the company, he points to the coming retirement of the remaining racist colleagues. His experiences of discrimination are similar to those of Hatice Yilmaz, but he is more inclined to conciliate.

Enes Demir is a practicing Muslim like Hatice Yilmaz and Tayfun Akgün, but does not experience his religion as complicating his relation to mainstream society. The personal relevance of religion is underlined by his choice of a mosque as the interview venue. During his guided tour through the building, he mentions that the municipality sponsored their central heating system, which may support a feeling of recognition. Unlike the case of Tayfun Akgün, his employer approves of both breaks for regular prayer and arrangement for Friday prayer. Apparently, this is an important ingredient to Enis Demir's accommodation. While his boundary perception is similar to that reported by other interviewees, he does not experience it as problematic. He has no intention of acquiring German citizenship, but the bright boundary apparently is not the main obstacle. Rather, incentives for citizenship acquisition are simply missing.

> Well, I am foreigner, but I haven't felt like a foreigner often. [...] We cannot adapt appropriately here in Germany, neither in Turkey, we are foreigners everywhere. And we've got to live like that, won't change. I repeat, even if I have German citizenship, I am foreigner, I will remain foreigner, hence, nothing will change. I don't object to German citizenship, but I don't need it. [...] (Enes Demir)

Interviewer: And could you tell me how you feel in this country?

Very well. I like living in Germany. I feel good, really. Also, I can practice my religion here.[xiv] (Enes Demir)

Enes Demir represents still another general response strategy to perceived exclusion from the majority group. While he perceives a bright boundary just like Hatice Yilmaz and Tayfun Akgün, he does not report experiences of racial discrimination. Consequently, the way he deals with symbolic exclusion is more laid-back. The whole range of response strategies is discussed in more detail in the next two sections.

Particular Responses

In order to analyse particular responses systematically, I again combined abductive and subsumptive coding. Since some of the responses were similar to findings by other researchers, I deemed it sensitive to use their categories where they fit (I draw on Bickerstaff 2012; Crystal M. Fleming, Lamont, and Welburn 2012; Lamont, Morning, and Mooney 2002; Wimmer 2008a). In this way, commonalities and differences between different minorities in different countries are more easily identified and the potential for a general theory of responses to symbolic exclusion and stigmatization can be assessed. However, some codes were impossible to subsume under known categories. Hence, my scheme builds on the categories applied in earlier projects, adding the sub-category of helplessness. I discuss the differences between prior taxonomies and mine at the end of this chapter. The broader categories of responses are (1) confronting, (2) deemphasizing, (3) ignoring / avoiding, and (4) boundary work (see Table 5.2). Whereas (1)-(3) are literally responses to stigmatization referring to *reactions* in specific situations, boundary work (4) refers to *proactive* strategies that are independent from concrete symbolic exclusion. In the rest of the section, I will describe these response categories in a more nuanced way. Particular responses are not mutually exclusive. Some respondents apply several of them depending on the context, while others have a more narrow strategy. Combinations of various particular strategies result in different general response strategies which are described in the following section. My analysis differs from former studies of responses to stigmatization not only in the particular case, but also by analysing the consequences of these responses for naturalisation intentions. In this chapter, I refer to the notion of everyday racism by Philomena Essed (1991). While she holds that racism is inscribed in the social order, I only share her conviction that making 'the other' is performed in common interactions. That can happen in harmless communications like asking a person of dark phenotype where she comes from or by labelling her Turk because of visual features. This is coherent with the concept of boundary making that I have elaborated above. The focus on perceived racisms renders a general definition of racism superfluous and is also in line with the boundary perspective.

Table 5.2 Particular Responses to Symbolic Exclusion

reactive			proactive
(1) Confronting	(2) Deemphasizing	(3) Avoiding/Ignoring	(4) Boundary Work
Teaching the ignorant	Assuming individual responsibility	Avoiding	Making b's within
Striking back	Relativizing stigmatization	Ignoring	Making b's between
	Blaming the perpetrator	Helplessness	Blurring b's

Table by author.

(1) Confronting

Under the broader category of confronting, I subsume 'teaching the ignorant' and 'striking back'. Both responses rebuff attempts of exclusion, but the former is a more patient reaction often to everyday racism or exclusion, e.g. discursive deconstruction of the term 'guest-worker' when addressed as one. The category of *'striking back'* subsumes instances as diverse as legal action against racist mobbing and talking back to colleagues' racist jokes. Tayfun Akgün simply questions his colleague's presumption, that non-Germans take Germans' jobs. "If someone says, for example, the foreigners take our jobs, then I reply, what about the German? He takes your job, too, right?"[xv] Persons that are regularly confronted with racism, tend to stop opposing it at some point. Among them, Hatice Yilmaz and Tayfun Akgün stick out in their awareness and designation of racist exclusion and their unabated efforts to strike back. Both are motivated by their religious belief in equality of all human beings and an interest in reciprocal recognition of minority and mainstream. As shown in detail above, both of them were victims of mobbing and fought cases at court. The apartment leasing contract of Hatice Yilmaz was cancelled because of her alleged death threat against her neighbour's children. Tayfun Akgün was fired for alleged anti-Semitic remarks at work.[70] She lost her case and her apartment but he won the trial, got back his job, and two of his colleagues who had given false testimony were replaced. Both decided to confront racist mobbing and respond similarly to the everyday racism they experience.

Serkan Demiroglu, a young member of the second generation, describes the situation of a failed application for German citizenship. The officer communicated that he was not eligible for naturalisation due to unemployment. He had the impression that she was talking to him in a disrespectful way and confronted her communication by calling for the person in charge.

<small>She only sees that I am unemployed and blares at me, well, we don't naturalise unemployed foreigners. Of course, I raised before I could not hold it anymore, I said, I want to talk to the head of department. As he comes, I tell him, listen, you wonder why persons freak out in public office.[xvi]</small>

'Teaching the ignorant' represents another more conciliatory but still confronting response category. Recep Dogan, a young marriage migrant with the prospect of staying in Germany for some decades, takes the time to explain the country's so called demographic problem to one of his classmates in response to his complaint about immigration. In his view, migrants are solving the problem by having more offspring than Germans, who are unwilling to establish families.

<small>There is, for example, this colleague in my course and he says, why do people come here with family asking for asylum? So I asked him, how old, are you? 35. Are you married? No. Will you marry? No. I say, there are many people like you in Germany. [...] I do have two daughters now, I tell him, they come after me. If you had a child somehow, you would be right. I'm not talking about that guy but generally.xvii (Recep Dogan)</small>

---

[70] Incitement to hatred (*Volksverhetzung*) is a criminal offence according to German Penal Law (*StGB*, §130).

A recurrent issue that provokes teaching the ignorant is prejudice. Persons are judged as unintelligent by their accent or simply by their appearance. Serkan Demiroglu is born in Germany and describes himself as a *Deutschtürke* (German-Turk). As a temporary agency worker, he is regularly given new assignments where he meets new co-workers. He describes a common issue.

[...] many situations where they treat me as if I was an asylum-seeker, who immigrated just a few years ago to Germany. Once they hear me talk, after some minutes, they are like, ehm. Then I say, yes. Well, because I actually use words that I have to explain to them first. I'm like, well, you haven't had German lessons at school, have you?[xviii] (Serkan Demiroglu)

His teaching the ignorant is certainly less patient and conciliatory than in the previous example. Still, it should be clear by now, that confronting does not necessarily imply an aggressive defence involving litigation in court. More often, it means dialogue over common misunderstandings and everyday racisms. However, the examples also show that the line between teaching the ignorant and striking back is not always clear-cut. One important commonality of responses of the confronting kind is their aim to change the state of affairs.

(2) Deemphasizing

The three deemphasizing responses are 'assuming individual responsibility', 'relativizing stigmatization', and 'blaming the perpetrator'. Those who assume individual responsibility imply individual control over stigmatization and thereby indirectly blame the victims. Those who blame the perpetrator purportedly do not care about it and attribute respective incidences to lack of knowledge on the discriminator's part. Finally, racism is often relativized by being presented as either normal ("exists everywhere"), as individual but not general ("some are racist, some are not"), or as represented by the "older generation". In addition, respondents express understanding for xenophobia ("if I were in his place") or take a pragmatic stance by laughing about colleagues' racist jokes. In those instances, the problem of stigmatization is deemphasized in the sense that responses do not aim at changing it.

Those who *assume individual responsibility* claim to control stigmatization by their own behaviour. Respondents who follow this strategy would often maintain they have "no problems" and go on to attribute this to personal virtues, like language-skills, honesty, friendliness, and decent work. For example, Lale and Erkan Yildirim, underline that they have had no issues with German society. They connect this to their decent live suggesting that those who encounter aggression have caused it.

I'd say I am friendly, I like being friendly. Well, so far I've been this way. Obviously [inaudible]. Some people are looking for fights, they create their own problems. For example someone has a drink goes out on the street and shouts, fucking foreigners and fucking Germans, and of course there will be problems. But calm people don't have problems.[xix] (Erkan Yildirim)

In line with that attitude, they feel guilty for their current unemployment. They argue that dual citizenship would be a way for them not to be a nuisance to the German state. Erkan Yildirim would like to leave for Turkey but would risk losing the permit of stay under current legal conditions.

Erkan Y.: Now, now this dual citizenship is good for us. People like us. We don't cost money and don't bother Germany and don't bother the unemployment office. I stay in Turkey.

Lale Y.: You mean burden. You wouldn't be a burden.

Erkan Y.: Yes.[xx]

Ibrahim Kaya also has "no problems" and explains this by his language adaptation and his decent work. "If you're foreigner or not, when your performance is good, you can achieve something."[xxi] By comparing his own lack of experience with racism with his friends' negative experience, he attributes it to his skills.

Well, I know people, acquaintances, who made negative experiences, like racism. Personally, I haven't had that, because I know how to talk to people. They don't get close to racism. For example, I have colleagues, I know they are racist, but I get along just wonderfully with them, because I am sure that language is essential here in Germany. If your language is right, everything's easier.[xxii] (Ibrahim Kaya)

His conviction about the internal locus of control (Rotter 1966) is mirrored in the education of his children and the judgement of his wife's headscarf. He and his wife spoke to their children in German and Turkish respectively in order to have them learn both languages and he takes pride in their language skills: "If you got them on the phone, that they are foreigners, you can't tell". Although he does not support language assimilation, he wants his wife to remove her headscarf. Instead of accusing the discriminator as one might expect, he expresses dissatisfaction with her refusal to drop the veil.

I am convinced that it's about language and how you present yourself that you don't have problems. Well, my wife has had some trifles, just because wears the headscarf. I gave you the example of the car. If I go by car or my sister in law, who's without the veil, she is regularly allowed in [in traffic; NW]. If it is for my wife, they accelerate. But you don't get them to drop the headscarf, because they say, my religion.[xxiii] (Ibrahim Kaya)

Blaming the perpetrator is a rather different strategy to deemphasize conflict. Since it is believed that racism is the racist's fault, there is no need to confront it. Those who blame the perpetrator doubt that confronting would change his mindset. Sometimes this strategy draws on former experience with perpetrators' reaction to confrontation. Ibrahim Kaya explains why he ignores persons who yell at him in the street.

> I had to deal with right-wing extremists when I was young. I tried to talk. It was an event by a communist club, I was there, the extremists arrived, the skin-heads, we came up to them with 3-4 guys and wanted to talk, and we did talk – no violence or such things – but after all you could see, no matter what you tell them, they have an attitude, they are stubborn, they don't change their mind. I am convinced that such people, you talk to them, eventually you have a beer together, you say, great, we get along after all, that this guy smashes your face next day.[xxiv] (Ibrahim Kaya)

Recep Dogan uses somewhat softer terms to describe the discriminator's ignorance. "Someone tells me, for example, go to Turkey, what do you do here with your knowledge? I think to myself: That's an inexperienced person without knowledge and that's why he says it. I think."[xxv] In the case of Tayfun Akgün, the strategy is similar, but his tone speaks of frustration with racist exclusion. He does not experience racism as coming from a radical minority but as lurking behind many corners in his everyday live. He refuses to deal with those who make racist remarks, branding them as idiots.

> You're adapting [orig. *sich integrieren*; NW], you're trying to stay on both tracks [German and Turkish culture; NW] and hope that, when you go shopping, that you don't get fierce looks or elbows and that you don't experience anything dire: Nobody taking your parking slot and swearing at you, fucking foreigners again or whatnot. You don't get that from the media, but it happens too often, that people, well, we don't care anymore, when we get that. We say, aha, another idiot and we walk on.[xxvi] (Tayfun Akgün)

Finally, *relativizing stigmatization* downplays the problem through reinterpretation. Ali Bilgic disagrees with the common claim that immigrants have to adapt to German culture. He contrasts the claim with descriptions of his son who plays with children from diverse origins who speak fluent German with each other. In his view, adaptation has already happened and politicians unfairly present a pessimist interpretation. However, they do so for non-xenophobic reasons.

> [...] probably that's why, when politicians are bored, or media and whatnot, they put things on the agenda at random, well integration and this and that, and this discussion is like, that is how they distract the people, media-wise at least. Maybe that's why.[xxvii] (Ali Bilgic)

Many interviewees report racist discrimination in public office. However, Recep Dogan relativizes this experience by reference to racist and non-racist officers. "As I said, there are nice public officers, nice guys and bad guys. One time you immediately note that the person doesn't want you in Germany and others don't care. For them we are all human beings."[xxviii] Serkan Demiroglu has been sent from one office to the next. Instead of suspecting racism, he attributes the treatment to bureaucratic idiocy: "Well, that's one thing that Germany is really good at, too, bureaucracy. World champion [laughs]."[xxix] Another common way to relativize racism is pinpointing it in those who are retarded in acknowledging the end of WWII or describing it as phenomenon of the 1990s. Tayfun Akgün takes a colleague's expertise in Turkish food as welcome proof of fading racism in the young generation.

That people still frame the world like in World War II and still don't accept that society becomes more heterogeneous and more colourful. When you ask, like 50 60 years ago, if you want to have a Kebab, perhaps nobody would have said yes. Nope, we don't want it because we don't know what it is. Well, this morning I learned, a colleague told me, the best Kebab you get there [...] you see, it's really only the older society, the laggards from WWII who haven't made their peace with it, who raised their children accordingly. That's really still, I don't know, ten or fifteen percent of society, but I don't care anymore.[xxx] (Tayfun Akgün)

The same person reflects a lot on his relation to Germany and discusses experiences with friends. One strategy they follow in their discussions, is trying to understand the motives of racism. Empathy then is a way to cope with experiences of discrimination internally.

And some would say, you should see it like this, what would you say, if you were in his position and he was you? Well, we do think about those things. What would it be like if Germans would come to Turkey and work there? And take your food, so to speak, comparing arguments roughly.[xxxi] (Tayfun Akgün)

A similar argument is that racism is common in all societies and prejudice is a general human flaw. Like some other respondents Erkan Yildirim considers street violence as normal and would attribute it to city size rather than to xenophobic sentiments.

Or like – you certainly heard that – a woman with headscarf took the metro and somebody punched her and stuff like that we haven't experienced but heard. But that's normal, so many people live here, three million people, that's normal. In Istanbul there are similar problems. Not only about foreigners, also against Turks. Such problems exist in all countries.[xxxii] (Erkan Yildirim)

The last relativizing approach of 'laughing with the racist' is applied as one of several strategies. Tayfun Akgün reports how his older colleague is complaining about foreigners when he is angry, "But in a nice way, and he's smirking too, and it doesn't hurt. And then you might joke with them. With tears in your eyes because it upsets you, but you're laughing."[xxxiii] While Tayfun Akgün pays attention to the nuances of racism, Ibrahim Kaya explicitly makes a stance against confronting racism. In order to deflate the conflicts, he chooses to reconcile.

If you know how to go along a bit, then it gets blurred. I mean, we live together in a foreign country although we are not too foreign to each other anymore and if you confront flat out and say, fucking Nazi or so then you trigger larger conflicts. But if you go along a bit and say, okay man, that is your view, your attitude, mine is a bit different, then it's not a big hurdle anymore and you get along with people.[xxxiv] (Ibrahim Kaya)

(3) Ignoring / Avoiding

The third kind of responses to stigmatization is summarized as ignoring or avoiding. Although similar to deemphasizing in not confronting conflict, the preventive character of this strategy is special. Interaction that might result in racial discrimination is avoided altogether. Hatice Yilmaz and Tayfun Akgün employ all kinds of particular responses. But from time to time, each of them likes to stay in their house. They portray this wish as a reaction to regular racial discrimination. Tayfun Akgün describes hostile reactions when he is in company of his wife and children. He is gazed at while shopping and elbowed in the fast-food restaurant. The presence of his wife's and daughters' headscarves makes him frame the situation as directed against their religious otherness. Hatice Yilmaz describes the general motivation for avoidance.

> I repeat, it's an everyday experience. Every day. And sometimes, imagine, like an old woman, I sometimes say I don't want to leave home. Well, I am somebody, I really enjoyed my youth, went out frequently, shopping, strolling, back then, you don't let it get close to you, I think, you don't really realise. But since I had my child, I really felt it. How inhumane actually, well how bad you can feel. Now I always say, best if I stay home, I cook, I iron, wash, I am there for my child, now for my husband, too. They are grateful for what I do. Everything I do outside, nobody is grateful. On the contrary, they hit you on the head, I mean like racism and whatnot.xxxv (Hatice Yilmaz)

Although her statement sounds like a definite retreat, it has to be judged in the light of her other responses. For example, she reports her experiences in a society of parents (*Elternschule*) where she tried to make conversation at the 'German table', felt rejected, and therefore prefers to sit with Muslim women henceforth. However, she proudly reports that her conversations are interesting enough to attract women from the 'German table' to join her. Similarly, Tayfun Akgün has some tolerance for his colleagues' racist jokes, but is sensitive to the spirit they are made in. Eventually, he refrains from events with colleagues who make racist jokes in an evil spirit but joins meetings with other colleagues.

In some cases, avoidance is not a reaction to racism but a way to live comfortably without having to deal with cultural barriers. Hüseyin Topcu and Ümit Okay both immigrated as adults for marriage with a Turkish-German partner.

> I haven't encountered many problems. I've been living here since 12 years. It is like Turkey; at the central station and elsewhere in Germany. Here, you can talk Turkish and whatnot, everything here. That's why I don't know German well, because I use to speak Turkish.xxxvi (Hüseyin Topcu)

The related response of ignoring is illustrated by Zuhal Özcan's report of everyday racism. She simply does not frame those experiences as stigmatization. The following passage shows, that she ignores stigmatizing questions and teaches the ignorant when necessary.

But I think I have never experienced anything. Well, sometimes, for example, when I worked and so on and how can you, they know Turks a bit different here I guess, and I grew up there and know our culture and they always said, how can you live like that? We always thought they all wear headscarves in Turkey. Or – I smoked for 3-4 years – how can you smoke here? Well such, I said, I am a real Turk.[xxxvii] (Zuhal Özcan)

Stereotyping 'the Turkish immigrant' in a similar way, others sometimes questioned that love was Zuhal Özcan's true motive to come to Germany. She struggles a bit with the poor image of Turks in Germany but tends to ignore it. For other respondents, ignorance is a conscious decision.

Interviewer: How does it materialise that they are racists here? How do you notice that?

Ibrahim Kaya: They harass you. I don't hear any of that, I pass by when something like that happens. You are harassed while queuing at the cash desk or when it's taking too long at the gas station. Then you notice that they are the ones who'd like to kill you. And real racism, personally, I haven't noticed. Like being punched or whatnot, I haven't.[xxxviii]

Instead of responding each time with confrontation Recep Dogan prefers ignoring stigmatization sometimes. "I don't talk much, someone laughs and insults and either I have to argue every day or – I don't know – not listen."[xxxix] Along these lines, Tayfun Akgün's friends advise him to ignore racial discrimination when he tells them about his experiences.

Finally, respondents sometimes report experiences of discrimination where they feel helpless and fail or refuse to react. Both subjectively and objectively, they often are in the weaker position with respect to the discriminator. Still, in most cases respondents mention solutions for the problem especially if they do not conceive of their position as weaker. The third mode of avoiding and ignoring summarizes responses that suggest a passive role and helplessness in interactions with discriminators. Enes Demir, for instance, holds that his phenotype and name cement his status as a foreigner. Even citizenship would not change this status. However, this everyday racism is relativized by his experiences of discrimination in Turkey. Enes Demir shares the impression with other respondents that he is a foreigner in both countries.

[…] If I am in the street or somewhere, here [pointing to his forehead; NW] it says foreigner, Turk, too. The way we dress, the way we move, you see it, let's put it this way, that we are […] no Germans. My name already, if you ask me, what's your name, I say Enes, oh, that's no German name, nope.[xl] (Enes Demir)

Ümit Okay responds to my questions in Turkish and his wife Meyrem translates. Not knowing German makes him feel helpless because people respond to his inability with rejection where he would hope for help and understanding. Still, he is unwilling to learn German and would prefer to leave the country.

Interviewer: Yes, if you have the time, one thing I would be interested in, did you sometimes experience being treated somehow differently?

[translation with partner]

Meyrem Okay: Yes, that is mainly because of the language. Here you are, you are foreigner, you come to my country and you ask for help sometimes, I'm sorry, I'm not that fluent yet, can you help me. This helpfulness does not exist, not at all, not at all. They look at you estranged, or ignore you, or like, learn German first, or learn the language. [...] Without language you are a nothing here and they sure make you feel it.[xli]

However, supposed indicators of successful structural assimilation like a nice car risk causing similar scepticism. Tayfun Akgün is both, frustrated and helpless, when it comes to everyday racism and humiliation. His experience is that even those who work hard to adapt and fulfil expectations of German society are ousted. He describes the scepticism that achievers face.

Same thing in society. If you look neat, you drive a Mercedes, you attract attention. Whether it's your father's or your own, they don't know but say, look at that, he's 20 and drives a big 5er BMW or Mercedes S-Klasse [expensive cars; NW] or whatnot. But that his father has been living here since the beginning and saved money and hasn't spent it in clubs, hasn't enjoyed it so to say, but saved and invested in insurance, insurance has paid him out in the meantime, people don't see that. Instead they see the young dude in a car and later it's the cliché, watch that, he's been selling drugs for sure, otherwise he wouldn't drive a 5er or Mercedes. Well you have that image and you are confronted with that image time and again, no matter at what level you are, if you went to university or not, people don't see that, but they frame things negatively.[xlii] (Tayfun Akgün)

Two more issues that make immigrants feel helpless are the way they are portrayed in German media and structural discrimination by the German state. Some mention media reports of so called 'honour killings' and scrutinize the different framing of murders by German and Turkish murderers. Otherwise, interviewees remember various examples for the pessimist angle media have on immigrants.

At the end of the day you talk about it, maybe you're fed up, and next morning everything's forgotten. And those who can't cope with it, who internalise it, we see them in the news. We see them stick out as negative news. Either, no idea, he does something evil, that comes in the [news]. Well, media do their part in that. [...] And that makes us increasingly unpopular. Well, if TV would show less of it, society would see us in a different light. And there media make a mountain out of a molehill and you are out because eventually you are part of that group, that thinks like that [referring to alleged honour killings by Muslims]. And then you are like, oh.[xliii] (Tayfun Akgün)

As for structural discrimination, some immigrants remember the former policy of preferential labour market placement of Germans and EU citizens before non-EU citizens. Some respondents compare Turks to Greeks or Bulgarians and resent those groups' superior legal status and their privilege of dual citizenship. Some respondents implicitly argue their religion would make them particularly vulnerable to discrimination. Hatice Yilmaz recalls having opened her doors to her neighbours until her trust had been betrayed in several ways. In one of the most consequential cases, her supposed friend mobbed her to achieve that the landlord would cancel the tenancy.

(4) Boundary Work

The responses to exclusion summed up as boundary work do not represent reactions in specific situations. They are more general discursive strategies of situating oneself within or outside certain imagined groups. Therefore, I categorized them as proactive strategies as opposed to the prior mentioned reactive ones. The proactive strategies include 'making boundaries within' the groups of 'Germans' and 'Non-Germans', 'making boundaries between' the two groups, and 'blurring' the boundaries between the two groups. Persons draw boundaries within by drawing attention to subgroups' deviance from the 'normal'. In this way, persons aim to underline their similarity with the 'standard'. Boundary deconstruction has the same goal but a different strategy. Differences between the mainstream and particular minorities are relativized by reference to social categories, norms of equality, or by directly deemphasizing national identity.

Those who want to underline their similarity with the dominant group sometimes draw boundaries between themselves and other groups that they present as inferior in some respect. I refer to this particular response as *making boundaries within*. The groups they refer to are other Turks, other groups of foreigners, Eastern Germans, and persons with lower socio-economic status. This comes close to individual crossing, except that none of the respondents refutes a Turkish identity. Ali Bilgic is opposed to immigration and argues against it based on labour market considerations. This is in line with popular beliefs (for Germany see Semyonov et al. 2004). His unemployment may explain why he opposes immigration. New labour migrants threaten to deteriorate his socio-economic situation.

Well, the whole foreign[er] politics, that makes me angry too, the unemployment, everything gets more brutal and tougher of course. Well, Germany is a humane country, a social country, but at some point, I say this although I am a foreigner myself, but at some point Germany doesn't bear any foreigners anymore, because it is impossible. If criminality increases or decreases, it likely remains unchanged, but there is no work, I know that.[xliv] (Ali Bilgic)

Further, he introduces a distinction between Turks from Istanbul and Turks from the Anatolian countryside, a strategy that can be found in other interviews, too. In his view, Istanbul Turks as opposed to Anatolian Turks can easily acculturate in Germany.

Yes, I enjoy being in Germany. Well, I do come from Turkey, but not like Anatolia in the mountains – I don't want to let down anybody – but, well, I am from Istanbul.[xlv] (Ali Bilgic)

Similarly, Zuhal Özcan reflects on educated Turks like herself and uneducated Kurds unlike herself. In addition, she denounces some Turkish asylum seekers of cheating when they apply in Germany. As many others, she suggests that dual citizenship could be a reward for those who are honest and perform nicely in adapting in Germany as she does. Hence, she makes distinctions similar to Ali Bilgic but draws different conclusions about the privileges that should follow.

> [...] well I understand that, if somebody comes from Turkey and cannot even, like Kurdistan, they don't even know Turkish. I once went to the German Consulate in Istanbul and had to apply for the visa. And there were people, they came from Turkey, went there but didn't even know Turkish. They first had to make Turkish translations and then they wanted to go to Germany. And I can understand that you don't want them. Or my former husband, they were here and took whole kinfolks here – not the normal way but asylum and they said, Turkey did this and that to them, but that was not the case. That was plain lie. And if I know that, you can treat people differently – like 'academic, this position' or not-academic – I just find that I don't belong in the same box, that you treat me the same way. That's not the case. Cause I do something here. I live like a German here.[xlvi] (Zuhal Özcan)

Serkan Demiroglu echoes a claim of the radical right and thereby makes a boundary within the group of non-Germans. "I always said, you can have your opinion, you're welcome to be proud on your country and you're welcome to say, normal, criminal foreigners out [of the country; NW]. I say so, too."[xlvii] Another strategy is to make boundaries within the dominant group. Murat Öztürk differentiates persons from Eastern and Western Germany as he knows them from work in construction. He finds Western Germans to be more like him and therefore easier to work with. This line of reasoning supports his stance that what you do is more relevant than where you come from.

> Well, it depends how the person is. I pay more attention to the personality. If the person is an asshole, then he is an asshole to me. If an *Ossi* [derogatory nickname for Eastern German; NW] is an *Ossi*, I tell him what I think right away. You got the manners of an *Ossi*. Fuck it. I won't hide anything. I worked a lot in the East [of Germany] and dealt a lot with folks from the East. There is just one point where they don't change. It's worse than anything else. When somebody shows the Eastern manner, forget about that guy. [...] Well, folks from the East are just really egoistic. Really egoistic.
>
> [...]
>
> Well, I've got much more problems when I work with East folks than with West folks. With West folks it actually doesn't matter much but with *Ossi* it does.[xlviii] (Murat Öztürk)

Ibrahim Kaya has experienced xenophobic insults from persons with lower socio-economic status. The fact that he has a job and they live on the street vaccinates him against their racism. Similar to Murat Öztürk, he attempts to blur the racial boundary by emphasizing social ones.

> [...] I have experienced that several times in Altona [name of a neighbourhood] that such bums, who sleep under the bridge, who carry along their bottle of wine, that it's rather them who say, fucking Turks. Either they don't think about it – let's put it this way – that the German disgrace says, fucking foreigner, although they suck themselves and rip welfare offices ad nauseam. Well the low level, talking about racism, it's higher than that of - I wouldn't say rich - but average income people. Maybe it's because they are worse off and they say, okay the foreigners are fine, social spongers, but that is actually them. Such people I just pass by and say, alright man. I pass by.[xlix] (Ibrahim Kaya)

These distinctions I label 'boundaries within' to differentiate them from the 'boundaries between' Turkish residents and German majority group. This research project is mainly interested in the minority's responses to German boundary making. However, all boundaries result from interactive processes. Interviews offer insight into minority members' *boundary making between*. In a very narrow sense, the boundary between Germans and non-Germans is made every time that the respective words are used. Paradoxically, the terms are sometimes used in a way that reinforces bright boundaries even where the aim is to blur them. Ali Bilgic's statement on immigrant integration illustrates this: "[…] Come on, the foreigners have been integrated long time ago. Only the Germans don't know that yet."[l] In this example, foreigners and Germans are differentiated in a thoughtless manner. The quote illustrates that even those who want to overcome ethnic categories may fail unconsciously. However, some explicitly defend an ethnic conception of nationality when reflecting on citizenship and belonging.

When I take up German citizenship, then I am German only on paper, but I am still a Turk. I am Turk, one cannot change that. One cannot change, you neither. You are German and remain so, no matter which documents you've got.[li] (Yakup Karadeniz)

In some cases, boundary making is even more explicit, referring to specific qualities of 'them' and 'us'. Those respondents characterize 'us' as kind, helping, sharing food with neighbours, honest, loyal, fair, and family-loving. At the same time 'they' are portrayed as cold, individualist, aggressive, insidious, and friendly with pets but unfriendly with human beings. This kind of boundary making tends to oppose Germans with an amalgam category of Muslims, Turks and foreigners. Hatice Yilmaz mentions Muslims' virtue as a sign of distinction: "Cause we've got many many small ideals, they are in us just like that. Well, certainly we are born like that, like genetically inherited."[lii] Tayfun Akgün observes different family aspirations between youth from his Muslim community and Germans: "What frightens me a bit is that this society wants to remain solo. Every time I ask, do you want a family? Well, I guess I don't."[liii] Less religious respondents echo differences in the personal meaning of family. Murat Öztürk observes, and is dismayed by, his friends' neglect of their parents. "They are 18, 20, 25 [years old] and I say, how's your father? And they go like, why? I don't see him. I don't mind if that geezer dies."[liv] Sometimes the distinction between groups is made by reference to the countries Germany and Turkey. Those who feel that they cannot adapt properly to 'German life' mention country characteristics as reasons. Erkan Yildirim praises Turkish easiness as opposed to German stringency while thinking of making barbecue in public space. When he goes on to describe the nature of neighbourhood relations, he explains them by national differences that remain relevant although he considers the urban-rural difference, i.e. if cities create anonymity, then cities are like Germany.

Erkan Y.: What changes is human interaction. In Germany it's not as friendly as in Turkey. For example, the neighbours, in Turkey now it's like in Germany.

Lale Y.: No.

Erkan Y.: Of course in big cities – in the village or small city it's always good – but Istanbul, 5-floor houses, all neighbours like in Germany, say good morning and that's it.[lv]

Another noteworthy aspect of boundary making is parents' advice to their offspring not to play with Germans. This was reported in only one interview; however, the voluntariness of participation in my research is likely to overlook those who followed their parents' advice. Serkan Demiroglu grew up in Germany and played with German kids against his parents' expressed will. He recounts some criminal adventures of his cousins to argue that playing with Germans is not necessarily bad influence.

I've seen a lot of that in my own family. Watching Turkish TV the whole day, buy only in Turkish shops, only in the Turkish neighbourhood. But then call us up - their children. Well, there are letters again and public office stuff. Read it, what do the Germans want again? I say, you've been living here for 30 years, 40 years. You can't even read a letter? And then they tell us, well, who have been born here as second or third generation, you adapted too much, you are too German.[lvi] (Serkan Demiroglu)

Finally, some respondents engage in boundary work by *blurring boundaries between*. They mainly do so by emphasizing social categories as opposed to national or ethnic ones, by relativizing their national identity, or by reference to moral criteria of general equality. Murat Öztürk's reflections on citizenship and belonging are noteworthy. By describing his identities as non-exclusive, he blurs boundaries between German and Turkish identity. "What can you do? I am a Turk and will always remain Turk. Maybe also in my head, I am Turkish, too, but German just as well. And I have to, politically spoken, find the right way."[lvii] Serkan Demiroglu's approach is more straightforward but still shows the restrictions of blurring strategies. He claims a hyphenated identity but implies that an attempt to claim a purely German identity would fail because of his phenotype. So crossing is not an option.

Interviewer: How is it when somebody addresses you as German?

I always say I am German-Turk. I add that. Because I say honestly, look at me, when I enter a room and say I am German, they say of course, but you are sure born. I say, of course I am Turkish, that's that. Then I say German-Turk. I give this hint. Because I use to say, you shouldn't deny your origin.[lviii] (Serkan Demiroglu)

Ibrahim Kaya relates the question of identification to cultural practices. Thereby he separates legal and symbolic belonging. He claims symbolic membership in German society that is independent of his legal Turkish membership. In his view, cultural adaptation has generated eligibility for legal admission into membership.

In fact, he is entitled to German citizenship, but what he means is an entitlement to hold both citizenships.

> I am still Turkish citizen, although I am, I've been here since 1973, that's 40 years, [...] since I was ten I've been here without interruption. Now the question is, what am I? Am I actually Turk or 40 years, after 40 years one should be a bit German, right? If you consider that I have a Christmas tree at home, that is decorated and windows with Christmas decoration, then you have somehow adopted this German tradition and then you could get German citizenship, right? After all you feel like a German.[lix] (Ibrahim Kaya)

A different blurring strategy is the emphasis of social categories opposed to national ones. This strategy seems similar to making boundaries within. However, the aim here is not to define the own group negatively through downgrading the other. As mentioned before, several respondents note that in public discourse being 'Turkish' is often associated with social problems. Murat Öztürk counteracts this tendency of scapegoating the Turks by questioning the relevance of ethnicity for those social problems.

> The government, I do find that their action is anti-Turkish. And the German government can't change it, the folks are there. Either you expel them, like they've done it in WWII with the Jews, or you accept such things and try to fix also the difficult persons, because – they aren't fixing it. They don't even fix it with Germans. Troublemaker remains troublemaker. If he is a Turk or not, that has got nothing to do with nationality.[lx] (Murat Öztürk)

Still, this sequence also illustrates how hard it is to relinquish the language of ethnic categories. He refutes the notion of nationality more clearly when it comes to his own work. In his view, social relations at work are all about integrity and trust as opposed to ethnicity.

> This man is a technician [colleague at the site]. He depends on me and I depend on him. And if you play the game right, you ain't got problems. I screw him only one time, then he's done with me. [...] It's normal life. And in Turkey that wouldn't be different. I'd have to work with people and they'd have to trust me and I'd have to trust them and where you have trust, you have no problem. But if you're a prick, you always have a problem.[lxi] (Murat Öztürk)

Another entity that allows for replacing national categories is the local environment. Some respondents find it easier to express affection for Hamburg compared to Germany. At the same time, identification with the city may catalyse identification with the country because symbolic membership in the city is less exclusive than membership at the national level. In the words of Murat Öztürk, "I love Hamburg. And that's, that's my Germany, Hamburg."[lxii] Finally, some migrants blur boundaries by reference to general equality of human beings. Tayfun Akgün takes the example of organ transplantations from his biography to stress his point that nationality is a secondary category. "And when I need an organ or when a German needs a liver, and there is a donor from Turkey, he won't say, thanks, I don't take the liver."[lxiii] If he could choose, he would define himself simply as a human being. He is convinced that everybody can learn from each other and gives an example for the benefits of approaching even racists: "For example someone who has always lived as a Nazi, told me about a fish recipe. Well, and then I prepared it and he even brought me a chunk of fish."[lxiv]

Particular responses and the MFS

So far, I have merely identified and described particular responses. But what are the conditions of opting for one particular response? The aim of this section is to formalise the selection of particular responses according the Model of Frame Selection that was introduced above. The crucial differentiations of the MFS are two modes of information processing (automatic and reflective) and three selections (interpretational frame, behavioural script, and action). If we assume that experiences of symbolic exclusion recur, individuals are likely to process information in the automatic mode. They know which frame yields reliable interpretations of the typical situation. The interpretation is not necessarily valid, but it entails comparatively low costs and eventual benefits. In addition, their reaction has to be quick because discrimination often happens in quick and ongoing communications, especially in its softer forms of everyday racism. For example, unfair treatment in the presence of female family members with headscarves (salience of Muslim identifiers) makes selection of a frame that reads the unfair treatment as motivated by religious otherness more likely. An important implication is that persons who carry visible features of their ethnic or religious otherness are more likely to frame unfair treatment as directed against their otherness if such a frame has proven gainful. Indeed, framing unfair treatment as ethnic discrimination reduces costs for the victim because it relieves her from introspection in search of own wrongdoing. On the other hand, it causes costs. Discrimination based on ascribed qualities induces feelings of powerlessness and social exclusion which, as neuroscience shows, causes pain that is comparable to physical pain (Eisenberger, Lieberman, and K. D. Williams 2003; Kross et al. 2011).[71]

To prevent the pain of discrimination, actor X may apply two sets of frames. The first set of frames serves to question the discriminatory character of the situation. The second set of frames leads to acknowledgement of discrimination and often causes X to react. The first set of frames includes understanding the unfair treatment as unimportant or understandable (relativizing stigmatization),

---

[71] With the help of neuroimaging the referenced studies show that "social pain is analogous in its neurocognitive function to physical pain, alerting us when we have sustained injury to our social connections, allowing restorative measures to be taken" (Eisenberger et al. 2003, 292).

as not directed against X but against other members of the group (assuming individual responsibility), or as simply not discriminatory (ignoring). All of these frames reduce the costs of being discriminated against by challenging the status of victim, but only one leads to changing X's behaviour. The assumption of individual responsibility for being the subject of discrimination implies acting in a way that proves X to be different from the group she is associated with. This has the positive effect of avoiding pain and reducing feelings of powerlessness. Pain is avoided through self-exemption from being subject of discrimination and self-empowerment associated with individual responsibility reduces potential feelings of powerlessness. Where other minority members are victims of discrimination the one who assumes individual responsibility controls the situation. Obviously, the framing that goes with this kind of action is only stable if the struggles for recognition are acknowledged eventually. It is important to note at this point that frames are not the same as actions. Still, I have just associated each frame with a particular response because the MFS supports the assumption that particular frames make particular scripts and their implied actions more likely. However, the association of frames with actions is by no means deterministic; it is merely typical (see Kroneberg 2005).

The second set of frames is based on the acknowledgement of a particular situation as discriminatory. Once a situation is framed that way the costs of victimization bear heavily on the subject. If discrimination is acknowledged and remains unchallenged then the obvious interpretation of attendees is either that discrimination was legitimate or the victim was too weak to respond. Both interpretations are costly for X, thus, to reduce costs, X may attribute the discrimination to the incompetence of the source (blaming the perpetrator) or she may confront the perpetrator. While the first reaction could be merely cognitive, reactions of the second kind involve social action. However, the costs of social action against discrimination are high for a number of reasons. First, discrimination normally happens in contexts that provide social support for the perpetrator. If X confronts the perpetrator only to find out that indeed perpetrator's action is widely supported then costs of confronting increase. Second, the interpretation of discrimination is usually not straightforward. The perpetrator may deny the discriminatory character of her action upon confrontation, challenging X's interpretation. The most common way to do so is to frame it as 'just a joke'. Third, there is no repudiation of the stigma without hurting the perpetrator at least to some extent. If the confrontation is successful, it means exposing the discriminator's misconduct. Hence, for X to choose confrontation as a proper response, he should be self-confident, sure that he is right to suspect discrimination, and merciless towards inflicting costs on the perpetrator. The expected utility of confronting is per definition higher than the costs of not responding, before the probability of success is factored in. If the probability of successful confrontation is low, then X is likely to opt for a different script. The aforementioned characteristics of self-confidence, certainty of the definition, and mercilessness increase the probability of successful confrontation. Which one of the confronting strategies of 'teaching the ignorant' and 'striking back' will be chosen? This choice is a function of the costs of discrimination where higher costs render striking back more likely. Accordingly, I find few instances of striking back in the interviews and two of them are lawsuits indicating that the costs of discrimination were substantial. Another implication of the high costs of confrontation is that the reflective mode of information processing is more likely than the automatic one especially for the selection of a behavioural script.

If X is to prevent not merely the pain of discrimination, but discrimination itself, he is likely to resort to boundary work. There are three options from which to choose: making boundaries between, blurring boundaries, and making boundaries within. What choice is more likely under what conditions according to the MFS? Where refutation or confrontation of the stigma is difficult, X is least likely to make boundaries within and most likely to make boundaries between or blur boundaries. If she makes boundaries between, the stigma continues to apply, but the source of discrimination is defined as other and therefore irrelevant to X. The victim is turning the tables and discriminating against the other ethnic group to prevent being discriminated against. The second and third options of boundary making both aim at blurring the boundary between X and mainstream, both refute the stigma, but the first strategy is more individualistic than the second. Boundary blurring aims at refuting the stigma by reducing the salience of ethnicity. Again, the boundary between X and mainstream gets blurred, but in addition the boundary is blurred towards the whole ethnic minority. By 'making boundaries within', X dissociates from part of the ethnic group or part of the mainstream by creating new sub-groups instead. The positively valued of these subgroups encompasses X and a relevant fraction of the mainstream. In other words, the boundary between X and mainstream gets blurred. Examples that I elaborated on above include the division of the mainstream into *Ossis* and *Wessis* and the dichotomisation of Turkish origin into Western urban Turkey and Anatolian rural Turkey. Actors are expected to prefer the latter individualistic strategy because it is more likely to be successful. However, actors will consider success more likely if they have reasons to believe that they can refute the stigma. Their estimate will rely on past experiences of discrimination and the success of response strategies. According to my analysis, blurring by fission is most likely to coincide with deemphasizing strategies like excusing or relativizing racism and assuming individual responsibility. Actors who successfully apply these strategies are also more likely to make boundaries within. General actor strategies are the subject of the next section. A formalization of response strategy selections according to the MFS helps to understand why specific responses are likely to prevail under specific conditions.

General Response Strategies

What we can learn about boundary perceptions from the interviews is not so much that they exist, but in what way Turkish residents frame their accounts. Most persons have experienced everyday racism, some were subject to racial mobbing, but they deal with it in different ways. In this section, I present five general response strategies that I identified throughout the interviews and a sixth type that is logically possible and empirically likely. During the process of type construction, some of the dimensions initially identified have been dropped either because they did not allow for differentiation of the cases or because other dimensions made them obsolete. As described in more detail above, theorizing the responses to exclusion is understood as an intuitive and iterative process that goes back and forth between concepts and data before arriving at a reasonable result (see Kelle and Kluge 2010; Kelle 2008; Swedberg 2012). To make this process more transparent, tables A10 and A11 reveal some of the dimensions that were tested with regard to their potential of capturing the differences between cases. The aim was to develop a model that is parsimonious (as in Table A11) and describes the most relevant differentiations (as in Table A10). The final typology differentiates responses to exclusion along three dimensions. First, respondents either perceive a bright boundary, or they perceive none. Second, some struggle to blur the boundary they perceive while others do not. And third, some but not all respondents engage in boundary making between mainstream and Turkish residents. While a majority of respondents report being subject to discrimination or exclusion by the majority group, they deal with it in different ways. Some are reluctant to accept exclusion, leading to *frustration*; some understand exclusion as an evil that is driven by a minor part of the majority group, they feel capable of mastering it and strive to earn recognition by working hard (*bullish*); and some are *confident* and unaware of racial exclusion (may they be subject to any or not). Few respondents accept exclusion willingly in a spirit of *resignation* or in *light-hearted* toleration. Finally, there is an *insular* type that is not to be found among respondents but is theoretically possible and likely to exist.[72] Persons of this type do not perceive bright boundaries but still engage in

---

[72] See for example Arslan (2009) for an evaluation of Turkish nationalists in Germany or Souleimanov and Schwampe (2017) for ethnic nationalism among Chechen Salafis in Europe.

boundary making against the majority group. A detailed description of each type, including illustrative interview passages, follows.

The Frustrated Type (ID1, ID6, ID8, ID16)

Several interviewees are frustrated with their relation to the host society. They are persons who struggled hard in the past decades to live up to the ideal of assimilated migrants and frustrated because they are not recognised in return. They feel that their efforts to please German society are in vain. Yakup Karadeniz (ID1) and Hatice Yilmaz (ID6) have a strong boundary perception and both are frustrated with permanent exclusion, non-recognition, and discriminatory treatment compared to other immigrant groups. They share the assumption that they cannot change anything about this situation and see themselves as victims of particular discrimination against Turks that is unjustified. In their view, discrimination is both social and institutional. On the institutional side, Turks are not allowed to have dual citizenship, which is different for EU-migrants and North-African migrants.[73] Social discrimination happens wherever they meet members of the mainstream. Since institutional and social boundaries are perceived as congruent, those who make either kind of boundaries are addressed as 'they'.

I have a feeling: We Turks are not wanted in Germany – by many people.[lxv] (Yakup Karadeniz)

And dual citizenship: German law doesn't allow it. The German constitution says all citizens have equal rights. But when it comes to dual citizenship. Apart from Turkey they all may have it, only the Turks may not. What do they have against us? What do they have against us?[lxvi] (Yakup Karadeniz)

[…] well, I can't really describe it, this discomfort. You never feel homey here, even if you got citizenship. Well, if I had German citizenship it would be the same. Cause they don't recognise that here.[lxvii] (Hatice Yilmaz)

Rarely do frustrated migrants confront racial exclusion. Only those who have a strong Muslim identity resort to the particular response of confronting. Apparently, their religion provides them with sufficient self-esteem to counter stigmatization. At the same time, Islam is a popular target of discrimination by members of the mainstream. Women are easily identified as Muslim when they wear the headscarf and some employers do not accept the headscarf. The labour market is of particular relevance for experiences of discrimination against Islam.

Those are the stereotypes I face at work. I say, yes, my daughter, I need 400 Euros for a class trip and whatnot. Then they go, well, you don't send her anyway. I say, why? Yes, because you Muslims don't send them and neither do you send her to swimming lessons. I say, man, when have we talked

---

[73] One of the exceptions is citizenship acquisition by birth for those born after 1990 (see Ch. 1). However, this is a recent development that was not settled until the last interviews were finished in summer 2014.

about it and when have I expressed anything like that? Well, what do you do then? Well, of course do I do [send her], why shouldn't I? Back then I couldn't, for my father was single earner. Now, that it's possible, why should I constrain my kids?[lxviii] (Tayfun Akgün)

Discrimination that happens in the street is often attributed to the headscarf. Men in particular have the impression that their female family members are targeted more often be it because they are more vulnerable, or because they are easier to identify as Muslim, or both. As a consequence, these persons develop a tendency to avoid contexts where discrimination might occur.

You're sitting in Pizza Hut, eat pizza and when your wife has a headscarf and the kids wear headscarf too, then you're pushed with the arm and that are things where you go out less often. Also, while shopping you hear, look at them, a whole family, and that's when you retreat a little more and say, I prefer to have my peace in my milieu and then you stay in the Turkish community.[lxix] (Tayfun Akgün)

He summarizes the state of Germany as a country of immigration and the best way to deal with problems. He is not satisfied with the ongoing stigmatization but sees some signs of sluggish improvement.

I think Germany is on the right track. It has started with the right foot. But, it's like a baby that is still learning how to walk, stumbles a bit, but let's put it like this, I don't complain, that I live in Germany and get xenophobic comments from time to time. You almost accepted that, but you wish that it doesn't happen.[lxx] (Tayfun Akgün)

Persons of the frustrated type do not confront stigmatization unless they are faithful Muslims. They do not deemphasize stigmatization because they acknowledge the existence and see no excuse given their struggles to comply with assimilation demands. Eventually, they avoid situations where stigmatization might occur because they feel helpless after futile attempts to comply with German standards. Finally, in spite of struggling to blur boundaries, they also make boundaries by (unconsciously) assigning migrants and Germans to two distinct and coherent categories.

The Bullish Type (ID4, ID5, ID9, ID12, ID13)

Next to Ali Bilgic, several other interviewees refer to racism as an evil they can master; a failed attempt to make a bright boundary. They assume individual responsibility, showing that directing practices of symbolic exclusion against them is inappropriate. Ibrahim Kaya reports having worked with racist colleagues for many years with an attitude of toleration. When his racist superior retired, he got the position.

And it's a job that I like very much and it's fun. For 19 years I worked with somebody in this company, I have to be honest, he was a racist. He really was a true racist. Hence, I say, the man should never give up. He should do his work properly even if he doesn't get to grips with people. In the end you get the recognition, even if you are a foreigner.[lxxi] (Ibrahim Kaya)

Similar to Ibrahim Kaya, Murat Öztürk portrays himself as a self-made man who can control his fate. The place he chose for the interview is in line with his self-portrayal. For reasons of time-efficiency, he invited me to a construction site and switched between welding and talking. He characterizes racial discrimination as an unavoidable evil that one must be able to deal with. By playing the racial card, people expose weakness and inferiority.

Interviewer: Were there situations, when you were treated somehow differently?

Murat Ö.: Well, yes, but that's normal. I see it as normal. If the man cannot handle that ... A weak person attacks you right there, because he got stuck. But if you are determined, if you don't question yourself, well, I don't question myself, I enter everywhere, I can make a difference everywhere. And if somebody is getting offensive, like, you fucking Turk, or something of that kind, I can't but laugh about it.[lxxii]

Bullish persons feel responsible for proving racists wrong by working hard. By doing so, they also set themselves apart from those who deviate from the norm of decent citizens. Where they explicitly define themselves negatively through downgrading of other minority members, I speak of making boundaries within. The following example of making boundaries within is noteworthy for its ambiguity. The respondent reifies ethnicity while proving the futility of ethnic markers.

In the meantime, we have all kinds of nationalities here in Germany: Arabs, Syrians, Afghans, and the Baltic states [presumably Balkan states; NW]. Thus many that look similar to Turks but are no Turks and no matter who does something, who looks a bit southern [the orig. term südländisch means black hair, darker phenotype; NW], it's always the Turk. And therefore I think we Turks will never win acceptance, because the German, who sees a foreigner, for him it's the Turk. And indeed the Arabs do a lot of shit and the credit always goes to the Turks.[lxxiii] (Ibrahim Kaya)

Persons of the bullish type express a strong work ethic and often gain self-esteem from success in their professional career. Considering their particular responses, three regularities seem to hold. First, they are more likely than persons of the other types to confront racism. Teaching the ignorant and striking back are equally likely responses, although not all of them apply them. Second, persons of the bullish type sometimes ignore but never avoid symbolic exclusion and none of them expresses helplessness when facing racial exclusion. Third, they tend to blur the boundary towards the mainstream by making boundaries within the Turkish and the German group.

The Confident Type (ID2, ID3, ID7, ID14, ID15)

The confident type is similar to the bullish one. As persons of the insular type, confident migrants do not perceive any exclusionary practices that would form a boundary between Turks and Germans. Like the bullish, they do not make boundaries between, and like the light-hearted, they do not struggle to blur boundaries. Lale Yildirim arrived when she was 13 years old. She and her husband both did unskilled work in the past and earned some extra money as self-employed retailers of household ware. Their current unemployment troubles Erkan Yildirim while his partner, Lale Yildirim, feels comfortable in Germany: "Well, I don't feel as a foreigner here. No, I feel well here."[lxxiv] She compares Germany to Turkey claiming that she is lost when it comes to bureaucratic affairs in Turkey whereas she is more autonomous in Germany. Similarly, Zelife Arslan arrived as a young woman when she married, did unskilled labour for some time after divorce, and is currently unemployed. Her children are the only reason for her to stay in Germany. She feels lonesome in Germany and wants to move to her Turkish family. Still, she has not experienced stigmatization: "I never had any issues. Well, I don't know, because I didn't go to school, because I didn't know how to speak German well. Children, I was always busy with my children."[lxxv] Although Zuhal Özcan's biography is rather different, her general response strategy is similar. She arrived in Germany as an undergraduate student and is now franchisee of a gym. She does not report any experiences of discrimination and presents herself as a self-confident person in full control of her fate.

I cannot say I am a foreigner and I don't know German, I never experienced it that way. I can't remember that. I think everything came about smoothly. I worked as a waitress during university and my German was poor but that is how I learned it. [...] Well, I just did it, I was afraid of course, but I had to do it. I am not a person to sit around and wait. I have to do something, that's how I learned German and I think in that way, by working as a waitress, I was encouraged and here at university I had no problems anyways.[lxxvi] (Zuhal Özcan)

Zuhal Özcan is similar to bullish type respondents in her self-confidence and her pragmatism. However, her case is particular in certain respects. She arrived in Germany as an adult in a multicultural academic environment and has not experienced racial discrimination. In her view, those who live a decent life will not encounter racism. Following the same logic, she makes 'boundaries within' in order to underline her difference to migrants who do not live a decent life.

I have my business here, I am like, ok, maybe they have had bad experiences [Germans with immigrants; NW], I can understand that, but I don't want to be in the same box. And I want them to see me differently and to distinguish me from the others.[lxxvii] (Zuhal Özcan)

Summing up, persons of the confident type are mostly first (or 1.5) generation immigrants but have otherwise different socio-economic backgrounds and different reasons for migration. In some cases, sparse contact with mainstream society may explain why they have not experienced stigmatization. They sometimes ignore soft forms of everyday racism. Generally, persons of the confident type never respond by confronting. This finding is coherent with their unawareness of racial exclusion. Also, they never relativize racism. The only deflecting response that can be found in this group is the assumption of individual responsibility. This is sometimes paralleled by making boundaries within the minority against those who deviate from the norm.

The Light-Hearted Type (ID 11)

Enes Demir, who holds that "we are foreigners everywhere [and] we got to live like that", fits neither with the frustrated nor with the bullish type. His approach is best described as light-hearted. It is similar to the bullish one in its prioritization of work over symbolic inclusion, but similar with the frustrated one in taking a passive role rather than feeling empowered to change the boundary. However, he does not aspire to recognition because he has no impression of being disadvantaged by his status as a foreigner. Similarly, the change of legal status through naturalisation does not yield incentives. "I don't have problems with the state, nor with the police, I don't need this paper in order to show that I am German, because it doesn't help me much."[lxxviii] Since he does not conceive symbolic exclusion as problematic, he has little reason to engage in boundary work. His responses to racism are of the deemphasizing kind. He has not experienced personal discrimination. In his view, after the threatening xenophobic events of 1990s, some directed against Turks, racism belongs to the past. He wants to comport like a good citizen but does not aim to blur ethnic boundaries. All he hopes for in return for his structural assimilation is accommodation of his religion. Legal benefits of German citizenship or cultural membership are not among his goals.

The Resigned Type (ID10)

The resigned perceive a bright boundary and have accepted that it will not change, making them similar to the light-hearted. However, they differ from the light-hearted type in their affirmation of ethnic boundaries. They clearly separate themselves from mainstream society both verbally and physically, moving into ethnic neighbourhoods. The only case of this kind among my interviews is the couple of Hüseyin Topcu and his wife. Being more fluent in German, the partner frequently answered for the in spite of not being the interviewee. However, as a

German-born second generation Turkish resident, she is part of the survey population and resigned persons are unlikely to be part of the sample. Therefore, it seemed sensitive to include them as a case of the resigned type even if differences between the two cannot be fully discerned. Hüseyin Topcu could as well be of the confident type, but he does not state his opinion clearly enough to allow unambiguous typification. Instead, he tends to agree with his wife. They hold that living in a neighbourhood with many of "our people" and few "Germans" eliminates many problems. In this case, "our people" are specified as foreigners and implicitly as Turks.

Partner of Hüseyin T.: It's not like 20 years ago. 20 years ago, there were no foreigner shops where you could go. I mean, foreigners expanded, too. At each corner, you find something now. In the past, it wasn't like that. That's why it's a whole different story.

Interviewer: Does that make it more comfortable, or...?

Partner of HT: Well, that our people have expanded, that everyone goes somewhere, Kebab shops, Turkish shops, feels like at home. In the past, it just wasn't like that.[lxxix]

So resigned persons do feel at home in Germany, but they do so because they live in ethnic neighbourhoods. They do not perceive racial exclusion, because they avoid places where they might encounter it. If they do experience everyday racism, they relativize it by reference to its universal character. They make a bright boundary between (Turkish) migrants and mainstream referring to "us" and "them".

Insular Type

Persons of this type do not perceive symbolic exclusion but make a boundary of their own against the cultural mainstream. They may resort to negative and positive self-definitions to build that boundary. Although no person with an insular strategy has been interviewed, the type is theoretically possible and empirically likely to exist. Above, I reflect on the selectivity of my sampling method and suggest that persons who distance themselves from the majority culture and society are less likely to be among my interviewees. Still, I find two hints to the existence of this general response type in my interviews. First, Serkan Demiroglu reports his parents' stance towards intermingling with Germans. They criticize their son for having German peers and accuse him of cultural assimilation. From the interview with their son it cannot be known, whether they promoted ethnic segregation from the outset or reacted to experiences of symbolic exclusion. If their attitude was non-reactive but proactive, they would fit the type of an insular strategy. Second, Ümit Okay that has been categorized as confident might as well fall into this insular category because he makes no effort to learn German.

However, his case is peculiar, because he arrived in Germany rather recently to please his wife who is second generation and assimilated structurally and culturally. Emre Güner has some insular qualities as Ümit Okay but is not adverse to German culture. Cultural assimilation is simply secondary to both interviewees' economic priorities. To assure Muslim education of his children Emre Güner sends his children to a private school. For the first case of Serkan Demiroglu's parents, I cannot disentangle reactive and proactive boundary making and the other two cases are not typically insular. Thus, the differentiation of resigned and insular strategies remains imperfect. It is a challenging task for future research to interview members of this group for they are particularly difficult to recruit for interviews.

General Response Strategies and the MFS

Although interviewees belong to the specific sub-group of un-naturalised immigrants, it is noteworthy that only persons of the confident type feel that they are recognised as members of German society. Given that some interviewees have lived in Germany for several decades, I had expected to find more cases of no- or blurred-boundary perception. Some cases that fall into the no-boundary category based on the survey do actually perceive a boundary but do not subject themselves to it. Namely, they may perceive discrimination of Turks generally but not personally. If the majority of Turks perceives symbolic exclusion, the assessment of boundary perception becomes less relevant. Instead, the identification of particular and general responses to stigmatization is more decisive. Before I analyse the implications of response strategies for citizenship acquisition, I want to reiterate the question I made after analysis of particular responses. What can we learn from the MFS about the preference of general response types for particular responses? How does the MFS account for actor types' preferences for particular response strategies?

General response strategies develop in repeated interactions of minority members with the mainstream. Individuals apply combinations of particular responses that have proven to be successful in the past (Bandura 1977). If, for example, teaching the ignorant has not been successful once, because the perpetrator claims he has been joking, the subject of discrimination may try a different strategy next time. The success of a strategy depends on too many factors for a general prediction of the choice. However, particular responses are not equally likely from the outset. I have defined above three preconditions that render responses of the confronting kind more likely and they include personality traits. Actors are more likely to confront discrimination when they are self-confident, convinced to have the right definition of the situation, and merciless towards the perpetrator. This is the case for persons of the bullish type and Muslim's of the frustrated type. As elaborated above, the same type of actor is also likely to excuse or relativize racism and assume individual responsibility. Hence, self-confidence seems to be lower in persons of the resigned and the light-hearted type and in persons of the frustrated type who have no strong religious identity. As the label suggests, confident persons are rather high in self-confidence, but are not confronting since they perceive nothing to confront. For persons of the insular type, responses to stigmatization are not relevant since they have a preference to stigmatize the mainstream proactively.

What regularities are there between general response strategies and the proactive responses of boundary work? Since boundary work is a strategy to prevent discrimination, it is likely to result from past experiences of symbolic exclusion unless migrants have an insular strategy. When refutation or confrontation of the stigma is difficult, migrants are likely to affirm symbolic boundaries or to blur them by making non-ethnic categories salient. Hence, these strategies are more likely for persons who carry visible markers of their otherness, like dark phenotype or a headscarf. Muslim's, for instance, would either affirm the boundary towards Germans or deconstruct it by making non-ethnic qualities salient. Further particular responses in their repertoire include confronting, and avoiding or ignoring. If refutation of the stigma is an option, they are more likely to make boundaries within and combine that response with the assumption of individual responsibility to expose compatibility with the mainstream. High self-confidence is most likely to result in bullish, frustrated, or confident strategies. In the next section, I discuss general strategies' implications for naturalisation intentions.

Meanings of Citizenship

This section presents respondents' conceptions of citizenship. The focus is on the interaction of symbolic and rights-oriented motives for and against naturalisation. Is it possible to separate the two kinds of motives or are they in fact impossible to treat as clearly distinct? In most interviews, it is rather clear if a respondent reflects upon citizenship in instrumental or in symbolic terms. However, their lines of argument are not necessarily straightforward. Some interviewees seemed to hide their naturalisation intentions from the interviewer. In some extreme cases, respondents conveyed disinterest in German citizenship and revealed their intention to naturalise only towards the very end of the interview or even after the interview was finished while they stressed symbolic exclusion all along. It appears as if they felt uncomfortable with applying for membership in a state and a society that reject them in a number of ways. However, in most interviews the interest in citizenship was rather transparent. Interviewees declared right away whether and for what motives they were interested in naturalisation or not.

Exemplarily, I describe one case that equally considers legal and symbolic motives, one where symbolic motives prevail, and one where legal motives prevail. Finally, I depict the citizenship conceptions of light-hearted and resigned types for whom naturalisation is not an option. I connect the lines of reasoning with general response strategies. Hatice Yilmaz (*frustrated*) emphasizes symbolic exclusion but is aware of the legal upsides of citizenship. Recently, she convinced herself of acquiring German citizenship for practical reasons in spite of feeling discriminated against and excluded from symbolic membership. Most frustrated respondents do not intend to naturalise unless dual citizenship is introduced. Like Hatice Yilmaz, Ali Bilgic (*bullish*) underlines the symbolic character of citizenship acquisition. He wants to naturalise irrespective of dual citizenship toleration. Indifference towards dual citizenship prevails in the bullish type, but some postpone their naturalisation. Emre Güner (*confident*) has an interest in both German and Turkish citizenship for practical reasons. He and his family would naturalise if dual citizenship was tolerated. Enes Demir (*light-hearted*), and Hüseyin Topcu and his wife (*resigned*), have no intention to naturalise whatsoever. German citizenship is neither practically nor symbolically relevant for them.

Frustrated – Symbolic vs. Legal Motives

Hatice Yilmaz presents a bunch of reasons for and against naturalisation. She experiences strong exclusion from mainstream society. Experiences of discrimination are predominant in her narration. Exclusion along with a lack of recognition by the host society is the reason not to naturalise. However, her lasting concern with these issues shows that she has not resigned in her struggle for recognition. At some point, she admits feeling well in Germany in spite of discrimination. Furthermore, she has a sense of duty and wants to participate in elections. That is reflected by her concern with naturalised family members' participation in German elections. Eventually, family related reasons will be decisive. After divorce, she found a new Turkish-German partner recently and they agree that family travels are more comfortable if everybody has the same passport. Hatice Yilmaz justifies why she wants to naturalise in spite of feeling discriminated against. Her line of reasoning is that, as a German citizen she might have a better position in her fight against discrimination. The fact that she feels a need to justify underlines that the passport has a symbolic meaning for her. It seems to be more than a bureaucratic act of legal membership acquisition.

Interviewer: Could you say more generally, how do you feel in this country?

Definitely as a foreigner. Also, I feel, I'm sorry I've to say that, very discriminated against. It may sound contradictory that in a country where I am discriminated against, I want to become citizen. But especially persons who are strongly excluded, discriminated against, they always have to fight for their rights, nothing is self-evident.[lxxx]

[…] I feel good [in Germany] after all, I can't deny that.[lxxxi] (Hatice Yilmaz)

Her experiences of discrimination make her generally suspicious of racial discrimination. Namely, she was subject to racist mobbing by her neighbours who collaborated with her landlord, a housing association, in order to make her leave the house. On the societal level, she is concerned that the immigrants' contributions to the economy tend to be ignored. Turks are supposed to function and never get unemployed. She connects her experience of rejection to her naturalisation intentions. "That's why I don't become German. Well, I haven't acquired German citizenship. They keep offering it to me, to us, written and whatnot."[lxxxii] Reflecting on the reasons for her reluctance to give up her Turkish passport, Hatice Yilmaz uses the metaphor of a mother and father who raised and fed her referring to Turkey. In the same breath, she notes her positive emotions towards Germany.

However, I think that it might hurt my country that cared for me a long time. Maybe I have a disadvantage if I do it. I don't want them to be disadvantaged. It's like my mother, like my father, I will always be grateful to them. That is the same with Germany. I would never commit a crime here, or never, I cannot leave here either after all.[lxxxiii] (Hatice Yilmaz)

Well, one two three small friendly people, and you forget the negative. And that makes me able to say again and again, I still want the citizenship.[lxxxiv] (Hatice Yilmaz)

Next to these symbolic aspects of citizenship, Hatice Yilmaz is aware of legal aspects of naturalisation. These legal aspects make it more relevant to her. Namely, she is interested in having equal rights as Germans, specifically franchise and travel options. Hatice Yilmaz perceives a bright symbolic boundary with the Germans. Although she does not hope to change the boundary by naturalisation, she still wants to apply. The legal advantages of German citizenship motivate her to take this step.

Bullish – Symbolic Motives

Ali Bilgic, the unemployed fitness coach, frames citizenship acquisition in symbolic terms. Also, some of the legal benefits he mentions are rather symbolic since he is not likely to enjoy them. He praises the advantage of German diplomatic protection, although the dimension of his debt may inhibit travel for the rest of his life. For him, naturalisation is a symbolic act that follows from having lived in Germany for many years: "Actually, nothing changes. But anyhow, I live here, I've been here forever. I might even die here. Of course I want to take it."[lxxxv] Since he has no acute practical reasons to naturalise, he refers to symbolic meanings and hypothetical benefits of Turkish and German citizenship.

I know that, if you have a German passport, you have a reputation in the world, in Europe. You are German. No matter, you have the German passport, you can go anywhere. If something happens, the German embassy, the German government backs you. They don't abandon you. If something happens to me here, if somebody cries at all in Turkey, it is my mother, but the government, or the Turkish consulate here, they don't care.[lxxxvi] (Ali Bilgic)

Later in the interview, he also mentions that he has insufficient funds for naturalisation at the moment. He feels a little uncomfortable talking about it. For once, he prefers to portray himself as a strongman who gets things done, second, he seems to feel obliged to the interviewer to naturalise. In the context of new immigration, he also mentions the possibility to cast a vote as something favourable. By having a vote, he hopes to prevent immigration of new labour seeking migrants. He repeatedly emphasizes his political interest but overall symbolic motives for naturalisation dominate.

Confident – Legal Motives

Emre Güner (39) arrived in Germany 18 years ago and he runs his own small Turkish restaurant. German citizenship would be valuable to him, but he also needs Turkish citizenship. His motivation to have both passports is mainly instrumental. The symbolic boundary to German society is not extremely relevant for him, with the exception of religion. Interestingly, his response to my question of how he feels in Germany is an episode about his daughter's education. He sends her to a private Turkish Muslim school (*Gülen*), where Islamic traditions are respected. Among the cultural habits he wants to be respected is separation of genders in swimming lessons and on school trips. In his view, some aspects of public schools are problematic for his daughter since she became older. The lack of Muslim education in public schools forces his children, as he sees it, to spend weekends in the mosque (4-5 hours) in order to learn about Islam. However, schools are not the only place of religious discrimination. He perceives strong Islamophobia in Germany more generally. Specific experiences are not personal, but by friends and family. He recounts the story of a relative who applied for the position of a police officer, passed all tests, and was not accepted after he told the employer about his regular prayers.

Emre Güner mentions practical reasons for his interest in both passports. He has worked in Turkey and can receive his pension only as a Turkish citizen. German citizenship would be very helpful to avoid trouble with public administration, banks, and when travelling. The question of easy access to loans is relevant for him as a self-employed businessman. In addition, he feels that officers treat German citizens better than they treat non-Germans. "If, for example, I go to public office and show a German passport, then automatically, well psychologically, they treat you in a different way. Because we are foreigners. We experience this story. We know that. It always makes a difference."[lxxxvii] This example illustrates how, in fact, symbolic and practical motives are often intertwined. Namely, the symbolic meaning of citizenship is instrumental in public office. Although he talks about party positions towards dual citizenship in the beginning of the interview, he would not mention political rights as a reason to have either citizenship. Emre Güner could be described as a transnational citizen. Having both citizenships seems apt for his plan to live in both countries. He conceives of citizenship mainly in instrumental terms. However, part of the instrumentality lies in the symbolic meaning of citizenship.

Light-Hearted / Resigned – No Motivation

Enes Demir (*light-hearted type*) says repeatedly that naturalisation would not change anything. The status of permanent residence is sufficient. Enfranchisement would be a motive for him, but Turkish citizenship is more important because he intends to move to Turkey as a pensioner. He would endorse dual citizenship but does not bring up the issue by himself. The symbolic boundary he perceives is unlikely to change by naturalisation: "I wear it on my head, that I am foreigner."[lxxxviii] However, this is not the main reason that keeps him from naturalisation. He just does not see any advantage in acquiring German citizenship.

No. No. As I said, otherwise I would stand up somehow, I as a foreigner, as a Turk, I am not recognised, then I'd need this German ID. Then I could say at least, listen, I am German, watch out. Well, I haven't had this impression.[lxxxix] (Enes Demir)

He feels at ease in Germany and admits missing it when he is in Turkey: "Well, I say Germany, not my son or my friends here, I say Germany."[xc] His homesickness directed towards Germany is stronger than the one towards Turkey. The stability of his employment is one reason for his wellbeing. He has been working in the same company ever since he moved from Munich to Hamburg for marriage 20 years ago. He highlights that he can practice his religion in that company and that his work schedule allows for visits of the Friday prayer. The most likely scenario for his future as a pensioner is spending summers in his house in Turkey and winters with his son's eventual future family in Germany, an arrangement chosen by many retired Turkish migrants. For this arrangement naturalisation is not necessary. Likewise, Hüseyin Topcu and his wife (*resigned type*) agree on the irrelevance of German citizenship for a decent life in Germany. They deny having considered naturalisation and mention only drawbacks of citizenship acquisition in Germany.

> Wife of HT: Sometimes you get documents, that you can apply for it [citizenship], but you don't do it. And anyhow, you got to work fulltime, many things, for me it wouldn't be the case. I don't know. Why would you pay 550 Euros in order to naturalise? That's the question. Therefore. Well, we haven't considered it.[xci]

She also translates from Turkish his ethnic conception of citizenship. "Well, he says, nothing changes with the passport. Also, when a German becomes Turk, ultimately he becomes German. Nothing changes. The person remains the same. [...] You've got no, I don't know. It's of no help."[xcii] Hence, the couple sees neither legal nor symbolic motives for naturalisation.

5.4 Summary and Discussion

Analysis of the qualitative interviews provides answers to the three sets of questions introduced above. How do immigrants come to perceive symbolic boundaries? How do they deal with it? And how consequential are symbolic motives and legal motives for naturalisation? In this section, I summarize the answers that this chapter provides to each of these questions respectively and discuss them in light of the literature. Further, I briefly point to the explanatory value of the MFS.

What is immigrants' perceived exclusion based on? As shown, symbolic exclusion draws on ethnic and religious otherness. The social construction of *ethnic otherness* is based on the visibility and audibility of Turkishness. Dark skin, black hair, foreign accent, Turkish name, and headscarf are perceived as irreconcilable with Germanness. It is noteworthy that one interviewee claims to be exempt from stigmatization thanks to his fair phenotype. Similar to ethnic othering, the construction of *religious otherness* draws on visibility. Muslim women wearing a headscarf are particularly affected by symbolic exclusion. Other issues relevant to symbolic exclusion based on religious otherness include the (non-)permission of religious practices by employers, institutional accommodation of Islam in public schools, and labour market discrimination against Muslims. Religious accommodation reduces migrants' feelings of exclusion compared to cases where religious needs are the subject of discrimination. As a mere description of boundary perception, these findings resonate with anthropological studies that are concerned with German identity and everyday nationhood. These studies support the notion of a relatively exclusive German identity that tends to be defined in cultural and in ethnic terms (Mandel 2008; Ehrkamp 2006; Miller-Idriss 2006; Schneider 2002). Two quantitative studies corroborate these findings (Kühnel and Leibold 2003; Mäs, Müller, and Opp 2005). They show fluency in German language and German decent to be central qualifications for passing as German. However, none of these studies finds religion to be definitive of German identity. Neither is Christian confession a precondition, nor is Islam an obstacle to identification as German. Still, Spielhaus (2013) argues that Muslims are per se conceived of as the other and according to Amir-Moazami (2005) Muslims describe themselves as *Ausländer* even when they are German citizens. Helbling's (2014) study of natives' attitudes towards Muslims and towards Muslim religious practice yields an interpretation of this seeming paradox. He shows natives to be more hostile towards wearing the headscarf than towards Muslims per se. The curious implication is that Germans can be Muslims but only as long as they forego religious practice. Potential proactive boundary making by immigrants against Germans is an aspect that is neglected in the aforementioned anthropological studies. Ehrkamp (2006) reads Turkish immigrants' reifying understanding of ethnicity as an adaptation to German mainstream discourse. However, the conception of the migrant as a relatively passive object of mainstream definitions is simplistic. In boundary perspective, both groups take part in negotiation of the definitions. While I cannot say much about migrants' proactive boundary making, the perspective adopted in this study allows for taking *re*actions of migrants to symbolic exclusion into account. I next consider migrants' responses to symbolic exclusion as their contribution to the negotiation of boundaries.

How do migrants respond to symbolic exclusion? I identified four broad categories of responses to symbolic exclusion: Confronting stigmatization, deemphasizing stigmatization, avoiding or ignoring stigmatization, and boundary work. This typology is inspired by the literature on responses to stigmatization and on symbolic boundaries. I adopt the strategies of confronting and deemphasizing conflict and the one of ignoring and avoiding from prior studies. Fleming et al. (2012) applied them in a study of African Americans and Bickerstaff (2012) did so in her study of first generation French Black. The strategies I summarized as 'boundary work' are inspired by and partly analogous to Wimmer's 'elementary strategies of boundary making' (2008a). Although Wimmer accounts for most boundary making strategies in his book (2013), Lamont's concept of responses to stigmatization is more useful for the study of alternating responses. Here, the focus is on the process of boundary negotiation; the ways actors respond to exclusion while combining several strategies. For example, my categories of confronting and deemphasizing could both aim at boundary blurring in Wimmer's taxonomy. But additionally, confronting may aim at status equality of migrants and non-migrants and deemphasizing could aim at individual crossing. I would argue that the 'responses perspective' allows for a clearer look at the means employed by minority members, while Wimmer's perspective is more suited for analysing the strategic goals they pursue. Along these lines, Lamont is interested in 'how group formation is dependent on the quest for cultural citizenship and dignity, especially in the face of racialization and stigmatization' (2014, 816). Wimmer considers the means of boundary making of dominated and dominant groups in his book as he remarks in reply to Lamont (Wimmer 2014). Also he stresses the heterogeneity of ethnic groups and their members' strategies. Still, his taxonomy assumes coherent actor strategies. When it comes to the analysis of immediate and context-dependent responses to symbolic exclusion Lamont's model is more helpful. However, the risk in a pure Lamontian approach lies in neglecting subordinate group members' potential for making boundaries against others. Therefore, I propose a combination of both approaches to study subordinate group members' strategies for dealing with symbolic exclusion.

Figure 5.1 Responses, Strategies, and Boundary Outcomes

general strategy	resigned insular light-hearted	bullish frustrated confident	
outcome	stasis / bright boundary	crossing (individual)	blurring or shifting (collective)
reactive particular responses *proactive*	avoiding / ignoring making boundaries between	deemphasizing making boundaries within	confronting blurring boundaries between

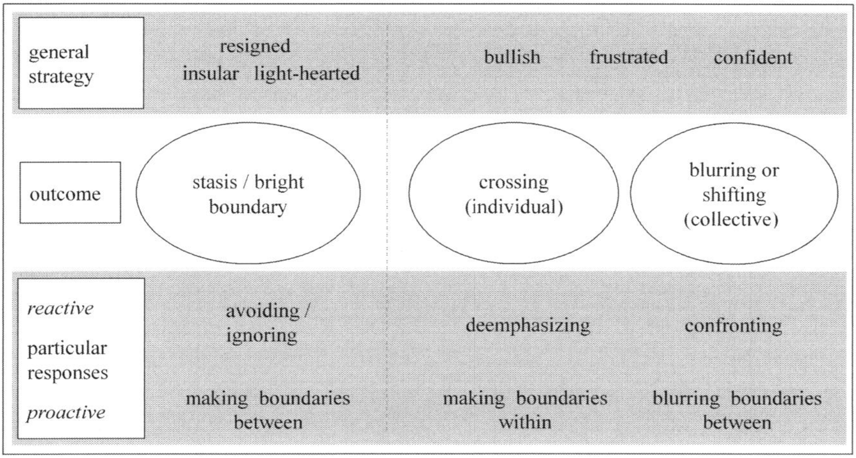

Figure by author.

Figure 5.1 illustrates how general strategies and particular responses relate to particular boundary outcomes. There are no simple causal relations between particular responses, general strategies, and boundary outcomes. Certain general strategies are more likely to encompass particular responses of a certain kind and they are more likely to result in certain boundary outcomes than in others. In short, the relations are probabilistic as opposed to deterministic. However, general strategies and particular responses are more clearly related to bright boundary outcomes than to the other two outcomes. Crossing and blurring/shifting may result from the same strategies. For example, bullish strategies tend to aim for individual boundary crossing but may also aim at blurring. Making boundaries within typically is a means to improve one's social status, which points to individual crossing. At the same time, status improvement applies to all fellow members of the group that is defined by the new boundary within, pointing to a collective strategy. In other words, if ego claims to assimilate more easily because he comes from Istanbul, then he, willingly or not, makes a claim for all migrants from Istanbul. That shows why Wimmer's classification is not tailored to my analytical problems. Moving down the level of abstraction as I do, it becomes more difficult to assign actions to categories of Wimmer's taxonomy. My analytical approach is tailored towards assessing boundary negotiation in a specific context referring to specific (latent) groups.

Next, I present a brief review of the responses to stigmatization I identified before I compare them to research findings. *Confronting* responses include teaching the ignorant and striking back. They aim at changing the stigma. *Deemphasizing* responses include the assumption of individual responsibility and relativizing or excusing racism. The assumption of individual responsibility is one of the predominant responses of interviewees. Sometimes migrants prefer to *ignore or avoid* stigmatization and sometimes they are just helpless and passive. This is usually one of several strategies that are applied depending on the context. The responses summarized under the category of *boundary work* are proactive strategies that pre-empt symbolic exclusion. The category of making boundaries *within* refers to differentiations within groups that aim at underlining similarities with the mainstream and thereby blur the boundary between a sub-minority and majority, or a sub-majority and minority. Making boundaries *between* does the opposite by pronouncing differences of the minority to the mainstream. However, this is not necessarily a primary strategy. Ethnic differentiations are so common that even those who want to eliminate them may refer to these concepts unconsciously. When responses aim at blurring without making boundaries within, they do so by making non-national categories salient. The predominant boundary work found in the interviews is making boundaries between.

Since this is the first German study of responses to stigmatization, I can only compare my findings to studies of other countries. That seems useful where the minority-majority constellation is similar to the one studied here. Most of the constellations are similar in their contrast of a structurally empowered group discriminating against a disadvantaged group. Often the disadvantaged group is an ethnic minority with visual markers that allow for distinguishing them from the mainstream. Turks' assumption of individual responsibility resonates with North African immigrants in France who describe themselves as 'the good Arabs' (Lamont 2000, 202) and African Americans' 'managing the self' (Crystal M. Fleming, Lamont, and Welburn 2012). Different from African Americans, however, Turkish residents would not dress up in order to reduce stigmatization. Similar to them, they claim to control racism by their own behaviour. As for North Africans in France, hard work is a major way of assuming responsibility. The case of Middle Eastern immigrants in Sweden (Bursell 2012) is particularly interesting because of cultural proximity between Germany and Sweden. Apparently, these migrants experience their original name as an instrument of exclusion and report improved social recognition and job chances once they change their name to a Swedish one. Germany does not provide the institutionalised opportunity to change names. However, when it comes to naming their offspring, German Turks tend to prefer Turkish names (Becker 2009; Gerhards and Hans 2009) although labour market discrimination against Turkish names promises pay-offs for ambiguous names.[74] Mizrachi and Herzog (2012) study three Israeli groups that are discriminated against based on their ethnic otherness. Their phenotype makes group membership visible for Ethiopian Jews and Arab Israelis whereas Mizrahi Jews are harder to recognise based on visual features. Although they are legal citizens, all three groups are subject to symbolic exclusion. The two Jewish groups deemphasize racism and emphasize similarity by referral to Zionist values. Arab Israelis instead admit racial discrimination and respond by assuming individual responsibility, showing that they are good Arabs, or they try to blur boundaries by making reference to universal human traits. It is noteworthy that the cultural script of Zionism is a potential resort to symbolic exclusion while religion serves as an indicator of difference in many contexts. North African migrants in France are shown to draw on their Muslim religion in order to respond to symbolic exclusion (Lamont 2000; Lamont, Morning, and Mooney 2002). Islam variously serves here as a script for two opposite purposes: To argue for equality of mankind or to argue for North African superiority. Turkish migrants in Germany are less likely to argue for their equality or superiority based on Islam. Although religion is a recurrent issue in many interviews, respondents rarely refer to it as a moral script. Like North Africans in France, African Americans, and Arab Israelis they usually rely on their performance as good citizens. Notably, the only interviewee to argue for Muslim superiority has

---

[74] According to Lucassen (2005) German citizens from former Polish territories often changed their names to avoid stigmatization (ibid, 72). Today, some immigrant groups chose bi-cultural names that are common in the country of origin and in Germany (Gerhards and Hans 2009).

retreated from the labour market after frustration of her aspirations. However, the scarcity of Muslim superiority may partly result from the selectivity of the sample.

If cultural contexts yield different scripts for responses to stigmatization, as Lamont, Welburn, and Crystal Fleming (2013) argue, then Germany offers a meritocratic script of earning recognition by patience, civic duty, and labour market performance. This resonates too well with the proverbial Calvinist work ethic (Weber 1947) and with identity constructions around work among North African and White working class members in France and White and Black workers in the US (Lamont 2000). However, this finding is likely to be biased by the absence of cases of downward assimilation in my sample.[75] Future research should therefore include migrants and their offspring whose struggle for meritocratic achievement has been in vain.

After analysis of responses at the level of action, I proposed six general response types to describe ideal typical respondents. Starting with the two prevailing ones, I described six different types as frustrated, bullish, confident, light-hearted, resigned, and insular respectively. Whereas migrants combine particular responses in non-exclusive ways, general response strategies refer to migrants' specific combinations of particular responses. Migrants of the *frustrated* type have been struggling for recognition for many years, but feel that their efforts remain unrewarded. Against the background of common portrayals of immigrants as lazy and living on social welfare, they assume individual responsibility by working hard. Since their hope for symbolic inclusion is in vain, they have a slight tendency to avoid contexts of potential stigmatization and retreat to their family and ethnic community. This is counterbalanced by strong political stakes that manifest in political action at the local level (e.g. school, neighbourhood, and mosque). *Bullish* persons conceive of symbolic exclusion as an unavoidable feature of life that they fortunately know how to deal with. Besides relativizing racism, they assume individual responsibility through hard work. They often make boundaries within both groups to argue for their own similarity with the cultural mainstream. They never avoid but sometimes ignore stigmatization. Persons of the *confident* type do neither perceive symbolic exclusion nor make boundaries against the mainstream culture. They emphasize non-ethnic categories such as professional achievement to argue for similarity with the German mainstream. They do not conceive of negative stereotypes against Turks as everyday racism. Persons of the *light-hearted* type assume a passive role in the given topography of boundaries. They conceive of ethnicity as primordial and feel comfortable with the situation although it may not be ideal. The comfort is

---

[75] Lamont (2000) acknowledges this as a potential selectivity of her interviews, too (ibid, Appendix A, fn.13).

partly explained by the absence of experiences of discrimination and some sense of recognition, although not as symbolic members of society. The *resigned* type is similar to the light-hearted one, but differs in one important respect. While light-hearted persons do accept bright boundaries willy-nilly, the resigned ones seem to endorse ethnic boundaries. They avoid symbolic exclusion by moving into neighbourhoods with predominantly non-German inhabitants. Persons of the *insular* type do not *perceive* a boundary that mainstream society makes towards them but *make* one against German mainstream culture. They refuse to assimilate to the mainstream and want to preserve their original Turkish culture.

How are these general response strategies reflected in the literature? Whereas former research has analysed particular responses, it has not assessed general strategies at actor-level. Hence, the literature on responses to stigmatization yields no material for comparison with my six types. However, some findings resonate with the psychological literature on resilience to stigmatization (see review by Son Hing 2013). These experimental studies find persons who believe in meritocratic ideals to be less resilient to stigmatization. A finding that fits with the frustration in those whose struggles for recognition through structural and cultural assimilation have been in vain. Generally, these studies find higher self-esteem, as in my bullish and confident types, to foster resilience. In addition to psychological research, there are some interesting parallels of general response types with updated versions of assimilation theory (for overviews see Alba and Nee 1997; Esser 2008). Portes and Zhou (1993) pointed out that there is no single path of assimilation that all immigrants uniformly follow (see also Portes and Rumbaut 2001). Instead, immigrants assimilate selectively to certain segments and aspects of mainstream society, and their assimilation is conditioned by incorporation at multiple levels. The three levels Portes and Zhou (1993) differentiate include receptiveness of state policies, hostility of the host society, and the strength of the ethnic community. They find empirical evidence for three of the potential outcomes generated by the variation at all three levels. These three outcomes are summarized as full-scale assimilation to the white middle class, downward assimilation into underclass, and economic upward mobility combined with cultural preservation. While they use that scheme to differentiate assimilation trajectories of different second generation ethnic groups, my study makes differentiations inside a single group across generations. For a comparison of both concepts, I categorize German government policies towards Turks as receptive and societal reception according to the boundary perception of each type as (not) prejudiced (see Table 5.3). The assessment of perceived societal perception is an essential difference to Portes and Zhou's scheme. It allows for variation inside one immigrant group whereas in the original scheme societal reception is allowed to vary only between immigrant groups. I have not assessed the strength of ethnic communities, but would assume that they vary according to the location. Overall, the extent of ethnic segregation in German is not comparable to the US (e.g. Alba and Nee 1997 for an overview). The only mention of ethnic neighbourhoods was by a person of the resigned type who pointed to high ethnic concentration. But even here, the partner's job was with a German employer. I have not assessed the causal connection between response strategies and assimilation outcomes but I would expect causality to work both ways. General response strategies might explain variation in segmented assimilation pathways where variation in the three levels of incorporation is absent. Most general response strategies I identified among interviewees are parallel to structural assimilation to the middle class. Namely, that applies to bullish, frustrated, and light-hearted types. However, diverging from the type of middle-class assimilation Portes and Zhou (1993) describe for the US, all of these three response types preserve their original culture. Also, those who drop out of the labour market at some point do not find new employment at higher age.[76] Those persons' former structural assimilation to the middle-class can be said to fail on the long run. The resigned strategy coincides with structural downward assimilation and a countercultural attitude, sometimes termed reactive ethnicity (Portes and Rumbaut 2001). The insular strategy might also coincide with structural downward assimilation, but I lack evidence on this type. It is theoretically possible that, in presence of strong ethnic networks, resigned and insular strategies could correlate with more economic success although educational assimilation is likely to be imperfect. Putnam (2007) has coined the term 'hunkering down' for this strategy of building ethnic islands. Finally, confident types perceive societal reception as unprejudiced and assimilate to both cultures, but are not necessarily successful in structural assimilation. Table 5.3 summarizes the comparison of my findings on general response strategies with the theory of segmented assimilation. This tentative comparison shows how the 'responses'-approach accounts for variation within ethnic groups and thereby contributes to broader theories of assimilation. Societal reception is perceived variously within ethnic minorities and structural assimilation and cultural assimilation/preservation may vary independently of macro-level incorporation.

Once I identified particular responses and general strategies, I also assessed the potential of the MFS to define conditions that make one or the other response more likely. The MFS-based explanation of responses to stigmatization rests on two basic assumptions. First, actors are expected to maximize the SEU of their actions, hence symbolic exclusion causes discomfort (Eisenberger and Lieber-

---

[76] I cannot discuss the flexibility of the German labour market here, but J. Mollenkopf and J. Hochschild (2010) argue, that the stronger regulation in Europe hampers incorporation of immigrants.

man 2004; Kross et al. 2011). Second, the calculation of SEU builds on past experiences with responses' consequences (Bandura 1977). Based on these assumptions, I identified the conditions that render particular responses more likely and explain why certain actor types prefer certain responses over others. I explained, for example, why confronting responses are rare, why persons with strong Muslim identities of the frustrated type are more likely to respond by confronting than those with weak or no religious identity, and why persons who are easily identifiable as others are more likely to attribute unfriendly treatment to their otherness. For encompassing explanations of responses, three kinds of information are needed: information about the context of symbolic exclusion, information about the history of prior responses' consequences, and information on the general response type.

Table 5.3 Segmented Assimilation and General Response Strategies

Government Policy	receptive				
Co-ethnic Community	varies by location (not assessed)			strong	
Perceived Societal Reception	prejudiced			not prejudiced	
General Response Strategy	resigned	bullish	frustrated / light-hearted	confident	insular
Cultural Assimilation	no	yes	yes	yes	no
Cultural Preservation	yes	yes	yes	yes	yes
Structural Assimilation	downward	middle-class / downward		various	ethnic economy

Table by author. Adapted from Portes and Zhou (1993).

The third and last set of questions is concerned with the consequentiality of legal and symbolic motives for naturalisation intentions. What do we learn about the intertwining of legal and symbolic motives of naturalisation? And what are the consequences for naturalisation intentions? The answers are given in the light of the response strategies I identified. At first glance, we do not learn much in terms of simplification. Naturalisation decisions imply myriad costs and benefits of material and symbolic kind. Often it is impossible to predict an outcome of the idiosyncratic negotiations of pros and cons. In order to provide an answer here, I analysed what citizenship means to migrants as the last step of interview analysis. Exemplarily, I presented one vignette for each general response strategy with empirical representation (all except insular). The five vignettes illustrate that reasons for and against naturalisation result from complex individual considerations. Individuals' experiences and interests differ, and sometimes the resulting intention to acquire host country citizenship is surprising given the indifference towards citizenship interviewees convey. Sometimes the wish to naturalise remains unrealised and some migrants want to naturalise although they do not want to become symbolic members. Still, naturalisation intentions appear somewhat less haphazard once general response strategies are accounted for.

Table 5.4 summarizes naturalisation intentions of the six response types as conditional upon dual citizenship toleration vs. unconditional and reports the dominant motivation of immigrants (symbolic vs. legal). Two findings stick out: Few persons want to naturalise under the condition of renouncing their former passport and all but persons of the bullish type have a dominant legal motivation for naturalisation, while insular people would refute to naturalise for symbolic reasons. The implication is that only persons of the bullish type are motivated to naturalise by the aspiration of symbolic membership. At the same time bullish type persons are the only ones with an unconditional interest in German citizenship and current non-eligibility is the reason why they have not naturalised yet. However, some bullish type persons, next to frustrated and confident ones, would only naturalise under dual citizenship toleration, whereas light-hearted and resigned persons are generally uninterested in German citizenship.

Table 5.4 Intention to Naturalise and Dominant Motivation by General Response Strategy

	naturalisation intention			dominant motivation	
	no	yes, if DC* tolerated	yes, unconditional	symbolic	legal
frustrated		▓			▓
bullish		▓	▓	▓	
confident		▓			▓
light-hearted	▓				
resigned	▓				
insular	▓			▓	

*DC=dual citizenship; table by author.

Why then are unconditional naturalisation intentions so rare? Three main factors render German citizenship unattractive. For once, relatively expansive rights for alien permanent residents reduce the value added of German citizenship. This is a reason why some migrants conceive German citizenship to be superfluous. Second, the requirement to renounce Turkish citizenship makes naturalisation relatively costly, keeping those with a conditional interest from naturalisation. Third, to most respondents it seems impossible to be recognised as full symbolic members reflected by the emptiness of the column 'dominant symbolic motivation' in Table 5.4. As shown above, symbolic membership tends to be inaccessible for Turkish immigrants because of phenotypical, language-related, and religious discrimination. This is irrelevant for migrants who have instrumental conceptions of citizenship. These persons either immigrated rather recently or have lived in Germany for many years without huge efforts of cultural assimilation. Symbolic recognition is more relevant to those who have been living in Germany for a longer period of time, often decades, and made efforts to assimilate. Those who feel that they are recognised as symbolic members, namely the confident and the bullish type, may still decide against German citizenship, as long as it means renunciation of the Turkish one. Those who feel excluded from symbolic membership, the light-hearted, the resigned, and the frustrated type, do not intend to naturalise unless there are strong legal motives. Their symbolic membership is at risk in Turkey in case of renounced citizenship and possibly unattainable in Germany even after naturalisation. The combination of non-tolerated dual citizenship and symbolic exclusion keeps that group from naturalisation unless there are legal incentives. Only among persons of the bullish type, symbolic motives for naturalisation prevail. However, their emotional attachment to citizenship often includes the Turkish one. Hence, even some persons of the bullish type postpone their decision until dual citizenship is eventually tolerated. The relation of legal and symbolic motives can be summed up as follows. Legal incentives are conducive to naturalisation intentions although sometimes the decision to naturalise can be based on symbolic reasons. Symbolic boundaries are an obstacle to naturalisation only if legal incentives are absent or irrelevant for an individual. In that case, the boundary threat is aggravated by the requirement to renounce the former citizenship. Symbolic exclusion would be less relevant for naturalisation if dual citizenship was tolerated.

Table 5.5 Sampling and General Response Types

	Weak legal motives	Strong legal motives
Blurred/shifted/no boundary perception	Bullish, confident, light-hearted, resigned	Bullish, confident[a]
Bright boundary perception	Insular, resigned[a]	Frustrated, confident, bullish

[a]No interviews/hypothesised. Table by author.

There is one caveat we have to keep in mind while analysing the interviews. Purposeful sampling intentionally focused on certain participants and disregarded other potential ones. The sample includes ideal cases with bright boundary perceptions and strong legal motives one the one hand, and no perceived boundary but weak legal motives on the other hand. Naturalisation motives of the two remaining ideal cases of bright boundary perception combined with weak legal motives, or no boundary perception combined with strong legal motives are rather obvious. The former have no reason to naturalise whatsoever, and the latter have all reasons to naturalise. Responses to stigmatization could have been analysed only for persons of the former type, who feel excluded. They are likely to be of the insular or resigned type because they react to symbolic exclusion with indifference. Those without boundary perception and strong legal motives are likely to be of the bullish or confident type because these are the only types to perceive no exclusion that are willing to naturalise for legal reasons. However, most persons are to be categorised somewhere between these ideal types with intermediate legal motives and more ambivalent perceptions of inclusion or exclusion. It should be kept in mind that the sampling and interview analyses are based on extreme cases.

While recent research on naturalisation in Germany often accounts for legal and symbolic motives (Diehl and Blohm 2001; 2008; 2003; Hochman 2011; Wunderlich 2005) it has failed to define the conditions that render the one or the other motivation more relevant. This is more obvious where immigrants originate from different countries and citizenship constellations are different. Below the level of groups, some familiarity with individual cases is necessary to understand diverging perceptions and motives. The aim was to identify regularities among these individual strategies. My systematization of individual strategies into types is a small advance in that direction. The 'responses'-approach shines a light on ethnic minority members as active stakeholders in the negotiation of symbolic boundaries. The taxonomy of particular response strategies is a variation of the known ones. However, the identification of general response strategies at the actor level goes beyond past approaches. The application and adaptation of these taxonomies to other groups and contexts promises theoretical development. The analysis of responses' consequences for naturalisation intentions provided here, shows how they are relevant for integration outcomes. Further research is needed to see how responses are causally connected to other dimensions of assimilation.

6. General Discussion and Conclusion

In this chapter, I first discuss the value added of approaching the subject of naturalisation from two angles using two different methods. The first section closes with directions for future surveys and a short excursion on the epistemological pitfalls of my research design. In the second section, I summarize main findings and reflect on their implications. I conclude with directions for future research on symbolic boundary negotiation and naturalisation.

6.1 Insights from Mixed Methods

What is the value added of applying two methods to answer my twofold research question? The aim of this research was to understand low naturalisation rates in spite of dwindling legal hurdles. The theory-driven idea was to think of legal and symbolic dimensions of citizenship as intertwined and to understand naturalisation as motivated by legal and symbolic considerations. Certainly both parts of the study illuminate aspects of legal and symbolic membership and their role in naturalisation intentions, but what are the concrete advantages of the mixed methods design?

A major gain of the sequential mixed methods design as applied here is its reflexivity aiming at objectivation of the researcher and at overcoming the dualism of structure and agency (Fries 2009; Robbins 2007; Bourdieu 2004). For once, in-depth interviews objectivate the researcher and his perspective by accounting for the subjects' perspectives and questioning the results of quantitative analysis. In other words the quantitative constructions can be deconstructed before the abstractions are reconstructed based on qualitative analysis and used to build new typologies. Second, mixing of quantitative and qualitative methods mirrors Bourdieu's dialogical understanding of interacting social and individual structures. Individuals are influenced by, but at the same time, producers of social structure. While the survey confronts them with structural givens that shape their naturalisation, in-depth interviews focus on minority members' subjective perceptions of those structures and their involvement in stabilizing or changing them. Put differently, the application of several methods allows for identification of clashing and reinforcing evidence (Bryman 2003). Along these lines, this chapter shows how the quantitative and the qualitative approach complement each other. The survey had a twofold goal. The first one was to develop an understanding of the general significance of symbolic motives (related to symbolic membership) compared to legal motives (related to legal membership). I aimed to develop an index variable of boundary perception and experienced exclusion based on the survey. However, it proved impossible to summarize the respective items into a single coherent index. Consequentially, the interviews aimed at refining the theoretical understanding of symbolic boundaries. I found respondents to vary in the ways they perceive symbolic exclusion and in the responses they provide. Ethnic minorities' 'responses to stigmatization' in other countries are relevant landmarks for this research. In-depth interviews compared to survey questions account more explicitly for the agency of migrants. Overall, the particular strengths of each method should complement each other leading to better understandings of symbolic boundaries and naturalisation intentions.

Complementary Qualitative and Quantitative Findings

The comparison of the quantitative and the qualitative part of my research project yields two major results. First, both elements of the study support the notion that a joined consideration of legal and symbolic motives yields a better understanding of naturalisation intentions than either kind of motives in isolation. Second, the theoretical model I tested in the quantitative analysis is unfit to account for migrants' responses to stigmatization. Qualitative interviews expose this theoretical shortcoming and provide input for a more fine-grained view of symbolic boundary perception. These interviews are no adequate instrument to check the effects established in multivariate analysis of survey results one by one. Their main purpose was to complement survey findings with a more subjective perspective of migrants. In-depth interviews allow for the interpretation of selected inconsistencies between theoretical predictions and empirical findings in multivariate analysis. Taking into account insights from in-depth interviews, I interpret anew the effects for perceived discrimination, the interaction of feeling at home and perceived discrimination, and the interaction between family effects and age.

Personal vs. Group Discrimination

One curious multivariate finding concerning symbolic aspects of citizenship is that perceived personal discrimination is on average lower than perceived group discrimination ($\bar{x}_{\text{group}}=2.64$; $\bar{x}_{\text{personal}}=2.26$), a phenomenon that is well known from other studies. Qualitative interviews provide an interpretation here. Interviewees sometimes treat everyday racism as a distinct and less serious phenomenon than physical racist violence or structural racism. Some respondents denied negative experiences when I asked them if they had been treated differently. For example, Ibrahim Kaya added that xenophobic remarks were rather common but he got never beat. "You are harassed while queuing at the cash desk or when it's taking too long at the gas station. Then you notice that they are the ones who'd like to kill you. And real racism, personally, I haven't noticed. Like being punched or whatnot, I haven't."[xciii] But qualitative interviews do more than illustrate why perceived group discrimination tends to be higher than personal experiences of discrimination. As elaborated in chapter 5, the denial of personal discrimination may represent a conscious or unconscious particular response to racism. Turkish residents often deemphasize or ignore racism, at least in its more subtle non-physical form. In some cases, perceived group discrimination could be inflated since media reports and word of mouth easily create the impression of group discrimination in the absence of personal experiences. Indeed, qualitative interviews show that some migrants are very sensitive to the ways migrants are portrayed in the media, while others neglect xenophobic discourses and events.[77] Those who are more sensitive tend to refer to events of local relevance rather than to events that received national attention. They more often perceive stronger group discrimination. Also, some male respondents report more frequent everyday racism against their female family members than against themselves. This is another reason why they might report more group discrimination than personal discrimination in a questionnaire. However, the average discrepancy between the two levels of discrimination is similar for men and women and in half of the cases their perceived discrimination is similar at personal and group level. This is in accordance with the qualitative finding that respondents employ different responses to stigmatization.

The discrepancy between perceived personal and group discrimination resonates with other studies. Dian and Kawakami (1996) find higher perceived group discrimination than personal discrimination for ethnic minorities in Canada. Crosby (1984) reports similar findings for labour market discrimination of women. She offers a threefold interpretation for the divergence of admitting personal vs. collective discrimination in surveys. First, it is socially desirable not to be a victim who fails to change her situation. Second, individuals tend to explain the

---

[77] Paradigmatic events and discourses I refer to here include the so called NSU-affair seen by many as proof of racially biased police investigation, xenophobic sentiments stirred in 2010 by Thilo Sarrazin's bestselling book 'Germany does away with itself' (orig. *Deutschland schafft sich ab*; for an assessment of the book and the ensuing debate see Bade (2013)), and the arson attacks on foreigners' homes in the early 1990s. However, few respondents mentioned these incidences.

treatment they receive with their performance. This would lead them to attribute non-invitation to a job-interview to their application documents rather than to their ethnic otherness. Third, other than collective victims of discrimination, individual victims imply individual villains. Human beings feel uncomfortable with that because they like to believe in a just world. Therefore, "[c]ompared with the perception of individual suffering, the perception of group suffering arouses little psychological discomfort" (ibid, 380). Taylor et al. (1990) confirm the discrepancy in reporting collective vs. personal discrimination on a sample of immigrants in Canada. They offer two additional interpretations next to the denial of personal discrimination. Individuals may exaggerate group discrimination where it serves collective goals of political claims or personal goals like success in spite of group discrimination. In addition, information on discrimination against the group may be cognitively available more easily than personal experience because of gossip and media reports. Salentin (2007) discusses some of the problems resulting from the measurement of discrimination by perceptions. Based on an original survey of ethnic minorities in Germany (N=301) he shows perceived personal discrimination to be conditioned by ethnic identity, perception of general discrimination, gender, and employment status. Namely, persons with a strong ethnic identity, Turkish, males, and those with employment or in apprenticeship or in the educational system report more frequent discrimination than the respective counterparts. Those who are generally convinced of discrimination are more likely to find incidents of personal discrimination severe. Overall, these studies echo the finding of stronger perceived group than personal discrimination. However, interpretations of this finding vary and argue either that perceived personal discrimination is underestimated or exaggerated respectively. Based on my findings on responses to stigmatization, I would argue that both interpretations are justified. It needs information on individual attitudes in order to judge whether respondents over- or under-report personal discrimination. This study provides intellectual input for the formulation of respective items.[78] I develop initial ideas for such items below.

Feeling at Home in Germany

Symbolic boundaries were measured in quantitative analyses as a combination of feeling at home in Germany and feeling discriminated as a group. One might expect the two variables to correlate negatively but the correlation between the

---

[78] Kahanec and Tosun (2009) include information on the "positive nature" of respondents and find a positive effect on naturalisation in multivariate analyses. However, the measure relies on interviewer assessment.

two variables is only weakly negative (r=-.07) and only slightly higher between feeling at home and personal discrimination (r=-.16). Based on quantitative data it is difficult to provide an explanation for the independence of both variables. Again, the insight obtained from qualitative interviews that minority members apply diverse 'response strategies' provides an interpretation for the independence of feeling at home and feeling discriminated against (as a group). For example, Zelife Arslan of the confident type has had no experiences of discrimination whatsoever, but still she feels lonely and not at home in Germany because she has no friends and her family is in Turkey. At the other extreme, Tayfun Akgün of the frustrated type has often felt discriminated against, but still feels at home in Germany. Again, qualitative interviews allow for an association of those cases with particular response strategies. Namely, those of the frustrated and the bullish type apply a whole range of particular responses to racism in order to protect a basic comfort with living in Germany. Those of the confident or resigned type on the other hand, sometimes would not experience exclusion because they have little or no contact with Germans. In some cases, the result is feeling not at home in Germany although discrimination is absent. Hence, feeling at home apparently is a good predictor of naturalisation intentions in multivariate analysis, but it is imprecise as an indicator of accommodation. Perceived discrimination reduces migrants' feeling at home in Germany sometimes but not necessarily.

Age & Family-Effects

In multivariate analyses, I found a negative age effect on naturalisation *intentions* and pointed to the positive age effect on *being* naturalised that other studies find. Further, the share of German family members was shown to have an unexpected negative effect on naturalisation intentions. Qualitative interviews show how the interaction of age and family contributes to an answer. Most of my qualitative interviewees are either over 40 years old or immigrated rather recently and are much younger then. Those who are older tend to have naturalised German children. In one interview, a father reported having prepared citizenship applications for the whole family but had withdrawn his personal application at the very last moment. In that light, the negative effect of having German family members might be an artefact of researching a particular population, namely, the unnaturalised. A sample of naturalised persons would be likely to reveal families that naturalised jointly. Just like studies that find positive age effects on being naturalised, such a sample might yield a positive impact of naturalised family members on being naturalised. Put differently, having naturalised family members might be a good indicator of being naturalised, even if it is a negative correlate of the intention to naturalise. Finally, those who migrated more recently for marriage are sometimes but not always more willing to naturalise. This inclination is independent of their partners' citizenship.

Theoretical Refinements and Lessons for Future Surveys

Few of my findings utterly diverge by the method of data collection. Qualitative interviews allow for a refinement of my theoretical concepts. In line with the rationale of the sequential mixed methods design, qualitative interviews allowed for questioning quantitative findings. As Erzberger and Kelle (2003) argue, "divergent empirical findings should not always be considered as an indicator of a poor research design; instead, they may be considered as a pointer to new theoretical insights" (ibid, 475). The theoretical refinements concern the theoretical idea of perceived symbolic boundaries as illustrated in Table 2.1. Boundary perception is not as straightforward as expected. As qualitative interviews show, even those who experience symbolic exclusion of their group by the mainstream do not necessarily perceive a bright ethnic boundary. Symbolic exclusion is an attempt the success of which is contingent on the response by the migrant. In other words, symbolic boundary perception is a function of experienced symbolic exclusion that is mediated by migrants' responses to stigmatization. Hence, researchers interested in boundary perception should assess those responses in addition to measures of perceived exclusion. I deal with the issue of operationalizing responses to stigmatization in the next section.

The main insight from the qualitative interviews is that the excluded respond to practices of exclusion in various ways. The question is whether those particular responses are relevant for quantitative studies and if yes, how they could be assessed. As discussed in chapter 5, there are hardly obvious causal connections between response strategies and naturalisation decisions. Hence, one might argue that it is not necessarily insightful to evaluate responses to stigmatization if the aim is to understand naturalisation decisions. However, response strategies allow for a more realistic description of naturalisation motives and they could be interesting even as a mere description of immigrant populations. Table 6.1 presents some ideas for an operationalization of particular response strategies as items in a questionnaire. General response strategies could be deduced from the answers according to type descriptions in chapter 5. To complete information for the resigned and the insular type, it would be necessary to collect information on the residential situation of the respondent, i.e. the ethnic concentration and whether living in a segregated neighbourhood is a deliberate choice. Generally, there are certain limits to the operationalization of responses to stigmatization. In qualitative interviews, respondents set the relevance of certain responses. Once the questionnaire makes potential responses salient, respondents are overall more likely to agree with them. Hence, standardized question-formats may lead to different results compared to open-ended formats.

Table 6.1 Operationalization of Particular Responses

Concept	Item (response scales)
	How often have you felt that you are treated differently because of your ethnic origin?
	How often have you reacted in one of the following ways?
Teach the ignorant	Explained the perpetrator that he is wrong
Strike back	Verbal attack against the perpetrator
	Legal means against the perpetrator
Ignore	Tried not to listen to the perpetrator
Avoid	Avoid places where I might be treated differently
	How much do you agree with the following statements
Ind. responsibility	Those who work hard are not discriminated against
	Those who behave like decent citizens are not discriminated against
	I work hard / I am a decent citizen
	If [ethnics] are discriminated against that is because they deserve it
Excuse /relativize racism	Racism exists in all countries
	Racism exists only among old persons
Blame the racist	People who discriminate against [ethnics] are stupid
Blurring b's betw.	Ethnic identities (e.g. German, Turkish) don't matter for who we are
Making b's betw.	[Ethnics] are overall superior to [nationals] / [Nationals] are overall superior to [ethnics]
	Overall, how similar you think you are to [include option: no answer]
Making b's within	Other Turkish citizens living in Germany
Making b's within	Other Turkish citizens living in Turkey
Blurring b's /	Other German citizens
Making b's betw.	Citizens of [city of residence]

Table by author.

Next to 'responses', it would be interesting to evaluate different forms of discrimination such as structural discrimination, everyday racism, and racial violence. This would allow for more thorough descriptions of the nature of symbolic boundaries. The main differentiation of symbolic exclusion that have been identified in the interview analysis is between ethnic and religious otherness. The concrete manifestations of exclusionary practices refer to deviation from 'the normal German' in phenotype, name, accent or language skills, or by exposing culturally suspicious behaviours like going shopping with the whole family, not drinking alcohol, eating halal meat, wearing the headscarf, taking breaks for prayer at work, and going to the mosque. Table A12 presents items that would cover relevant issues of symbolic exclusion. Since questionnaires are normally constrained in the number of items they can account for, I also want to give guidance for the most parsimonious solution. When it comes to predicting naturalisation intentions, the most effective items from a broader range were 'feeling at home' and 'perceived group discrimination' even if they may not provide a realistic assessment of symbolic boundary perception.

Even if the measurement of symbolic boundary perception is improved, determining the relevance of symbolic membership for naturalisation remains difficult. The reason is more substantial than measurement. Qualitative interviews show many Turkish residents to find cultural membership out of reach. There is nothing they can do to be recognized as Germans and they do not expect German citizenship to support recognition. These persons are unlikely to naturalise for symbolic reasons and will base their naturalisation decisions on instrumental considerations instead. Based on multivariate analysis of survey results one would find symbolic motives to be less relevant than instrumental motives. As for naturalisation decisions this finding is correct, but it would be wrong to conclude that migrants are not interested in symbolic recognition. Motives for naturalisation are instrumental because the hope of symbolic recognition is in vain. Those who naturalise may have an interest in becoming symbolic members, but they do not maintain hopes to be recognized thereafter. Qualitative interviews support this interpretation. Therefore, interpretations of migrants being uninterested in symbolic membership are misguided.

Like many mixed methods studies, the present one implies a clash of philosophical worldviews. Following the simple differentiation by Creswell (2009, 5) my approach fits best with a pragmatic worldview.[79] The point of departure was a twofold research question and the methodical repertoire was exploited in pragmatic fashion transgressing paradigmatic boundaries. The approach of my quantitative research is postpositivist in its determinism, reductionism, and in the idea of theory-testing based on empirical observation. In the in-depth interviews constructivist ideas of theory generation from participants' multiple constructions of meaning predominate. Instead of subscribing to either philosophy, I defend the oscillation between theoretical construction, empirical testing, theoretical deconstruction, and empirically guided reconstruction of theory. When it comes to the choice of methods, this study follows Bourdieu's dictum that "it is forbidden to forbid" (Bourdieu and Wacquant 1992, 227) the use of any. Obviously, this approach can be criticized for being opportunistic, or, worse, for neglecting fundamental contradictions between the epistemological foundations of the methods mixed (Small 2011, 77). For example, recruitment of survey participants follows the logic of randomized sampling while participants of qualitative interviews have been sampled purposefully. However, I would argue that

---

[79] Creswell differentiates postpositivism, constructivism, advocacy, and pragmatism (ibid, 6).

each method follows a particular logic for good reason and the logic of randomized sampling, for instance, simply does not fit small-N studies like the in-depth interviews. Further, each method has its weaknesses and its blind spots. Multi-method research supports the reflexivity of science regarding those flaws. Hence, and here I agree with Small (2011), the best thing we can do is to lay the deficits and possible incommensurability bare. It remains with the reader to judge whether mono-method research was a better answer to the concerns raised against pragmatic combination of research methods and their philosophies.

I can think of various methods to get a more comprehensive understanding of symbolic boundary negotiations. An assessment of boundary definitions by mainstream members would complement the analysis in fruitful ways. Longitudinal data would allow for studying long-term dynamics, and focus groups with migrant and mainstream participants, for instance, would allow for the observation of actual boundary negotiations. Still, my qualitative interviews are an advance from the static perspective I was compelled to apply, just like most quantitative studies, in the analysis of survey results.

6.2 General Conclusion

This book seeks to elucidate the motives of Turkish citizens to naturalise in their country of residence Germany. A considerable share of this group refrains from naturalisation although they are legally eligible. I argue for a differentiation of legal and symbolic membership to improve the understanding of naturalisation. While legal membership follows in a straightforward manner from citizenship, symbolic membership is subject to ongoing negotiations between citizens and non-citizens with stakes in the host country. I show how the concept of symbolic boundaries helps to account for the dynamic nature of these negotiation processes. When it comes to the empirical assessment of these boundary negotiations, the study of minority members' responses to stigmatization is particularly insightful. This moves us from mere 'lazy boundary talk' – to paraphrase Hedström and Ylikoski (2010) – to actual analysis of dynamic boundary negotiations. To my knowledge, this is the first mixed methods study at the intersection of boundary negotiations and naturalisation intentions.[80] Based on multivariate analyses of original survey data, I establish the empirical significance of legal and symbolic motives in naturalisation intentions. Naturalisation is best under-

---

[80] Street (2014, 2013) has combined qualitative interviews with secondary data to assess the role of family in naturalisation decisions. However, Street assigns a merely illustrative function to his interviews.

stood by accounting for both kinds of motives. Qualitative follow-up interviews reveal various strategies that minority members deploy in response to (attempts of) symbolic exclusion. Alien residents' general response strategies provide no comprehensive explanation of naturalisation intentions but enlighten certain aspects.

Insights from the Survey

The aim of the survey was to assess the relative relevance of various legal and symbolic aspects of citizenship for naturalisation. Overall, legal aspects of citizenship contribute more than symbolic aspects to the prediction of naturalisation intentions, but the combination of both aspects yields the best predictions. Persons with an interest in franchise in Germany are more inclined to naturalise. The same is true for those who expect job-related, or travel-related benefits, feel at home in Germany, were born in Germany, and are younger. Interest in rights connected to the Turkish passport concerning voting and property negatively affect the intention to naturalise. In addition, persons who think that Turks are discriminated against in Germany are less inclined to naturalise. These findings are all in line with the expectations formulated in chapter 4 but there are some caveats that I address in the next paragraph. The effects of political interest in Germany, age, being born in Germany, feeling at home in Germany, and perceived discrimination resonate with past research findings. The effects of expected job- and travel-related benefits and interest in rights in Turkey have not been assessed quantitatively before. Thus, the analyses provided here corroborate many quantitative findings and complement qualitative studies that identified these factors as relevant for naturalisation decisions.

Next to the confirmed hypotheses, there are three kinds of surprises: no effects where I hypothesised them, effects contrary to what I hypothesised, and effects where I had not expected to find any. I start with a discussion of the last kind of surprise because therein lies some explanation of the other surprises. Separate regressions by gender prove the robustness of major effects but also reveal gender differences that I had not expected. Generally, predicted probabilities for naturalisation intentions are similar between both genders. Also, central legal and symbolic motives have similar effects for each gender, but the significance varies. Among legal aspects, the effect of interest in citizenship-specific rights in Turkey is only significant for women. The expectation of job- and travel-related benefits on the other hand is only significant for men. Apparently, women are more attached to the Turkish passport for legal motives. Among symbolic aspects, the negative effect of naturalised family members is only significant for men. Drawing on findings by Street (2014, 2013) I pointed to the sampling procedure in order to understand this finding. Before the 2000's reform of citizenship law, migrant families often naturalised collectively because naturalisation with a parent was the only way for minors to acquire citizenship.[81] The parent who deliberately refrained at that moment is unlikely to change his mind later on. After his deliberate choice, he is less likely to intend to naturalise.[82] Indeed, in qualitative interviews there were some cases of un-naturalised parents with naturalised children. Thus, the effect of naturalised family members might still be positive in a sample of naturalised persons and my findings can be read as support for Street's. Not to find effects where I hypothesised them is the third surprise. This is true of the identity-relevance of passports. Neither does the emotional attachment to the Turkish passport decrease the inclination to naturalise, nor does the prospect of enhancing emotional attachment to Germany increase the inclination to naturalise. The same is true for the share of naturalised friends. There is no effect where I expected a positive one. Apparently then, role models for naturalisation are not as relevant as expected. A post hoc interpretation that would find support in qualitative interviews is that some naturalised friends regret naturalisation in retrospect because symbolic inclusion does not follow legal membership. By drawing on those friends' experience, one would abstain from naturalisation. In spite of these three surprises, the theoretical models make decent predictions of the inclination to naturalise. I next set out to qualify results with the help of in-depth interviews.

Insights from Qualitative Interviews

The analysis of in-depth interviews is organized around three issues: The content of symbolic exclusion, the responses to that exclusion, and the intertwining of legal and symbolic motives in naturalisation intentions. Perceived symbolic exclusion is based on construction of the other on ethnic and religious grounds. Turkish minority members feel that visibility and audibility of their Turkishness and their Muslim religion are seen as incongruous with being German. Concretely, phenotypical features like dark skin and dark hair, a foreign accent, a foreign name, and the headscarf are impediments to being recognized as symbolic members. It is noteworthy that visibility of Muslim religion is often a means of symbolic exclusion. With the headscarf as a common and visible marker, women are subject to exclusion more often than men. That leaves Tayfun Akgün with the impression that the rules of recognition are dictated as he plays the game. "But

---

[81] This is changed through the jus soli provision in place since 2000 (*StAG*, §§4, 29, 40b).
[82] At the same time he might be more willing than others to reflect on his decision by answering survey questions.

back then at the door nobody said, wait, if you enter here, you've got to leave your clothes, change your skin colour, change your hair colour, and then you can enter and belong to us."[xciv] Ali Bilgic's experience of not being discriminated against thanks to his fair complexion is a case in point. In principle, this echoes former research findings. However, quantitative studies that assessed the meaning of various cultural aspects for German identity found no effects for religion. Helbling's (2014) finding that Muslims are better received than Muslim religious practice could explain this seeming inconsistency. Seemingly, religious diversity is accepted as long as it does not materialize. It is important to note that not all migrants perceive symbolic exclusion and those who do, respond in different ways.

The analysis of these responses was the next step in the project, starting with particular responses at the level of action and continuing with general response strategies at the actor level. Four categories of particular responses are identified: confronting stigmatization, deemphasizing stigmatization, avoiding or ignoring stigmatization, and boundary work. The last category comprises proactive strategies and the former response strategies are classified as reactive. This categorization combines elements from two literatures. One source are the studies inspired by Lamont's 2000 book *The Dignity of Working Men* (Bickerstaff 2012; Fleming et al. 2012; Lamont, Morning, and Mooney 2002). The second source is Wimmer's (2008a) set of 'elementary strategies of boundary making', some of which I adapted for my category of boundary work. Confronting responses have more conciliatory forms like teaching the ignorant on his flawed views harsher versions of striking back including legal action. These responses aim at overcoming symbolic exclusion. Deemphasizing responses are most often realised by assuming individual responsibility and sometimes by relativizing or excusing racism. The assumption of individual responsibility, a dominant response among Turkish migrants, is well known from other groups in other contexts and usually means struggle for recognition by hard work (Lamont 2000). However, different from African Americans, Turks in Germany do not manage the self by dressing up and showing material wealth. They rather work hard and perform decently similar to minority members in France and Israel comporting like 'good Arabs' (Mizrachi and Herzog 2012; Lamont 2000). Deemphasizing responses aim at overcoming symbolic exclusion by denying its significance. When the desire and the opportunity for confronting are not given and the discriminated are unwilling to deemphasize stigmatization, they ignore or avoid it. These somewhat fatalistic responses often go along with helplessness or frustration. The last category of boundary work subsumes three strategies that in fact pre-empt symbolic exclusion. Some minority members make boundaries within their own group or within the mainstream in order to blur the differentiation between a fraction of the minority and the mainstream, or between a fraction of the mainstream and the minority respectively. Here, socio-structural differentiations (employed vs. welfare receiver) and socio-cultural differentiations (urban Turk vs. rural Kurd) function to replace the boundary between minority and mainstream. Sometimes minority members do the opposite by pronouncing differences between minority and mainstream. This often happens through unconscious reifying understandings of certain characteristics as ethnic and less often as deliberate boundary construction. In the latter case, Turks or Muslims are framed as superior by ascription of positive qualities such as family loving, humane, and forgiving whereas Germans are described as individualistic and egoistic. Lamont and colleagues have also found this phenomenon among African Americans and French North Africans (Lamont 2000, 77; Lamont, Morning, and Mooney 2002). Finally, minority members sometimes aim at blurring boundaries towards the mainstream by emphasizing commonalities between Turks and mainstream members. Minority members refer to their participation in the German Christian tradition of Christmas and to 'normal' comportment like working and paying taxes. Further, they question exclusive understandings of nationality.

While the identification of responses at the level of action is the endpoint for many studies, this book explores whether certain persons systematically prefer types of particular responses over others. As a result, I came up with six types of general response strategies: Frustrated, bullish, confident, resigned, light-hearted, and insular. Frustrated and bullish types prevail. Migrants of the frustrated type assume individual responsibility, but also confront stigmatization. They have been struggling for recognition for many years and feel that all efforts are in vain. Therefore, they sometimes avoid contexts where symbolic exclusion might occur and retreat to their home and family instead. However, strong political stakes prevent them from total retreat into the private sphere. Persons of the bullish type take symbolic exclusion as a given that they know how to deal with. They assume individual responsibility by working hard, and, depending on the context, they sometimes confront and sometimes relativize racism. Although they may sometimes ignore racism, they do not avoid contexts of potential stigmatization, and they never feel helpless. In order to blur the boundary between themselves and Germans, they often make boundaries within the minority or within the mainstream. Persons of the confident type do neither perceive nor make boundaries towards the mainstream. Their ignorance of negative stereotypes against Turks vaccinates them against symbolic exclusion and their positive professional experience supports their perception that they are equal to Germans. Light-hearted migrants do not cherish symbolic boundaries but conceive of them as unavoidable, given primordial ethnicity. Their comfort with the topography of ethnic boundaries is supported by the absence of experienced discrimination. Resigned persons are more supportive of the boundary landscape. Since nothing can be changed about it, they prefer to avoid symbolic exclusion by moving into ethnic neighbourhoods. Like the confident, persons of the insular type do not perceive symbolic exclusion. Insular type persons preserve their original culture, keep German culture at distance, and make a boundary with the mainstream. No person of this type was interviewed, but the type follows from the dimensional logic of the topology and can be traced in some interviews. These six types have implications for all dimensions of assimilation. Therefore, I showed how they refer to the theory of segmented assimilation (Portes and Rumbaut 2001, Portes and Zhou 1993). The differentiation of societal reception, co-ethnic community, structural and cultural assimilation, and cultural preservation is complementary with the six response types. However, in boundary perspective, the idea of societal reception of ethnic groups is under-complex. I complicate the perspective by invoking the *perceived* societal reception. The prevalence of cultural preservation among all response types is a noteworthy difference to the American context. Whether cultural preservation is stable in the third and fourth generation remains to be answered by future research. As for the consequences of general response strategies, I next explored whether they systematically affect naturalisation intentions.

While systemizing the connection between response types and naturalisation I invoked the differentiation of legal and symbolic motives. Further, it proved reasonable to differentiate unconditional naturalisation intentions from intentions that are conditional on the toleration of dual citizenship (see Table 6.2). As a matter of fact, only some persons of the bullish type want to naturalise unconditionally. Other bullish, but also frustrated and confident persons, would naturalise only if they could keep their Turkish citizenship. Persons of the bullish type are also unmatched in their dominant symbolic motivation. Their strong self-esteem provides autonomy from legal resources of citizenship. They would naturalise to reaffirm their symbolic membership in Germany. Diverging from that, persons of the frustrated type do not believe in symbolic qua legal membership. Confident persons are indifferent to the symbolic meaning of German citizenship and sometimes also to the symbolic meaning of Turkish citizenship. Instead, legal motives are dominant among frustrated and confident persons. The remaining types are not interested in German citizenship. This systematization resonates with my multivariate survey findings. First, it provides an explanation why many migrants do not naturalise in spite of the high share of persons interested in German citizenship. These people are waiting for the toleration of dual citizenship until they realise their intention. As long as the law remains unchanged, they prefer to make do with their status as alien residents unless there are strong legal incentives. Even those who are ready to renounce their Turkish passport struggle with the prospect of neglected symbolic membership in German society. Second, the systematization underlines the relative dominance of legal over symbolic motives in understanding naturalisation intentions. To most immigrants, symbolic membership aspiration is not a motivation because they are either uninterested (resigned, insular, confident), or do not believe that legal membership is conducive to symbolic recognition (light-hearted, frustrated). Table 6.2 summarizes central findings from both parts of the study. It connects response types to dominant motives, (un)conditional naturalisation intentions, perceived symbolic exclusion, and the consequentiality of perceived symbolic exclusion. As shown, persons of the frustrated type, who made strong efforts to earn recognition, are the only group of persons to consider symbolic exclusion problematic. The other types either know how to deal with exclusion (bullish), perceive none (confident, insular), or consider it irrelevant (resigned, light-hearted). The causal connection of responses and naturalisation intentions contributes to the literature that is seeking to understand naturalisation and to the one that is interested in responses to stigmatization. While quantitative studies of naturalisation are simply unable to provide sophisticated measurements of symbolic boundaries, no qualitative study has focused on the nexus of symbolic and legal membership. Among the two most serious qualitative explorations of naturalisation, one does account for various motives of persons of various origins (Wunderlich 2005), and the other one restricts the examination to Turks but accounts for multiple motives (Prümm 2004). My approach was different in restricting the analysis to one group, accounting for the multiplicity of motives in the quantitative analysis, and delving into the conundrums of symbolic membership in in-depth follow-up interviews. The literature on responses to stigmatization has only hinted to the consequences of responses for different dimensions of assimilation. Bursell (2012) indicates the positive effects of name change on labour market assimilation, various studies have pointed to the connection of response strategies and identificational assimilation (Bickerstaff 2012; Lamont 2000; Mizrachi and Herzog 2012), and some have argued that responses to stigmatization could mediate the effect of inequality on health (Lamont 2009; for a review see Son Hing 2013). My study adds to this growing literature by providing an analysis of systematic effects of 'responses' on naturalisation intentions.

Table 6.2 Central Mixed Methods Findings on Intended Naturalisation

QUANT	QUAL	Naturalisation	perceived symbolic exclusion	symbolic exclusion problematic
Instrumental motives	frustrated	conditional upon DC*	yes	yes
	confident	conditional upon DC*	no	-
	light-hearted	no	yes	no
	resigned	no	yes	no
Symbolic motives	bullish	some conditional upon DC, some unconditionally	yes	no
none	insular	no	no	-

*DC= dual citizenship. Table by author.

Religion is an aspect of symbolic exclusion that I have not given as much attention as some might expect. The analysis of public discourse might yield the result that symbolic exclusion is based on Islamophobia, but my empirical observation does not. Also, the argument risks reifying groups of Muslims and of non-Muslims who are associated with the rejection of Islam. That is exactly what the boundary perspective seeks to avoid in the realm of ethnicity, hence, the same caution is required in the realm of religion. My theoretical perspective implies a processual understanding of groupness that is incompatible with preconceived ethnic and religious groups. Obviously, religion is an issue when symbolic exclusion is based on religious markers. It is therefore little surprising that some minority members perceive their religion and especially the visible parts of it, to be grounds of discrimination. To support the claim that exclusion is based on religiosity, however, mainstream members would have to be interviewed concerning their attitude towards Islam and Muslims. One of the few serious quantitative analyses on this subject finds attitudes against wearing the headscarf to be more negative than attitudes against Muslims (Helbling 2014). That study further finds xenophobia to be the strongest predictor of negative attitudes against both, Muslims and the headscarf. Based on the information I gathered, all that can be claimed is that religious markers serve as pretext for symbolic exclusion. Certainly, the concept of 'Islamophobia' is often defined vaguely enough to see my findings as supporting evidence.[83] Still, I would argue that we gain conceptual clarity if we remain with the concept of symbolic boundaries and conceive of religion as one possible means of, and pretext for, social exclusion. In other words, Turks who are not (visibly) Muslim, are excluded for other haphazard reasons, e.g. because they have black hair. The logic of exclusion follows the stickiest stigmas. Also, we would lose from the theoreti-

---

[83] Bleich (2011) defines Islamophobia as 'indiscriminate negative attitudes or emotions directed at Islam or Muslims'. See also the discussion by (Helbling 2013).

cal presumption of Islamophobia because we would miss the variation of experiences and perceptions that Muslim minority members report.[84] In spite of the theoretical precaution, this study shows Turkish Muslims to be the target of discrimination. Turkish Muslim women are particularly prone to stigmatization when they wear a headscarf, making them easily identifiable as different. This finding echoes Helbling's (2014) finding that European natives are particularly intolerant towards Muslim religious practice. Employers are in a position not only to reduce discrimination at labour market-entry, but also when dealing with religious needs of their employees. In my interviews, there are examples of both extremes: an employer that is generous when it comes to accommodating religious needs and an employer that is particularly prohibitive. In addition, the prohibitive stance of the latter company apparently fuels employees' aversion against their Muslim co-worker. That exemplifies the potential impact of institutional on symbolic boundaries. The resulting feelings of recognition and religious discrimination of the respective Muslims translate to other contexts. Hence, employers bear a responsibility when it comes to the general accommodation of immigrants. Apparently, Muslim migrants who may pray at work feel generally recognised, whereas migrants who are prohibited religious practice at work feel that they are discriminated against in Germany. This point is worthwhile further exploration in future research.

Next to the employer, there are other actors with definitional power to change the chances of recognition. As elaborated in chapter 3, this was one of the reasons to study the case of Hamburg. The city-state has been running a campaign to promote naturalisation since 2011. Resident aliens who have lived in Hamburg for more than eight years are invited personally via mail and a PR-campaign features role models who naturalised in the past. Naturalisation is framed as membership acquisition in Germany, supplementing 'citizenship' of Hamburg. Posters display testimonials holding an anchor in the colours of the German flag, symbolizing membership in Hamburg and Germany. However, the brochures avoid literal mentions of becoming German or Hamburger and speak of *Einbürgerung* (naturalisation) instead. A ceremony in the venerable town hall underlines the exceptional character of citizenship acquisition and the friendly character of the invitation.[85] The campaign does not define symbolic membership in very explicit terms. The notion that is conveyed is one of inviting diversity for accommodation in a rather vaguely defined community of 'us'. Hence, the campaign can be seen as an elite attempt of boundary blurring and shifting.

---

[84] By that I do not intend that religion does not matter for the construction of boundaries. I find fruitful the macro-analysis of institutional support for religious boundaries (e.g. Amir-Moazami 2013; Lewicki 2014).
[85] See Jakob (2017) for a comprehensive discussion of naturalization ceremonies in Germany.

However, even aliens who cherish the gesture will not be convinced easily if they want to keep their former citizenship. Furthermore, the elite discourse will be of little consequence for the everyday experience of alien residents. In the worst case then, discursive blurring of the elite in spite of legal exclusiveness and experienced bright boundaries is understood as hypocritical and implausible. Along these lines, the elite discourse is most credible for aliens who perceive blurred boundaries and can keep their original citizenship after naturalisation. This study does not provide evidence for a positive effect of the campaign on Turkish residents' naturalisation intentions. However, this is no final verdict on the impact of elite blurring of boundaries since an encompassing evaluation of the campaign was not the central concern. Still, the campaign would potentially increase its credibility by parallel blurring of legal boundaries and by addressing mainstream society next to resident aliens.[86]

Contributions

This study speaks to several research strands and makes both empirical and theoretical contributions. I address these contributions one by one. *First*, my findings resonate with research on naturalisation and naturalisation intentions. Through the development of an issue-specific survey, I was able to synthesize qualitative and quantitative findings. Most quantitative studies resort to secondary data and are therefore restricted in their models to the items they find in what are usually general surveys. Kahanec and Tosun (2009) are an exception because the dataset they use has some more detailed information on the relationship between ethnic minorities and mainstream society. However, in my survey, I systematically accounted for research findings and translated them into corresponding survey items. I was in the comfortable situation to draw on two rather recent in-depth qualitative studies (Prümm 2004; Wunderlich 2005) next to an abundance of quantitative studies, including some on Germany. In addition, there was enough information on the peculiarities of Turkish residents since they are the most studied migrant group in the German context. This literature provided guidance for the assessment of aspects of legal and symbolic membership for Turkish residents. In this way, I was able to focus on the particular aspect of symbolic membership for citizenship in qualitative interviews. *Second*, insights from my qualitative interviews speak to a literature that is concerned with everyday nationhood. Although the concept of ethnic boundary does not figure prominently in this literature, it ultimately explores how symbolic boundaries are con-

---

[86] I am aware that citizenship law is decided at national level. However, interviews indicate that minority members are not necessarily aware of federalism's peculiarities.

structed in everyday interactions (Fox and Miller-Idriss 2008; Surak 2012). Everyday nationhood was not the focus of this study, but I analysed Turkish residents' construction of meanings of citizenship. Interviews indicate that naturalisation is only rarely seen as an avenue to symbolic belonging. *Third*, the analysis of responses to stigmatization and symbolic exclusion resonates with a literature that has gained momentum recently and is at the heart of Michèle Lamont's research agenda. Although the number of countries and minorities studied in this framework is quickly expanding (see Lamont and Mizrachi 2012), Germany and its minorities have been neglected so far. I show how comparison of the German Turkish minority to other minorities in Sweden, the US, France, and Israel can be made fruitful. But this is certainly not the last word on responses to stigmatization in various contexts, especially if the aim is to build an overarching theoretical framework (Lamont 2009; Lamont, Welburn, and Crystal Fleming 2013; Lamont et al. 2016). In a broader perspective, responses to stigmatization are but one of several 'cultural processes' that are relevant to the understanding of inequality (Lamont, Beljean, and Clair 2014). I have only considered here the consequences of stigmatization for citizenship acquisition. The agenda Lamont and her colleagues develop is much broader. In their perspective, stigmatization is at one level with other cultural processes of standardization, evaluation, and racialization that have consequences for material and symbolic resource allocation and location-based inequality. If citizenship is understood as a source of symbolic and material inequality, more theoretical and empirical work will be needed in order to establish the links between cultural processes of exclusion and the consequences for legal inclusion and for resource allocation. In this view, outcomes are open-ended and the research focus is on the ongoing (boundary) negotiations of dominant and dominated. *Fourth*, next to empirical contributions just described I make theoretical ones to the study of symbolic boundaries and the study of responses to stigmatization. My theoretical model makes a clear differentiation between macro- and micro-level implications of the boundary perspective. While institutional arrangements define the nature of boundaries at the macro-level, boundary perceptions at the micro-level are negotiated in interactions. My analysis of responses to stigmatization shows the reach and limits of Wimmer's (2008a) taxonomy of elementary strategies of boundary making. His model is useful for the categorization of boundary negotiations that have come to a settlement. Although he considers the strategy of individual crossing, his model is more suitable where group interests are homogeneous. My focus on the process of boundary negotiation at the micro-level requires a more flexible perspective because individuals often combine several sometimes contradictory strategies in a parallel manner. Lamont's concept of responses to stigmatization proved useful here. I show that Turkish residents' self-descriptions invoke the ideal of decent persons who work hard and pay taxes. They reject the notion of burdening or abusing the welfare state. Furthermore, I identify general response strategies at the actor-level and show how these general strategies refer to assimilation outcomes predicted by the theory of segmented assimilation. The German context, requires a more complex model that allows for variation in the *perceived* societal reception among persons from the same country of origin. Moreover, structural assimilation outcomes vary irrespective of the uniformity in cultural preservation and are not fully explained by the variation in cultural assimilation. It needs the general response strategies in order to fully understand structural assimilation outcomes. However, an empirical test with quantitative data would complement the qualitative analyses that has been provided here. *Fifth*, some political theorists call for interdisciplinary and empirical work at the nexus of migration and citizenship (e.g. Bauböck 1994b; Bosniak 2006; Carens 2013). For example, Bauböck (1994b) develops a tentative rational choice model to support his normative argument of how to incentivise naturalisation, but he leaves the empirical test to other researchers. My approach does not question the institution of national citizenship as some theorists would like to see (e.g. Bader 1995; Bosniak 2006; Shachar 2007), and indeed such perspectives are of little help for empirical studies. However, I do account for the social constructedness of national membership by exploring the link between socially negotiated and legally codified membership. This is what Joseph Carens is concerned with in his theory of social membership. He makes a normative claim to social membership qua residence:

"For citizens of immigrant origin to feel that they belong, they have to see that other citizens regard them as equals, take their concerns and interests seriously, and want to find ways of living together that are satisfactory to all. And the other citizens can reasonably expect to see the same attitudes and dispositions in the citizens of immigrant origin. But the power lies with the majority and the weight of the existing rules reflects that" (Carens 2013, 71).

The theoretical conception of legal and symbolic boundaries chosen in this book allows for an assessment of the empirical obstacles to that ideal. As described above, citizenship is conceptualised as institutional support of symbolic boundaries. Where Carens neglects the dynamic element of boundary negotiation, the boundary approach emphasizes the agency of minority members, even where they may be lead to assume symbolic exclusion. Hence, this study is an important supplement of normative perspectives on migration's consequences for citizenship. *Finally*, the study has important policy implications next to the academic contributions. In the introduction, I have echoed liberal theorists' claim that states have an obligation to incorporate residents into the polity, to turn permanently resident aliens into citizens, or, more precisely, to make acquisition optional (e.g. Bauböck 1994a; 1994b; Carens 2013; Walzer 1983). Past failure of political incorporation compounds deficient representation today (Jones-Correa 1998; Jennifer L. Hochschild and John H. Mollenkopf 2009). Although access to German citizenship has been liberalised throughout the 1990s, many permanent residents still refuse to naturalise in spite of eligibility. One remaining hurdle is the requirement to renounce the former passport. It is almost common knowledge among policy makers that the non-toleration of dual citizenship is the most significant remaining hurdle to naturalisation for Turks in particular. Proponents of dual citizenship have argued that toleration would be more coherent with the transnational practice of Turkish-German migrants (Kaya 2012) and that liberal ideals of universal associational and political rights should overrule plural citizenship's ostensible and diffuse threat to security, equality, and solidarity (Spiro 2010). However, the continued failure of left-wing parties' legislative proposals to find majorities leaves little reason to expect change in the near future. Taking this stalemate into consideration, one insight of this study is actually news because it invalidates an argument of exclusive citizenship's proponents. Qualitative interviews reveal that those who are interested in German citizenship but refrain unless they can keep their original passport are assimilated structurally and culturally. Adversaries of liberal access who are usually opponents of dual citizenship conceive of naturalisation as the last step of a successful assimilation process. This study shows that many migrants are stuck without German citizenship at the end of successful assimilation because they are not ready to disconnect with their country of origin. These persons have a strong work ethic, they send their children to German schools, and many of them are committed to the German polity. They are ready to endorse the link with their new home country through naturalisation under one condition: they want to keep their former citizenship which is already tolerated for many other immigrant groups in Germany. Their example should allay the fear of split loyalties in case of dual citizenship toleration. The larger concern in my view is that their striving for symbolic recognition is frustrated and their potential for political commitment is wasted.

This book focuses on a particular membership constellation, but I have developed ideas for a comparative framework in order to relate the case of Turks in Germany to other sending-country-receiving-country-constellations. This framework gives guidance for national and international comparisons of naturalisation motives. It shows that accounting for specific citizenship constellations is crucial because the constellations define opportunities and incentives for naturalisation. My quantitative analysis of motives for naturalisation gives directions for the consideration of respective items in future surveys. The qualitative analysis of responses to stigmatization is a starting point for the future assessment of particular strategies. Qualitative research should expand the analysis of boundary negotiations in several directions. First, I was unable to assess to what extend boundary work is proactive from the side of minority members. Interviews with persons of the insular type, who preserve their ethnic culture without mingling with the mainstream, have particular promise here. Second, boundary making by the mainstream has been assessed only indirectly in the perceptions of minority members. Hence, interviews with mainstream members would be a helpful complement. Third, boundary definitions evolve over time; thus, longitudinal studies are needed to assess their change dynamics. Varying boundary perceptions promise insights from the systematic comparison of generations of immigrants and their different approaches to the negotiation of boundaries. Fourth, comparative studies will allow for disentanglement of the role (dual) citizenship has for symbolic recognition in countries with different conceptions of cultural belonging. And finally, I want to underline that naturalisation is not the panacea for political inclusion of immigrants. Their legal inclusion is a necessary condition for their political incorporation. To what extent it increases their participation through the exercise of political rights remains may depend on context and groups (Hainmueller, Hangartner, and Pietrantuono 2015; Levin 2013; Street 2017). Once they become citizens, they are on the right track to political incorporation, but there is no automatism. However, the primary challenge to Western democracies is more substantive. At the beginning of the 21st century, high proportions of the population are not even part of the polity. After several decades of post-war immigration, it is time to blur legal and symbolic boundaries; time to recognise the new residents as citizens and embrace their dual attachments.

Original Interview Passages

[i] Bin schon eigentlich recht gut eingedeutscht, wenn man das Wort mal so verwenden kann, ne. Hab auch schon mehr die deutsche Mentalität und hör mir auch deswegen öfter an, bist gar kein Türke mehr undso. Kennt man ja, ne. Wenn man als Türke in der Türkei ist, ist man eigentlich n Deutscher. Wenn man hier ist, ist man eigentlich immer n Ausländer.

[ii] Also wenn man von Ausländern spricht, spricht man automatisch vom Türken. Wenn im deutschen Staat irgendetwas nicht richtig ist - und gegen Ausländer ist - dann ist es meistens gegen Türken. Türken sind die- es gibt ein Wort dafür - die Sündenböcke. Egal welche Nationalitäten irgendwelchen Scheiß machen, das sind eben immer die Türken. Das finde ich eigentlich schade, weil es gibt tatsächlich genug Türken, die lange genug hier sind und sich etabliert haben und die sich selbstständig gemacht haben eventuell, einen guten Job machen aber trotzdem wird das alles über einen Kamm geschert.

[iii] Denn die Person selber wird sich nicht ändern - das heißt, wenn ich jetzt die deutsche Staatsbürgerschaft hätte- dann wär ich für meine Kollegen oder für meine Freunde immer noch der Ibrahim. Ich habe zwar den deutschen Personalausweis aber ich bin immer noch der Türke, oder der Kanake wie einige Kollegen sagen - auch Spaß natürlich - und das werde ich auch bleiben. Das werde ich 100 % bleiben.

[iv] Die deutsche Gesellschaft möchte die Ausländer nicht so sehen wie sie sind als Mensch, sondern sie gucken nur auf dem Ausweis, dass man die Staatsangehörigkeit hat. Und das ist sehr ärgerlich. Und nur deswegen möchte ich nicht Deutscher werden weil ich - davon hab ich nichts. Ich kann arbeiten, ich verdiene mein Geld, ich bezahle meine Steuern ich bin seit 42 Jahren in Deutschland. Seit 42 Jahren in Deutschland! Und ich darf nicht wählen. Warum nicht?

[v] Dadurch werde ich meine Staatsangehörigkeit nicht ändern. Weil, ich bleib immer Türke. Weil auf meinem Ausweis steht mein Name. Ich bin [Name] also bleibe ich auch [Name]. Auch wenn hinten Deutscher steht. Ich kann doch gar nicht Deutscher sein, ich habe einen anderen Namen.

[vi] Ja, und wie gesagt, ich habe keine großen Probleme gehabt in Hamburg sag ich mal, weil ich hab immer hell ausgesehen. Ich zeig Dir nachher mal ein paar Bilder von mir. Die Leute haben immer gesagt, ich sei Italiener oder Grieche, ich wüsste nicht was der Unterschied zwischen Griechen und Türken ist, optisch das gleiche Ding.

[vii] AB: Das war ein super netter Typ. Hätte ich vielleicht keinen Mut gehabt und wäre ich nicht hingegangen, hätte ich den Job verloren. Also echt, wir haben uns fantastisch verstanden. Ich hab korrekt gearbeitet. Er war auch korrekt. Ich hab ihn nochmal drauf angesprochen. Du hast mir gesagt, Du willst einen deutschen Trainer. Ich weiß gar nicht mehr was er gesagt hat. Reden wir da nicht drüber. Oder, vergiss es.
Interviewer: War ihm unangenehm, hmm.
AB: Jaja. War auch nicht wichtig. Hat mir auch nicht wehgetan. So ist es ja nicht. Er kannte mich ja nicht. Und später hat er mir mehr bezahlt, oder war großzügig.

[viii] Dadurch, dass ich auch bedeckt bin, dass ich ne Türkin bin, und dass, also mir ist leider hier aufgefallen, dass Türkinnen oder, vor allem Musliminnen, also die bedeckt sind, die so offen sind, die sind sehr angenehm, gewollt undso weiter, aber wenn man so bedeckt ist und noch selbstbewusst

oder irgendwie aus sich was gemacht hat, das merk ich immer, das kommt nicht gut an, also das ist nicht gewollt.

[ix] Wenn Du nicht wie ein Deutscher bist, sei es vom Glauben her, sei es vom Feiern her, und dies und das, dann wird man immer abgestempelt als Türke Ausländer, das ist das halt. Und wir heißt immer: Wir, die abgestempelt werden als Ausländer, egal ob man deutsche Staatsbürgerschaft hat oder nicht.

[x] Für mich ist dieses Land nicht unser Land aber es ist auch nicht anders für mich, also ich nehme es nicht anders auf. Ganz im Gegenteil, ich würde mich vielleicht in meinem Land ein bisschen anders verhalten, weil ich mich vielleicht einfach wie zu Hause fühlen würde. Hier geb ich mehr Acht, Respekt natürlich, das ist bei mir dann noch höher. Weil wir dürfen hier leben, wir dürfen hier alles, wie jeder andere auch machen, deswegen schätze ich dieses Land. Aber leider muss ich sagen so werden wir nicht behandelt. Das wird an uns nicht geschätzt. Und das ist das, was einen immer traurig macht [...] Das ist wirklich, wenn man alles versteht, dann tut einem das immer weh, wenn angesprochen wird, angemacht wird, diskriminiert wird und dann fühlt man sich auch nicht wohl hier ehrlich gesagt.

[xi] Die Deutschen, Deutschland akzeptiert mich nur so lange ich arbeite. Wenn ich arbeitslos bin und Sozialfall bin, dann bin ich ja negativ. Wenn ich arbeite, dann bin ich positiv und in den Medien kursiert das ja immer wieder. Wieder ne Ausländerfamilie, die vom Sozialamt lebt. [...] Aber man merkt dann in der Gesellschaft, auch wenn man positiv ist, gehört man mit zu dieser Gruppe. Man ist Ausländer.

[xii] Also eine Sache, immer wieder, ich finds eklig aber er sagt das immer wieder, die Juden habens hinter sich und euch steht das noch bevor. Sowas sagt er immer öfter. Und das sag ich auch Leuten, auch Vorgesetzten, auch Leuten, die ne bisschen bessere Position haben, denen ich ein bisschen traue, denen sage ich das. och, ist doch scheißegal, lass ihn doch sagen.

[xiii] Da hab ich gefragt, ob ich da denn Möglichkeit hätte zur Gebetszeit auszustempeln. Also nicht auf Kosten der Firma. Auszustempeln und dann einfach meine 5 Minuten oder 10 Minuten Körpergymnastik zu machen und seelische Stabilität zu bekommen, danach wieder weiterarbeiten. Haben die gesagt, nee, das ist was privates und das geht nicht. [...] Ja, also sie können gern was anderes machen, aber beten geht nicht.

[xiv] ED: Gut, ich bin Ausländer, aber ich habe mich nicht so oft als Ausländer gefühlt. [...] Wir können uns hier in Deutschland nicht richtig anpassen, auch in der Türkei nicht, wir sind überall Ausländer. Und so müssen wir leben, wird sich nicht ändern. Wie gesagt, auch wenn ich die deutsche Staatsbürgerschaft habe, bin ich auch Ausländer, werde ich auch Ausländer bleiben, also wird nichts ändern. Ich hab nichts gegen deutsche Staatsbürgerschaft, aber ich brauche das nicht.
Interviewer: Und kannst Du noch mal sagen so, wie fühlst Du Dich in diesem Land?
ED: Sehr wohl. Ich lebe gern in Deutschland. ich fühle mich wohl, wirklich. Ich kann auch meinen Glauben hier ausleben.

[xv] Wenn einer sagt zum Beispiel, ja, die Ausländer nehmen uns den Arbeitsplatz weg, dann frag ich, was ist denn bei den deutschen? Nimmt der dir den Arbeitsplatz nicht weg?

[xvi] Die sieht nur, dass ich arbeitslos bin und schmettert mir gleich den Satz entgegen, ja, arbeitslose Ausländer werden nicht eingebürgert. Hab ich natürlich, bin ich erstmal aufgestanden, bevor ich auf 180 war, hab gesagt, ich will jetzt sofort den Abteilungsleiter sprechen. Kam der, da hab ich erstmal gesagt, passen Sie mal auf, und Sie wundern sich, dass hier in den Behörden und Dienststellen Leute ausrasten.

[xvii] Es gibt z.B. in der Schule einen Kollegen in der Klasse und einer sagt, warum kommen die Leute hierher mit Asyl und mit Familie? Und ich habe gesagt wie alt bist Du, habe ich ihn gefragt. 35. Bist Du verheiratet? Nein. Willst du heiraten? Nein. Ich sage, es gibt in Deutschland viele Menschen wie Dich. [...] Ich habe jetzt zwei Töchter, sag ich ihm, die kommen hinter mir. Wenn du auch irgendwie ein Kind bekommen würdest, dann hättest du Recht. Ich rede nicht über ihn sondern allgemein.

[xviii] Mir ist das auch oft hier aufgefallen. Also ich bin ja wie gesagt hier geboren aufgewachsen. Also so viele Situationen in denen man immernoch mit mir umgegangen wär, als wenn ich son Asylant wär, der gerade erst seit n paar Jahren in Deutschland eingewandert ist. Wenn die Leute aber erst mich reden hören, nach n paar Minuten, dann - öh. Dann sag ich, ja. Ne, weil ich auch wirklich Wörter gebrauche, die ich in den Leuten erstmal erklären muss. Ich sag, sag mal, habt ihr keinen Deutschunterricht gehabt?

[xix] Ich würde so sagen ich bin freundlich, ich mag freundlich sein. So, ich habe bis jetzt immer so gemacht. Natürlich, [unverständlich]. Manche Leute suchen Streit, machen ihre Probleme selber. Zum Beispiel geht jemand auf die Straße und trinkt und ruft, scheiß Ausländer und scheiß Deutsche, und natürlich gibt es dann Probleme. Aber ruhige Leute haben keine Probleme.

[xx] Jetzt, jetzt dieser Doppelpass für uns ist echt gut. Genau für Leute wie uns und einfach hier kein Geld und ich störe Deutschland nicht und ich hier störe Arbeitslosenamt, Jobcenter. Ich bleib in der Türkei.
IP: Du meinst belasten. Wärst Du keine Belastung.
PIP: Ja.

[xxi] Ob man Ausländer ist oder nicht, wenn die Leistungen stimmen, dann kann man auch was erreichen.

[xxii] Also ich kenne Leute aus meinem Bekanntenkreis, die negative Erfahrungen gemacht haben - sprich Rassismus. Ich persönlich habe das nicht erlebt weil ich kann mit den Leuten reden. Man kommt gar nicht dazu in die Richtung Rassismus zu gehen. Ich habe z.B. Arbeitskollegen, da weiß ich, dass sie Rassisten sind, aber mit denen komme ich wunderbar klar, weil ich bin mir sicher, dass die Sprache hier in Deutschland das wichtigste ist. Wenn die Sprache stimmt, dann kommt man wesentlich besser klar.

[xxiii] Und ich bin davon überzeugt, dass es an der Sprache und daran wie du auftrittst liegt, dass man keine Probleme hat. Also meine Frau hat da schon Kleinigkeiten schon öfter erlebt, weil sie eben ein Kopftuch hat. Als Beispiel habe ich dir das Auto gegeben. Also wenn ich mit dem Auto fahre oder meine Schwägerin, die ohne Kopftuch durch die Gegend läuft, die wird gerne mal rein gelassen. Bei meiner Frau da geben die Leute noch Gas. Aber, du kriegst ja auch die Frauen nicht dazu das Kopftuch abzulegen, weil die sagen, meine Religion.

[xxiv] Ich habe es auch mal mit Rechtsradikalen zu tun gehabt in meinen jungen Jahren. Hab dann auch versucht zu reden. Da war so eine Veranstaltung von einem kommunistisches Club, da bin ich auch gewesen, und dann kamen die Rechtsradikalen, die Glatzköpfe, da sind wir mit 3-4 Mann nach vorne und haben eigentlich das Gespräch gesucht, wir haben auch miteinander geredet - keine Gewalt oder so- aber man hat am Ende gemerkt, egal was du den sagst, die haben eine Einstellung, die haben etwas festgesetzt im Kopf, die kriegst du davon nicht weg. Ich bin überzeugt davon, dass solche Leute, dass du heute mit denen redest, vielleicht ein Bier trinkst, und sagst, mensch, wir kommen ja doch klar miteinander, dass der dir am nächsten Tag die Fresse einschlägt.

[xxv] Einer sagt zum Beispiel, geh doch in die Türkei, was machst du hier mit diesen Kenntnissen? Und ich sage mir: das ist ein unerfahrener Mensch ohne Kenntnisse und deswegen sagte er das. Denke ich mal.

[xxvi] Man integriert sich, man versucht das soweit auf beiden Bahnen eben zu halten und hofft dann, wenn man mal einkaufen geht, dass man nicht scharf angesehen wird oder nicht angerempelt wird und nicht irgendwas Schlimmes erlebt. Nicht einer den Parkplatz wegnimmt und nachher pöbelt, immer diese scheiß Ausländer oderso. Man hört zwar in den Medien davon nichts, aber im Leben kommt das zu oft vor, dass die Leute, also uns nervt das gar nicht mehr, wenn wir sowas begegnen. Dann sagen wir, ah , noch ein Spinner und dann gehen wir weiter.

[xxvii] [...] wahrscheinlich liegt das daran, wenn die Politik Langeweile hat, oder Medien undso, irgendwas werfen sie in die Mitte, also Integration und dies und jenes, und diese Debatte ist so, damit lenken sie das Volk ab, zumindest Medien-mäßig . Vielleicht liegt das daran.

[xxviii] Es gibt, wie gesagt, in den Behörden nette Beamten, nette Menschen und schlechte Menschen. Bei einer Person merkst du es sofort, dass sie dich nicht in Deutschland haben möchten und anderen ist das egal. Für den sind wir alle Menschen.

[xxix] Also das ist eine Sache wo ich sage, da ist Deutschland auch super top darin, Bürokratie. Weltmeister [lacht].

[xxx] Dass Leute immer noch nicht aus dem 2. Weltkrieg raus sind und immer noch nicht akzeptieren, dass die Gesellschaft mehrschichtig wird und auch bunter wird. Wenn man mal fragt, so vor 50 Jahren oder 60 Jahren, ob man hier einen Döner haben möchte, dann hätte vielleicht keiner ja gesagt. Nee möchten wir nicht, weil wir wissen ja nicht was das ist. So, jetzt habe ich heute morgen erfahren, ein Kollege hat gesagt, den besten Döner gibt's da und da [...] und da sieht man, das ist wirklich nur die ältere Gesellschaft, die Nachzügler vom Zweiten Weltkrieg, die halt mit dem ganzen noch nicht abgeschlossen haben, die ihre Kinder danach erzogen haben. Das sind wirklich noch, weiß ich nicht, 10 oder 15 % in der Gesellschaft, aber mir macht das mittlerweile nichts mehr aus.

[xxxi] Und von einigen heißt es dann, Du musst es auch mal so sehen, was würdest du denn sagen, wenn Du an seiner Stelle wärst und er wär du? Also wir machen uns da schon Gedanken. Was wär das denn wenn in der Türkei jetzt die deutschen einwandern würden und da arbeiten würden? Und dir das Essen wegnehmen würden in Anführungsstrichen. So die Argumente von denen jetzt grob verglichen.

[xxxii] Oder solche - das hast du bestimmt auch gehört- eine Frau mit Kopftuch ist in der U-Bahn gefahren und jemand hat geschlagen und solche Probleme haben wir nicht erlebt aber gehört. Aber das ist normal so viele Leute leben hier, 3 Millionen Leute, das ist normal. Auch in Istanbul gibt es solche Probleme. Nicht nur gegen Ausländer auch gegen Türken. Solche Probleme gibt es in allen Ländern.

[xxxiii] Aber mit einer freundlichen Art und Weise und grinst auch dabei und das tut nicht weh. Und da macht man auch mal Scherze darüber. Kriegt zwar Tränen in den Augen, weil das einen beleidigt, aber man lacht dann darüber.

[xxxiv] Und wenn man ein bisschen mitgehen kann, dann wird das verwischt. Ich meine wir leben so zusammen in einem fremden Land obwohl wir eigentlich gar nicht mehr so fremd sind und wenn man volle Pulle dagegen hält und sagt, du scheiß Nazi oder so dann entstehen größere Konflikte. Aber wenn man ein bisschen mitgeht und sagt, ok mensch das ist deine Einsicht, deine Einstellung, meine ist ein bisschen anders, dann ist es auch keine große Hürde mehr dann kommt man auch mit den Leuten klar.

[xxxv] Aber wie gesagt, ich erlebe das tagtäglich, tagtäglich. Und manchmal, stellen Sie sich mal vor, wie eine alte Frau, ich sag manchmal, ich möchte nicht von zu Hause raus. Also ich bin ein Mensch, der, also ich hab meine Jugend sehr stark ausgelebt, ich bin immer viel ausgegangen, einkaufen, bummeln, damals, das lässt man nicht so an sich ran, denk ich mal, man kriegt das nicht so mit. Aber so nachdem ich mein Kind hatte, da habe ich das richtig so erlebt. Wie unmenschlich das eigentlich, also wie schlecht es einem gehen kann. Nun sag ich immer, ich bleib am besten zu Hause, ich koche, bügel, wasche, ich bin meinem Kind nützlich, oder jetzt noch meinem Mann dazu. Die sind alle dankbar für das was ich mache. Alles was ich draußen mache, da ist keiner dankbar. Ganz im Gegenteil, da wird noch ordentlich auf den Kopf gehauen, ich mein jetzt wegen Rassismus und so.

[xxxvi] Ich hab nicht hier Probleme gehabt. Seit 12 Jahren wohne ich hier. Hier ist es wie eine Türkei. Am Hauptbahnhof und anderswo ist Deutschland. Hier kann man türkisch reden undso, alles hier. Deswegen kann ich nicht gut deutsch reden, weil immer ich immer türkisch rede.

[xxxvii] Aber ich glaube, ich habe nie etwas erlebt glaube ich. Manchmal schon, z.B. wenn ich gearbeitet habe und so weiter und hatte du - die kennen glaube ich die Türken hier anders- und ich bin ja dort aufgewachsen und kenne unsere Kultur und da haben sie mir immer gesagt: wie kannst du so leben so? wir haben immer gedacht in der Türkei tragen alle Kopftücher. Oder -ich habe mal 3-4 Jahre geraucht- wie kannst du rauchen hier? Also solche - ich habe gesagt ich bin eine richtige Türkin.

[xxxviii] Interviewer: Fällt dir hier noch was ein wie es sich hier äußert dass es hier Rassisten sind? Woran merkst du das?
IK: Du wirst dumm angemacht. Ich höre das alles nicht, ich gehe daran vorbei, wenn sowas ist. Du wirst dumm angemacht, wenn du an der Kasse stehst oder es an der Tanke zu lange dauert - dann merkst du es schon, dass es die Leute sind, die dich am liebsten einmal erwürgen würden. Und so richtigen Rassismus an meiner Person habe ich so nicht gemerkt. Dass ich mal Schläge gekriegt habe oder was weiß ich- habe ich nicht.
[xxxix] Und ich rede nicht so viel, einer lacht und beleidigt und entweder muss ich jeden Tag streiten oder weiß ich nicht - nicht hören.
[xl] [...] Wenn ich auf der Straße bin oder irgendwo hier steht [deutet auf seine Stirn] Ausländer, auch Türke, so wie wir uns anziehen, so wie wir uns bewegen sieht man das, dass wir, sag ich mal, echte deutsche sind, keine deutschen sind. Schon mein Name, wenn Du mich fragen würdest, wie heißt du, ich sag Kackar, oh, das ist kein deutscher Name, nee. [...]
[xli] Interviewer: Ja, wenn Sie noch Zeit haben, ein Punkt, der mich noch interessieren würde, ob Sie manchmal die Erfahrung gemacht haben, dass sie irgendwie anders behandelt werden.
[Übersetzung der Partnerin]
MO: Ja, das kommt überwiegend durch die Sprache. Hier wird man, Du bist Ausländer, Du kommst in mein Land, und Du bittest manchmal um Hilfe, Entschuldigung ich kann das noch nicht so gut, können Sie mir behilflich sein, diese Hilfsbereitschaft ist nicht da, gar nicht, gar nicht. Da wird man doof geguckt, oder wird man ignoriert, oder man wird dann halt so, lernen Sie mal deutsch, oder lernen Sie mal die Sprache. [...] Ohne Sprache ist man hier ein nichts und das bekommt man auch sehr zu spüren.
[xlii] Genauso ist das in der Gesellschaft, wenn man gepflegt ist, wenn man Mercedes fährt, dann fällt man auf. Ob das vom Vater ist oder sein eigenes, das wissen die ja nicht, aber sagen, hier guck mal, der ist 20 und fährt nen dicken 5er BMW oder Mercedes S-Klasse oder sonstwas. Aber dass der Vater schon von Anfang an hier gelebt hat und immer nur gespart und das Geld nicht in der Diskothek ausgegeben hat, nicht ausgelebt hat sozusagen, sondern gespart hat und auch in Versicherungen angelegt hat, die Versicherung jetzt auch bezahlt hat, das sehen die Leute ja nicht. Sondern sehen nur den jungen Typen da im Auto drin und das ist dann nachher das Klischee, ja guck mal, der hat bestimmt mit Drogen gedealt sonst würde er den *5er* oder den *Mercedes* nicht fahren können. Also dass man dieses Bild hat und mit diesem Bild immer wieder konfrontiert wird, egal in welcher Ebene man ist, ob man die Uni besucht hat oder nicht, das sehen die Leute ja nicht, aber es wird immer so negativ argumentiert.
[xliii] Am Ende eines Tages redet man darüber, ist vielleicht genervt, und am nächsten Morgen steht man auf und alles ist vergessen. Und die Leute, die das dann nicht verkraften, die das dann verinnerlichen, die sehen wir dann leider in den Nachrichten. Die sehen wir dann immer als negative Nachricht herauspieken. Entweder, keine Ahnung, begeht er irgendeine schlimme Sache, oder es ist dann in den Dings kommt, aber da tun die Medien ja auch ihr nötigstes. [...] Und das macht uns auch immer unbeliebter. Also, wenn das Fernsehen viel weniger davon zeigen würde, dann würde die Gesellschaft auch ein anderes Ansehen für uns haben. Und da machen die Medien halt aus einer Mücke einen Elefanten und dann steht man vor der Tür, weil man vielleicht zu einer Gruppe gehört, die auch so denkt. Und dann denkt man sich oh.
[xliv] Ansonsten diese ganze ausländische Politik, was mich auch ärgert, diese Arbeitslosigkeit, es wird alles brutaler alles härter natürlich. Gut Deutschland ist ein humanes Land, ein soziales Land, aber irgendwann ist auch, ich sag das jetzt mal obwohl ich selber Ausländer bin, aber irgendwann ist ein Punkt da. Deutschland verträgt keine Ausländer mehr, weil es nicht mehr möglich ist. Ob die Kriminalität weniger wird oder nicht, sie bleibt gleich womöglich, bloß, es gibt keine Arbeit, ich weiß das.
[xlv] Gut, ich komm aus der Türkei, aber ich komm nicht so aus Anatolien in den Bergen - ich will hier nicht die Leute herablassen - aber ich bin schon aus Istanbul.

xlvi [...] also ich kann das verstehen wenn jmd. aus der Türkei kommt und nicht mal, Kurdistan so, die können ja auch nicht türkisch, ich habe ja mal in der Türkei in Istanbul war ich im deutschen Konsulat da musste ich hier dieses Visum nehmen. Und da waren Leute, die aus der Türkei kommen und da hingegangen sind aber nicht mal türkisch konnten. Die mussten erst mal türkische Übersetzungen machen und dann wollten die nach Deutschland. Und das kann ich ja verstehen, dass man das nicht haben möchte. Oder mein Exmann, die waren hier und die haben ganze Verwandtschaften aus der Türkei hierhergeholt, aber nicht den normalen Weg, aber Asyl, und dass sie gesagt haben, die Türkei macht das und das und das aber das war gar nicht so, das war einfach die Lüge. Ja, die Türkei -keine Ahnung- schlechte Behandlung oder irgendetwas haben sie immer gesagt, um hier her zu kommen aber das war gar nicht so. Und wenn ich das weiß, dann kann man die Leute einfach anders - also Akademikerin diese Position oder nicht Akademikerin, so ich finde das ich gehöre nicht immer gleich, so dass man mich irgendwie mit jedem gleich behandelt. Das ist nicht so. Ich mache hier nämlich was. Ich lebe wie eine Deutsche hier.

xlvii Hab ich auch immer gesagt, du kannst Deine Meinung gerne haben, du kannst auch gerne stolz auf Dein Land sein und kannst auch gerne sagen, normal, kriminelle Ausländer raus. Sag ich selber.

xlviii Das ist. Also kommt drauf an. Wie der Mensch ist. Ich achte mehr auf die Menschlichkeit. Wenn der Mensch ein Arschloch ist, dann ist das für mich eben ein Arschloch. Wenn ein Ossi Ossi ist, dann sag ich auch gleich meine Meinung, Du hast Ossi Manieren. Da kenn ich nichts. Da bin ich schmerzfrei. Ich hab nichts zu verstecken. Ich hab viel im Osten gearbeitet und ich hab sehr viel mit Leuten aus dem Osten zu tun gehabt. Aber es gibt einen Punkt, da verändern sie sich nicht. Das ist ja schlimmer als alles andere. Wenn die Ost-Manier rauskommt, dann kann man den Typen vergessen. [...] Also die ausm Osten sind richtig egoistisch. Richtig egoistisch. [...] Also ich hab viel mehr Probleme, wenn ich mit Ost-Leuten zusammenarbeite also mit West-Leuten. Bei West-Leuten ist das eigentlich ein bisschen gut, aber bei Ossi nicht.

xlix [...] Ich habe das ein paar Mal in Altona erlebt dass so Penner, die unter der Brücke schlafen, die ihre Pulle Wein mit sich schleppen, dass die dann eher schon mal sagen, hier Scheißtürken. Entweder denken die nicht nach - ich sag jetzt mal - so dass die Schande von Deutschland, Scheiß-Ausländer sagt, obwohl sie eigentlich selber scheiße sind und die Sozialämter abzocken, bis zum geht nicht mehr. Also die untere Ebene, was Rassismus betrifft, ist höher als - betucht möchte ich nicht sagen aber - die normal verdienenden Menschen. Vielleicht liegt es auch daran, weil es denen ein bisschen schlechter geht und die dann sagen, ok den Ausländern geht es gut, Sozialschmarotzer, aber eigentlich sind das die selber. Aber an solchen Leuten laufe ich vorbei und sage, alles klar Mann. Da lauf ich dran vorbei.

l [...] ach die Ausländer sind schon längst integriert worden. [betont] Schon längst. Bloß die deutschen wissen das noch nicht.

li Wenn ich deutsche Staatsbürgerschaft annehme dann bin ich ein Deutscher nur auf dem Papier aber dann bin ich immer noch ein Türke. Ich bin Türke mich kann man nicht ändern. Sie kann man auch nicht andern Sie sind Deutscher und bleiben sie auch egal welche Papiere sie besitzen.

lii Weil wir haben ganz große viele viele auch kleine ideelle Werte, die sitzen in uns einfach drin, die werden uns fast angeboren. Also, die werden uns bestimmt so angeboren, genetisch so übertragen.

liii Was mich bisschen beängstigt ist, dass diese Gesellschaft Sologänger bleiben möchte. Und immer wieder wenn man mal fragt, willst Du denn ne Familie gründen? Nöö, ich will garnicht.

liv Die sind 18 20 25 und ich sag, Du wie gehts Deinem Vater? Und die sind so, wieso? Den sehe ich garnicht. Der alte Knacker, der kann doch von mir aus verrecken.

lv EY: Aber Mensch was verändert, was sich verändert ist der menschlicher Kontakt. In Deutschland ist es nicht so freundlich wie in der Türkei. z.B. die Nachbarn, in der Türkei ist es jetzt wie in Deutschland.
LY: nee

EY: Aber natürlich in der grossen Stadt - im Dorf oder in der Kleinstadt ist es immer gut- aber in Istanbul. 5-Stock Häuser alle Nachbarn wie in Deutschland, sagen vielleicht guten Morgen aber mehr nicht.
[lvi] Hab ich oft in meinem eigenen Familienkreis mitgekriegt. Den ganzen Tag nur türkische Programm kucken, immer nur beim Türken einkaufen, immer nur im türkischen Viertel. Aber dann uns Kinder ständig anrufen. Ja, hier sind schon wieder Briefe und Behördendings. Lies mal, was wollen die Deutschen wieder? Ich sag, seit 30 Jahren lebt ihr hier, seit 40 Jahren. Könnt ihr nicht mal nochn Brief lesen? Deswegen. Und da hören wir uns dann an, also die Generation, die schon als zweite dritte hier geboren ist, ihr habt euch zu sehr angepasst, ihr seid zu deutsch. [...]
[lvii] Es ist nunmal so. Ich bin ein Türke und werd immer Türke bleiben. Kopfmäßig vielleicht auch noch, bin ich auch türkisch, aber genauso gut deutsch. Und ich muss immer, wenn man so politisch sagt, muss man immer den guten Weg finden nicht.
[lviii] Interviewer: Wie ist das wenn Dich jetzt jemand als Deutscher bezeichnet?
SD: Ich sag dann immer ich bin Deutsch-Türke. Das geb ich nochmal mit. Weil ich sag immer auch ganz ehrlich, guck mich an, also wenn ich in einen Raum reingehe und sage ich bin Deutscher, dann sagen sie natürlich, aber du bist aber doch geboren. Ich sag, bin ich natürlich Türke, das ist das. Da sag ich immer Deutsch-Türke. Diesen Hinweis geb ich immer. Weil ich immer sage, man soll ja auch nicht seine Herkunft verleugnen.
[lix] Ich bin nach wie vor türkischer Staatsbürger, obwohl ich - seit 73 bin ich - das sind 40 Jahre - [...] seitdem ich 10 bin, bin ich ununterbrochen hier und nun ist die Frage was bin ich? Bin ich jetzt tatsächlich ein Türke oder 40 Jahre nach 40 Jahren sollte man eigentlich schon ein bisschen deutsch sein oder? Wenn man überlegt, dass ich einen Tannenbaum zu Hause habe der geschmückt ist und die Fenster weihnachtlich geschmückt sind, dann hat man diese deutsche Tradition ja auch schon ein bisschen mitgenommen und dann könnte man eigentlich auch die deutsche Staatsbürgerschaft kriegen oder? Man fühlt ja schon irgendwann wie ein Deutscher.
[lx] Die Regierung. Ich finde schon, dass sie sehr türkenfeindlich damit umgeht. Und die deutsche Regierung kann daran nichts ändern. Die Leute sind da. Entweder man schmeißt sie raus, wie sie es damals im Zweiten Weltkrieg mit den Juden gemacht haben, oder man akzeptiert manche Sachen und versucht auch die schwierigen Personen hinzukriegen, weil - kriegen sie ja nicht hin. Das kriegen sie ja noch nichtmal bei den deutschen hin. Ein Querulant bleibt ein Querulant. Davon abgesehen. Ob das ein Türke ist oder nicht. Das hat mit Nationalität nichts zu tun.
[lxi] Der Mann ist ein Techniker [gemeint, Kollege auf Montage]. Der ist auf mich angewiesen und ich bin auf ihn angewiesen. Und wenn man das Spiel richtig spielt, hat man keine Probleme. ich bescheiß ihn nur einmal, dann bin ich unten durch. [...] Es ist ganz normales Leben. Und in der Türkei wär das auch nicht anders. Ich müsste auch mit Leute zusammenarbeiten und die müssten mir vertrauen und ich müsste denen vertrauen und wo das Vertrauen da ist, da hast Du auch kein Problem. Aber, wenn Du ein Schwein bist, dann hast Du immer ein Problem.
[lxii] Ich finde Hamburg ist ganz gut. Also ich, ich liebe Hamburg. Und das ist, das ist mein Deutschland, Hamburg. Hamburg ist mein Deutschland.
[lxiii] Und wenn mir ein Organ fehlt, oder wenn nem Deutschen zum Beispiel ne Leber fehlt, und da ist ein Leberspender aus der Türkei, der sagt nicht, nee ich nehm die Leber nicht.
[lxiv] Ich hab zum Beispiel auch von dem Typen, der als Nazi immer gelebt hat, hab ich auch n ganz leckeres Fischgericht erklärt bekommen. Ja und dann hab ich das einmal gemacht, hat er mir sogar ein Stück Fisch mitgebracht vom Stör.
[lxv] Ich habe ein Gefühl: wir Türken wir sind unerwünscht in Deutschland - von vielen.
[lxvi] Und die doppelte Staatsangehörigkeit. Das deutsche Gesetz erlaubt das nicht. In der deutschen Verfassung steht, alle Bürger sind gleichberechtigt. Aber wenn es um die doppelte Staatsangehörigkeit geht. Außer der Türkei dürfen sie alle - nur die Türken nicht. Was haben sie gegen uns? Was haben sie gegen uns?

[lxvii] Ist auch so, aber ich kann das irgendwie nicht beschreiben, dieses Unwohlsein. Man fühlt sich nie heimisch hier, also auch wenn man die Staatsbürgerschaft hat. Also, wenn ich die deutsche Staatsbürgerschaft hätte, wäre das genauso. Das erkennt man ja nicht an hier.

[lxviii] Das sind so die Vorurteile , die ich auf der Arbeit immer kriege. Ich sag, ja , meine Tochter, ich muss wieder 400 Euro für ne Klassenreise aufbringen undso. Dann heißt es, ja, du schickst sie ja sowieso nicht hin. Ich sag wieso? Ja, weil ihr Muslime ja sowieso nicht dahinschickt und Schwimmen schickst du sie auch nicht hin. Ich sag, Mann, wann haben wir mal darüber gesprochen und wann habe ich sowas geäußert? Ja, was, machst du das denn? Ja , natürlich mach ich das, warum soll ich das nicht machen? Ich konnte damals nicht, weil mein Vater Alleinverdiener war. Jetzt, wenn die Situation es ermöglicht, warum soll ich meine Kinder damit eingrenzen?

[lxix] Dann sitzt man bei Pizza Hut und isst Pizza und wenn die Frau Kopftuch trägt und die Kinder auch Kopftuch tragen dann wird irgendwie mit dem Arm gegen gestoßen und und das und so Sachen wo man sich dann nicht so oft nach draußen begibt. Auch beim Einkaufen hört man dann, guck mal, sind ne ganze Familie, also das ist dann wo man sich ein bisschen mehr zurückzieht und sich sagt, ich will lieber in meinem Umfeld meine Ruhe haben und dann bleibt man auch in der türkischen Gesellschaft.

[lxx] Aber ich glaub, Deutschland ist zwar aufm richtigen Weg. Hat auch mit dem richtigen Fuß angefangen. Aber, es ist wie ein Baby dass gerade noch laufen lernt, stolpert nochn bisschen, aber ich sag mal so, ich beschwer mich nicht, dass ich in Deutschland lebe und immer mal wieder Ausländische oder ausländerfeindliche Sprüche kriege. Das hat man fast schon akzeptiert, allerdings wünscht man sich, dass das nicht passiert.

[lxxi] Und es ist ein Job, den ich sehr mag und macht auch Spaß. 19 Jahre lang habe ich hier in der Firma habe mit jmd. zusammen gearbeitet, da muss man ganz ehrlich sagen, das war ein Rassist. Das war echt ein richtiger Rassist. Deswegen sage ich, der Mensch sollte nicht aufgeben, der sollte seine Arbeit vernünftig machen auch wenn er mit dem Menschen nicht klarkommt. Am Ende kriegt man doch die Anerkennung. Auch wenn man Ausländer ist.

[lxxii] Interviewer: Gabs denn mal Situationen, wo Du irgendwie anders behandelt wurdest?
MÖ: Schon. Aber das ist normal. Ich seh das als normal. Wenn der Mensch das nicht abkann. Ein schwacher Mensch greift an diesem Punkt an, weil er ja nicht weiterkommt. Aber wenn man ehrgeizig ist, wenn man an sich selbst nicht zweifelt, also ich zweifel an mir selber nicht. Ich komm überall rein. Ich kann überall was bewegen. Und wenn mir einer dumm kommt, du scheiß Türke, oder so. Da kann ich nur lachen.

[lxxiii] Aber inzwischen haben wir ja jede Art von Nationalitäten hier in Deutschland: Araber, Syrer, Afghane, und die Baltischen Staaten. Also sehr viele, die den Türken ähnlich sind, aber keine Türken sind und egal wer was macht, der ein bisschen südländisch aussieht, dann ist es immer der Türke. Und deswegen glaube ich, werden die Türken hier nie in Reine stehen, weil der Deutsche, der einen Ausländer sieht, für den ist das der Türke. Und die Araber machen natürlich auch viel Scheiß und dann bleibt das immer an den Türken kleben.

[lxxiv] Also ich fühle mich hier nicht als Ausländer. Nein ich fühle mich hier wohl.

[lxxv] Ich hab nie schlechte Erfahrungen gehabt. Also, weiß ich nicht, weil ich nicht in die Schule gegangen bin, weil ich konnte nicht gut deutsch sprechen. Mit Kindern, ich war immer mit meinen Kindern beschäftigt

[lxxvi] Ich kann nicht sagen ich bin jetzt hier Ausländerin und kann nicht so gut Deutsch, das habe ich nie so erlebt. Ich kann mich nicht daran erinnern. Lief alles ok glaub ich. Ich habe auch gekellnert parallel und da konnte ich auch nicht so gut deutsch aber dadurch habe ich es ja gelernt. […] Also ich habe es einfach gemacht, hatte Angst natürlich, aber ich musste es so machen, ich musste es, ich habe kein Mensch der sitzt und wartet und ich muss tun so habe ich deutsch gelernt also ich glaube ich habe dadurch, dass ich da gekellnert habe meistens habe ich mehr Mut bekommen und hier an der Uni hatte ich sowieso kein Problem.

[lxxvii] Ich hab mein Geschäft hier, ich bin ja, ok, haben sie vielleicht viele schlechte Erfahrungen damit gemacht - das kann ich auch verstehen - aber ich möchte nicht in dieser gleichen Schiene sein. Und ich möchte, dass sie mich auch mal anders sehen und von den anderen unterscheiden.

[lxxviii] Ich habe keine Problem mit dem Staat, mit der Polizei nicht, ich brauche nicht unbedingt dieses Papier, um zu zeigen ich bin deutsch, weil es nützt mir eigentlich nicht viel.

[lxxix] HTs Partnerin: Es ist alles nicht wie vor 20 Jahren. Vor 20 Jahren gabs auch keine Geschäfte von Ausländern, wo man reingehen konnte. Ich meine, die Ausländer haben sich auch erweitert. In jeder Ecke ist jetzt irgendwas. Früher war das nicht so. Deswegen ist es auch ganz anders.
I: Und ist es dadurch angenehmer geworden, oder?
HTs P.: Also, das unsere Leute sich auch erweitert haben, dass jeder irgendwo hingeht, ob es ein Dönergeschäft ist, ob es ein türkischer Laden ist, dass man sich wie zu Hause fühlt. Und früher war das ja nicht so.

[lxxx] Interviewer: Können Sie nochmal allgemein sagen, wie Sie sich in diesem Land fühlen?
HY: Als Ausländer auf jeden Fall. Ich fühle mich auch, ich muss das leider sagen, sehr diskriminiert. Das hört sich vielleicht widersprüchlich an, dass ich in einem Land, wo ich stark diskriminiert werde, dass ich trotzdem ein Staatsbürger werden möchte. Aber gerade Menschen, die sehr stark ausgegrenzt werden, diskriminiert werden, die müssen ja immer kämpfen für ihre Rechte, da ist nichts selbstverständlich.

[lxxxi] Ich fühle mich im ganzen auch wohl, ich kann das nicht abstreiten.

[lxxxii] Warum ich auch keine deutsche werde. Also ich bin nicht in die deutsche Staatsbürgerschaft eingetreten. Also mir wurde das immer wieder, es wird uns ja immer wieder angeboten, schriftlich undso.

[lxxxiii] Da denke ich jedenfalls, das kränkt vielleicht mein Land, das so lange für mich gesorgt hat, das hat vielleicht einen Nachteil für mich, wenn ich das mache. Ich gönne denen keinen Nachteil. Das ist so wie meine Mutter, wie mein Vater, denen ich immer dankbar bin. Das ist ja auch mit Deutschland so. Ich würde hier nie ein Verbrechen oder niemals, ich komm ja hier auch nicht weg.

[lxxxiv] Also 1 2 3 kleine freundliche Menschen, schon vergisst man das Negative. Und das bewegt mich dazu, dass ich immer wieder sagen kann, ich möchte doch die Staatsbürgerschaft.

[lxxxv] Es ändert sich in der Tat nichts. Aber nichts destotrotz, ich lebe hier, ich bin schon ewig hier. Womöglich würde ich auch hier sterben. Natürlich will ich das nehmen.

[lxxxvi] Aber ich weiß, dass wenn Du den deutschen Pass hast, Du deutscher bist, hast du Ansehen auf der Welt, in Europa. Du bist deutscher. Egal, du hast den deutschen Pass, du kannst überall hingehen. Wenn was passiert steht die deutsche Botschaft, die deutsche Regierung hinter Dir. Die lassen Dich nicht im Stich. Wenn mir hier etwas passiert, wenn in der Türkei jemand weint, dann meine Mutter, aber die Regierung, oder das türkische Konsulat hier. Interessiert die nicht.

[lxxxvii] Wenn ich zum Beispiel zum Amt gehe und einen deutschen Pass hingebe, dann automatisch, also psychologisch, wird man anders behandelt. Weil wir sind ja Ausländer. Wir erleben diese Geschichte. Das wissen wir. Das macht immer einen Unterschied. Hundertprozent.

[lxxxviii] Hier steht [deutet auf seine Stirn] Ausländer.

[lxxxix] Nein. Nein. Sag ich ja, sonst würde ich mich schon irgendwie dafür einsetzen, ich als Ausländer, als Türke, werde nicht akzeptiert, dann bräuchte ich also diesen deutschen Ausweis. Dann könnte ich wenigstens sagen, hier hör mal , ich bin deutscher, aufpassen. Also, das habe ich nicht, dieses Gefühl gehabt.

[xc] Also ich sag Deutschland, nicht meinen Sohn oder meine Freunde hier, ich sag Deutschland.

[xci] Man kriegt manchmal Unterlagen, dass man das beantragen kann, aber man macht das nicht. Und dann kommt ja auch noch, dass er Vollzeit Arbeit haben muss, alles mögliche, bei mir wäre das ja nicht der Fall. Weiß ich nicht. Wieso soll man 550 Euro bezahlen, um sich einbürgern zu lassen? Das ist ja auch die Frage. Und deswegen. Also, wir haben uns keine Gedanken darüber gemacht.

[xcii] Also er meint, wegen dem Pass ändert sich nichts. Auch wenn ein Deutscher Türke wird, im Endeffekt wird er Deutscher. Da ändert sich nichts. Der Mensch bleibt gleich. […] Man hat keinen, weiß ich nicht. Das ist keine Hilfe.

[xciii] Du wirst dumm angemacht, wenn du an der Kasse stehst oder es an der Tanke zu lange dauert - dann merkst du es schon, dass es die Leute sind, die dich am liebsten einmal erwürgen würden. Und so richtigen Rassismus an meiner Person habe ich so nicht gemerkt. Dass ich mal Schläge gekriegt habe oder was weiß ich- habe ich nicht.

[xciv] Aber damals hat keiner an der Tür gesagt, Moment, wenn Du hier reinkommst, dann musst Du alle Klamotten ablassen, die Hautfarbe ändern, die Haarfarbe ändern, und dann kannst Du hier reinkommen und dann gehörst Du mit zu uns.

References

AAPOR. 2011. *Standard Definitions: Final Dispositions of Case Codes and Outcome Rates for Surveys:* THE AMERICAN ASSOCIATION FOR PUBLIC OPINION RESEARCH.
Alba, Richard. 2005. "Bright vs. blurred boundaries: Second-generation assimilation and exclusion in France, Germany, and the United States." *Ethn. Racial Stud.* 28 (1): 20–49. doi:10.1080/0141987042000280003.
———. 2006. "On the Sociological Significance of the American Jewish Experience: Boundary Blurring, Assimilation, and Pluralism." *Sociology of Religion* 67 (4): 347–58.
Alba, Richard, and Michelle Johnson. 2003. "Measuring Contemporary Prjudice Toward Immigrants in Germany." In Alba, Schmidt, and Wasmer 2003.
Alba, Richard, and Victor Nee. 1997. "Rethinking Assimilation Theory for a New Era of Immigration." *International Migration Review* 31 (4): 826–74.
Alba, Richard, Peter Schmidt, and Martina Wasmer, eds. 2003. *Germans or foreigners? Attitudes Toward Ethnic Minorities in Post-Reunification Germany.* New York: Palgrave Macmillan.
Amir-Moazami, Shirin. 2005. "Reaffirming and Shifting Boundaries: Muslim Perspectives on Gender and Citizenship in France and Germany." In *Islam and the New Europe. Continuities, Changes, Confrontations*, edited by Sigrid Nökel and Levent Tezcan. Bielefeld: transcript Verlag.
———. 2007. *Politisierte Religion. Der Kopftuchstreit in Deutschland und Frankreich.* Bielefeld: transcript Verlag.
———. 2013. "Islam and geder under liberal-secular governance. The German Islam Conference." In *Religion, identity and politics: Germany and Turkey in interaction*, edited by Haldun Gülalp and Günter Seufert. New York: Routledge.
Anderson, Benedict. 1991. *Imagined Communities. Reflections on The Origin and Spread of Nationalism.* London: Verso.
Arrighi, Jean-Thomas, Rainer Bauböck, Michael Collyer, Derek Hutcheson, Madalina Moraru, Lamin Khadar, and Jo Shaw. 2013. *Franchise and Electoral Participation of Third Country Citizens Residing in the European Union and of EU Citizens Residing in Third Countries.* Brussels: European Parliament.
Arslan, Emre. 2009. *Der Mythos der Nation im Transnationalen Raum. Türkische Graue Wölfe in Deutschland.* Wiesbaden: VS Verlag.
Bade, Klaus J. 2013. *Kritik und Gewalt: Sarrazin-Debatte, "Islamkritik" und Terror in der Einwanderungsgesellschaft:* Wochenschau-Verlag.
Bader, Veit. 1995. "Citizenship and Exclusion: Radical Democracy, Community, and Justice. Or, What is Wrong with Communitarianism?" *Political Theory* 23 (2): 211–46.
Bail, Christopher A. 2008. "The Configuration of Symbolic Boundaries against Immigrants in Europe." *American Sociological Review* 73 (1): 37–59.
Bandura, Albert. 1977. *Social Learning Theory.* Englewood Cliffs: Prentice-Hall.
Barth, Frederik. 1969. *Ethnic Groups and Boundaries. The Social Organization of Culture Difference.* Bergen: Universitetsforlaget.
Bauböck, Rainer. 1994a. "Changing the Boundaries of Citizenship: The Inclusion of Immigrants in Democratic Polities." In *From aliens to citizens: redefining the status of immigrants in Europe*,

edited by Rainer Bauböck. Public policy and social welfare ; 17. Aldershot: Avebury; European Center Vienna.
———. 1994b. *Transnational Citizenship: Membership and Rights in International Migration.* Cheltenham: Edward Elgar.
———. 1998. "The Crossing and Blurring of Boundaries in International Migration. Challenges for Social and Political Theory." In *Blurred Boundaries: Migration, Ethnicity, Citieznship,* edited by Rainer Bauböck and Rundell, ‚John. Aldershot: Ashgate.
———. 2010. "Studying Citizenship Constellations." *Journal of Ethnic and Migration Studies* 36 (5): 847–59. doi:10.1080/13691831003764375.
Bauböck, Rainer, Eva Ersbøll, Kees Groenendijk, and Harald Waldrauch, eds. 2006. *Acquisition and Loss of Nationality Policies and Trends in 15 European States (2 Volumes).* Amsterdam: Amsterdam University Press.
Bean, Frank D., Susan K. Brown, James D. Bachmeier, Tineke Fokkema, and Laurence Lessard-Phillips. 2012. "The dimensions and degree of second-generation incorporation in US and European cities: A comparative study of inclusion and exclusion." *International Journal of Comparative Sociology* 53 (3): 181–209. doi:10.1177/0020715212457095.
Becker, Birgit. 2009. "Immigrants' emotional identification with the host society The example of Turkish parents' naming practices in Germany." *Ethnicities* 9 (2): 200–225.
Beckman, Ludvig. 2006. "Citizenship and voting rights: Should resident aliens vote?" *Citizenship Studies* 10 (2): 153–65.
Beine, Michel, Anna Boucher, Brian Burgoon, Mary Crock, Justin Gest, Michael Hiscox, Patrick McGovern, Hillel Rapoport, Joep Schaper, and Eiko Thielemann. 2016. "Comparing Immigration Policies: An Overview from the IMPALA Database." *Int Migr Rev* 50 (4): 827–63. doi:10.1111/imre.12169.
Bender, Stefan, and Wolfgang Seifert. 2003. "On the Economic and Social Situation of Immigrant Groups in Germany." In Alba, Schmidt, and Wasmer 2003.
Benhabib, Seyla. 1999. "Citizens, residents, and aliens in a changing world: political membership in the global era." *Social Research,* 709–44.
———. 2004. *The Rights of Others: Aliens, Residents, and Citizens.* The John Robert Seeley lectures: Cambridge University Press.
Best, Henning, and Christof Wolf. 2010. "Logistische Regression." In *Handbuch der sozialwissenschaftlichen Datenanalyse,* edited by Christof Wolf and Henning Best, 827–54: VS Verlag für Sozialwissenschaften.
Bickerstaff, Jovonne J. 2012. "All responses are not created equal. Variations in the Antiracist Responses of First-Generation French Blacks." *Du Bois Review* 9 (1): 107–31. doi:10.1017/S1742058X12000173.
Bleich, Erik. 2011. "What is Islamophobia and how much is there? Theorizing and measuring an emerging comparative concept." *Am Behav Sci* 55 (12): 1581–1600.
Bloemraad, Irene. 2006. "Becoming a Citizen in the United States and Canada: Structured Mobilization and Immigrant Political Incorporation." *Social Forces* 85 (2): 667–95.
BMI. 2009. *Vorläufige Anwendungshinweise des Bundesministeriums des Innern zum Staatsangehörigkeitsgesetz in der Fassung des Gesetzes zur Änderung des Staatsangehörigkeitsgesetzes vom 5. Februar 2009 (BGBl. I S. 158) (Anlage zu dem BMI-Rdschr. an die Innenministerien der Länder vom 17. April 2009).* Berlin.
———. 2015. *Vorläufige Anwendungshinweise des Bundesministeriums des Innern vom 1. Juni 2015: zum Staatsangehörigkeitsgesetz (StAG) in der Fassung des Zweiten Gesetzes zur Änderung des Staatsangehörigkeitsgesetzes vom 13. November 2014 (BGBl. I S. 1714).* Berlin.
Bosniak, Linda. 2006. *The citizen and the alien: dilemmas of contemporary membership.* Princeton: Princeton University Press.

References

Boudon, Raymond. 2003. "Beyond Rational Choice Theory." *Annual Review of Sociology* (29): 1–21.
Bourdieu, Pierre. 1984. *Distinction. A social critique of the judgement of taste*. London: Routledge & Kegan Paul.
———. 2004. *Science of science and reflexivity*. Chicago: University of Chicago Press.
Bourdieu, Pierre, and Loïc J. Wacquant. 1992. *An invitation to reflexive sociology:* University of Chicago Press.
Brettell, Caroline B. 2006. "Political Belonging and Cultural Belonging Immigration Status, Citizenship, and Identity Among Four Immigrant Populations in a Southwestern City." *Am Behav Sci* 50 (1): 70–99.
Brubaker, Rogers. 2009. "Ethnicity, race, and nationalism." *Annual Review of Sociology* 35: 21–42.
———. 2010. "Migration, membership, and the modern nation-state: Internal and external dimensions of the politics of belonging." *Journal of Interdisciplinary History* 41 (1): 61–78.
Bryman, Alan. 2003. *Quantity and quality in social research:* Routledge.
Bursell, Moa. 2012. "Name change and destigmatization among Middle Eastern immigrants in Sweden." *Ethn. Racial Stud.* 35 (3): 471–87. doi:10.1080/01419870.2011.589522.
Çağlar, Ayşe. 2004. ""Citizenship Light": Transnational Ties, Multiple Rules of Membership, and the "Pink Card"." In *Worlds on the move: Globalization, Migration, and Cultural Security*, edited by Jonathan C. Friedman and Shalini Randeria. London: Tauris.
Calder, Gideon, Phillip Cole, and Jonathan Seglow. 2010. *Citizenship acquisition and national belonging: migration, membership and the liberal democratic state*. Migration, minorities and citizenship. Basingstoke: Palgrave Macmillan.
Carens, Joseph H. 2013. *The Ethics of Immigration*. Oxford: Oxford University Press.
Chappell, David L. 1996. *Inside Agitators: White Southerners in the Civil Rights Movement*. Baltimore: JHU Press.
Constant, A. F., L. Gataullina, and K. F. Zimmermann. 2007. "Naturalization Proclivities, Ethnicity and Integration." *DIW Discussion Paper 755*.
Council of Europe. 1993. *Second Protocol amending the Convention on the Reduction of Cases of Multiple Nationality and Military Obligations in Cases of Multiple Nationality: European Treaty Series, No. 149*. Strasbourg.
Creswell, John W. 2009. *Research Design: Qualitative, Quantitative, and Mixed Methods Approaches (3rd ed.)*. Los Angeles: Sage.
Crosby, Faye. 1984. "The denial of personal discrimination." *Am Behav Sci* 27 (3): 371–86.
Deding, Mette, Torben Fridberg, and Vibeke Jakobsen. 2008. "Non-response in a survey among immigrants in Denmark." In *Surveying Ethnic Minorities and Immigrant Populations: Methodological Challenges and Research Strategies*. Vol. 2, edited by Joan Font and Mónica Méndez, 107–21. Amsterdam: Amsterdam University Press.
DeSipio, Louis. 1987. "Social Science Literature and the Naturalization Process." *International Migration Review* 21 (2): 390–405.
Diehl, Claudia. 2002. "Wer wird Deutsche/r und warum? Bestimmungsfaktoren der Einbürgerung türkisch-und italienischstämmiger junger Erwachsener–Ergebnisse des Integrationssurveys des BiB." *Zeitschrift für Bevölkerungswissenschaft* 27 (3): 285–312.
Diehl, Claudia, and Michael Blohm. 2001. "Apathy, adaptation or ethnic mobilisation? On the attitudes of a politically excluded group." *Journal of Ethnic and Migration Studies* 27 (3): 401–20. doi:10.1080/136918301200266149.
———. 2003. "Rights or Identity? Naturalization Processes among "Labor Migrants" in Germany." *International Migration Review* 37 (1): 133–62. doi:10.1111/j.1747-7379.2003.tb00132.x.
———. 2008. "Die Entscheidung zur Einbürgerung: Optionen, Anreize und identifikative Aspekte." In *Kölner Zeitschrift für Soziologie und Sozialpsychologie, Sonderheft 48 Migration und Integration*. Vol. 48, edited by Frank Kalter, 437–64. Wiesbaden: VS.

———. 2011. "Naturalization as boundary crossing: Evidence from labour migrants in Germany." In *Identity and participation in culturally diverse societies: a multidisciplinary perspective*, edited by Assaad E. Azzi, Xenia Chryssochoou, Bert Klandermans, and Bernd Simon. Oxford: Wiley-Blackwell.

Diehl, Claudia, and Patrick Fick. 2012. "Deutschsein auf Probe: Der Umgang deutsch-türkischer junger Erwachsener mit dem Optionsmodell." *Soziale Welt* 63 (4): 339–60.

Diehl, Claudia, and Rainer Schnell. 2006. ""Reactive Ethnicity" or "Assimilation"? Statements, Arguments, and First Empirical Evidence for Labor Migrants in Germany." *International Migration Review* 40 (4): 786–816. doi:10.1111/j.1747-7379.2006.00044.x.

Diehl, Claudia, and Ingrid Tucci. 2011. "Fremdenfeindlichkeit und Einstellungen zur Einbürgerung." *DIW Wochenbericht* 31: 3–8.

Dillman, Don A. 2007. *Mail and Internet Surveys: The Tailored Design Method. 2nd Ed. 2007 Update with New Internet, Visual, and Mixed-Mode Guide.* Hoboken, NJ: Wiley.

Dion, Kenneth L., and Kerry Kawakami. 1996. "Ethnicity and perceived discrimination in Toronto: Another look at the personal/group discrimination discrepancy." *Canadian Journal of Behavioural Science/Revue canadienne des sciences du comportement* 28 (3): 203.

Dronkers, Jaap, and Maarten P. Vink. 2012. "Explaining access to citizenship in Europe: How citizenship policies affect naturalization rates." *European Union Politics* 13 (3): 390–412. doi:10.1177/1465116512440510.

Dumbrava, Costica. 2014. *Nationality, Citizenship and Ethno-cultural Belonging: Preferential Membership Policies in Europe.* Basingstoke: Palgrave Macmillan.

Edlin, Aaron, Andrew Gelman, and Noah Kaplan. 2007. "Voting as a Rational Choice: Why and How People Vote To Improve the Well-Being of Others." *Rationality and Society* 19 (3): 293–314. doi:10.1177/1043463107077384.

Edwards, Phil, Ian Roberts, Mike Clarke, Carolyn DiGuiseppi, Sarah Pratap, Reinhard Wentz, and Irene Kwan. 2002. "Increasing response rates to postal questionnaires: systematic review." *BMJ* 324 (7347): 1183.

Ehrkamp, P. 2006. ""We Turks Are No Germans": Assimilation Discourses and the Dialectical Construction of Identities in Germany." *Environ. Plan. A* 38 (9): 1673–92. doi:10.1068/a38148.

Ehrkamp, Patricia, and Helga Leitner. 2003. "Beyond National Citizenship: Turkish Immigrants and the (Re)Construction of Citizenship in Germany." *Urban Geography* 24 (2): 127–46. doi:10.2747/0272-3638.24.2.127.

Eisenberger, Naomi I., and Matthew D. Lieberman. 2004. "Why rejection hurts: a common neural alarm system for physical and social pain." *Trends in cognitive sciences* 8 (7): 294–300.

Eisenberger, Naomi I., Matthew D. Lieberman, and Kipling D. Williams. 2003. "Does Rejection Hurt? An fMRI Study of Social Exclusion." *Science* 302 (10): 290–92.

Elias, Norbert, and John L. Scotson. 1965. *The Established and the Outsiders. A Sociological Enquiry Into Community Problems.* London: Frank Cass & Co.

Elster, Jon. 1983. *Sour Grapes: Studies in the Subversion of Rationality.* 1. paperback ed. Cambridge: Cambridge Univ. Press.

———. 2007. *Explaining social behavior. More nuts and bolts for the social sciences.* New York: Cambridge University Press.

Ersanilli, Evelyn, and Ruud Koopmans. 2010. "Rewarding integration? Citizenship regulations and socio-cultural integration of immigrants in the Netherlands, France and Germany." *Journal of Ethnic and Migration Studies* 36 (5): 773–91.

Erzberger, Christian, and Udo Kelle. 2003. "Making Inferences in Mixed Methods: The Rules of Integration." In *Handbook of Mixed Methods in Social and Behavioral Research*, edited by Abbas Tashakkori and Charles Teddlie, 457–90. Thousand Oaks, CA: Sage.

Essed, Philomena. 1991. *Understanding Everyday Racism: An Interdisciplinary Theory.* London: Sage.

Esser, Hartmut. 2002a. *Soziologie. Spezielle Grundlagen. Band 1: Situationslogik und Handeln.* Frankfurt/Main: Campus.
———. 2002b. *Soziologie. Spezielle Grundlagen. Band 6: Sinn und Kultur.* Frankfurt/Main: Campus.
———. 2006. *Sprache und Integration: die sozialen Bedingungen und Folgen des Spracherwerbs von Migranten.* Frankfurt/Main: Campus.
———. 2008. "Assimilation, ethnische Schichtung oder selektive Akkulturation? Neuere Theorien der Eingliederung von Migranten und das Modell der intergenerationalen Integration." *Migration und integration* 48: 81–107.
———. 2009. "Rationality and Commitment: The Model of Frame Selection and the Explanationa of Normative Action." In *Raymond Boudon. A Life in Sociology. Essays in Honour of Raymond Boudon*, edited by Mohamed Cherkaoui and Peter Hamilton. Oxford: Bardwell Press.
Euwals, R., J. Dagevos, M. Gijsberts, and H. Roodenburg. 2007. "Immigration, Integration and the Labour Market: Turkish Immigrants in Germany and the Netherlands." *IZA Discussion Paper* 2677: 1–39.
Evans, M. D. R. 1988. "Choosing to be a Citizen: The Time-Path of Citizenship in Australia." *International Migration Review* 22 (2): 243–64.
Farahat, Anuscheh. 2013. "Naturalisation Procedures for Immigrants. Germany." *EUDO Citizenship Observatory*, 1–36.
Feskens, Remco, Joop Hox, Gerty Lensvelt-Mulders, and Hans Schmeets. 2006. "Collecting data among ethnic minorities in an international perspective." *Field Methods* 18 (3): 284–304.
Festinger, Leon. 1957. *A Theory of Cognitive Dissonance.* Stanford: Stanford Univ. Press.
Fleming, Crystal M., Michèle Lamont, and Jessica S. Welburn. 2012. "African Americans respond to stigmatization: the meanings and salience of confronting, deflecting conflict, educating the ignorant and 'managing the self'." *Ethn. Racial Stud.* 35 (3): 400–417. doi:10.1080/01419870.2011.589527.
Foner, Nancy, and Richard Alba. 2008. "Immigrant religion in the US and Western Europe: Bridge or barrier to inclusion?" *International Migration Review* 42 (2): 360–92.
Fox, Jon E., and Cynthia Miller-Idriss. 2008. "Everyday Nationhood." *Ethnicities* 8: 4.
Freeman, Gary P., and Nedim Ögelman. 1998. "Homeland citizenship policies and the status of third country nationals in the European Union." *Journal of Ethnic and Migration Studies* 24 (4): 769–88. doi:10.1080/1369183x.1998.9976665.
Fries, Christopher J. 2009. "Bourdieu's Reflexive Sociology as a Theoretical Basis for Mixed Methods Research: An Application to Complementary and Alternative Medicine." *Journal of Mixed Methods Research* 3 (4): 326–48. doi:10.1177/1558689809336660.
Gathmann, Christina, and Nicolas Keller. 2014. "Returns to Citizenship? Evidence from Germany's Recent Immigration Reforms." *IZA Discussion Paper* 8064: 1–59.
Gerhards, Jürgen, and Silke Hans. 2009. "From Hasan to Herbert: Name-Giving Patterns of Immigrant Parents between Acculturation and Ethnic Maintenance." *American Journal of Sociology* 114 (4): 1102–28.
Gesemann, Frank, and Roland Roth. 2014. *Integration ist (auch) Ländersache! Schritte zur politischen Inklusion von Migrantinnen und Migranten in den Bundesländern.* Berlin: Friedrich-Ebert-Stiftung.
Glaser, Barney G., and Anselm L. Strauss. 1967. *The discovery of grounded theory: Strategies for qualitative research.* Chicago: Aldine.
Goffman, Erving. 1963. *Stigma. Notes on the Management of Spoiled Identity.* Englewood Cliffs: Prentice-Hall.
González-Ferrer, Amparo. 2006. "Who do immigrants marry? Partner choice among single immigrants in Germany." *European Sociological Review* 22 (2): 171–85.

Goodman, Sara W. 2012. "Fortifying Citizenship: Policy Strategies for Civic Integration in Western Europe." *World Politics* 64 (4): 659–98. doi:10.1017/S0043887112000184.

Goodman, Sara W., and Marc M. Howard. 2013. "Evaluating and Explaining the Restrictive Backlash in Citizenship Policy in Europe." *Studies in Law, Politics, and Society* 60: 111–39.

Groves, Robert M. 2006. "Nonresponse Rates and Nonresponse Bias in Household Surveys." *Public Opinion Quarterly* 70 (5): 646–75. doi:10.1093/poq/nfl033.

Groves, Robert M., and Emilia Peytcheva. 2008. "The Impact of Nonresponse Rates on Nonresponse Bias: A Meta-Analysis." *Public Opinion Quarterly* 72 (2): 167–89. doi:10.1093/poq/nfn011.

Guglielmo, Jennifer, and Salvatore Salerno, eds. 2003. *Are Italians white? How race is made in America.* New York: Routledge.

Hailbronner, Kay, and Anuscheh Farahat. 2015. "Country Report on Citizenship Law: Germany. Revised and updated January 2015." *EUDO Citizenship Observatory*, 1–36.

Hainmueller, Jens, Dominik Hangartner, and Giuseppe Pietrantuono. 2015. "Naturalization Fosters the Long-Term Political Integration of Immigrants." *Proceedings of the National Academy of Sciences of the United States of America* 112 (41): 12651–56. doi:10.1073/pnas.1418794112.

Hall, Peter A., and Michèle Lamont, eds. 2013. *Social Resilience in the Neoliberal Era.* New York: Cambridge University Press.

Hammar, Tomas. 1990. *Democracy and the nation state: aliens, denizens and citizens in a world of international migration.* Reprinted. Research in ethnic relations series. Aldershot: Avebury.

Haug, Sonja. 2003. "Interethnische Freundschaftsbeziehungen und soziale Integration. Unterschiede in der Ausstattung mit sozialem Kapital bei jungen Deutschen und Immigranten." *Köln Z Soziol* 55 (4): 716–63.

Haug, Sonja, Stephanie Müssig, and Anja Stichs. 2009. *Muslimisches Leben in Deutschland. Im Auftrag der Deutschen Islam Konferenz.* Nürnberg: Bundesamt für Migration und Flüchtlinge.

Hechter, Michael, and Satoshi Kanazawa. 1997. "Sociological rational choice theory." *Annual Review of Sociology*, 191–214.

Hedström, Peter. 2005. *Dissecting the Social: On the Principles of Analytical Sociology.* Cambridge: Cambridge University Press.

Hedström, Peter, and Petri Ylikoski. 2010. "Causal Mechanisms in the Social Sciences." *Annual Review of Sociology* 36 (1): 49–67. doi:10.1146/annurev.soc.012809.102632.

Helbling, Marc. 2013. "Islamophobia in the West. An introduction." In *Islamophobia in the West. Measuring and Explaining Individual Attitudes*, edited by Marc Helbling. New York: Routledge.

———. 2014. "Opposing Muslims and the Muslim Headscarf in Western Europe." *European Sociological Review*, 1–16.

Helbling, Marc, Liv Bjerre, Friederike Römer, and Malisa Zobel. 2016. "measuring immigration policies: the IMPIC database." *European Political Science.* doi:10.1057/eps.2016.4.

Hellevik, Ottar. 2015. "Extreme Nonresponse and Response Bias." *Qual Quant*, 1–23. doi:10.1007/s11135-015-0246-5.

Hochman, Oshrat. 2011. "Determinants of Positive Naturalisation Intentions among Germany's Labour Migrants." *Journal of Ethnic and Migration Studies* 37 (9): 1403–21. doi:10.1080/1369183x.2011.623615.

Hochschild, Jennifer L., and Charles Lang. 2011. "Including Oneself and Including Others: Who Belongs in My Country?" *The ANNALS of the American Academy of Political and Social Science* 634 (1): 78–97. doi:10.1177/0002716210388990.

Hochschild, Jennifer L., and John H. Mollenkopf. 2009. "Modeling Immigrant Political Incorporation." In *Bringing Outsiders In. Transatlantic Perspectives on Immigrant Political Incorporation*, edited by Jennifer L. Hochschild and John H. Mollenkopf. Ithaca: Illinois University Press.

Holmes Cooper, A. 2002. "Party-Sponsored Protest and the Movement Society: The CDU/CSU Mobilises Against Citizenship Law Reform." *German Politics* 11 (2): 88–104.

Jacobson, David. 1996. *Rights across borders: immigration and the decline of citizenship*. Baltimore, Md. Johns Hopkins Univ. Press.

Jakob, Maria. 2017. *Einbürgerungsfeiern: Wie Zugehörigkeit praktiziert wird*. 1. Auflage. Baden-Baden: Nomos.

Janoski, Thomas. 2010. *The ironies of citizenship: naturalization and integration in industrialized countries*. New York: Cambridge Univ. Press.

Jeffers, Kristen, Iseult Honohan, and Rainer Bauböck. 2012. "Comparing Citizenship Across Europe: Laws, Implementation and Impact." *EUDO Citizenship Observatory*, 1–63.

Jenkins, Richard. 1997. *Rethinking Ethnicity. Arguments and Explorations*. London: Sage.

———. 2004. *Social identity*. London: Routledge.

Jones-Correa, Michael. 1998. *Between Two Nations. The Political Predicament of Latinos in New York City*. Ithaca: Cornell University Press.

———. 2001a. "Institutional and contextual factors in immigrant naturalization and voting." *Citizenship Studies* 5 (1): 41–56.

———. 2001b. "Under Two Flags: Dual Nationality in Latin America and Its Consequences for Naturalization in the United States." *International Migration Review* 35 (4): 997–1029. doi:10.1111/j.1747-7379.2001.tb00050.x.

Joppke, Christian. 1999. *Immigration and the Nation-State: The United States, Germany, and Great Britain*: Oxford University Press.

———. 2001. "The Legal-domestic Sources of Immigrant Rights." *Comparative Political Studies* 34 (4): 339–66. doi:10.1177/0010414001034004001.

———. 2005. "Exclusion in the Liberal State." *European Journal of Social Theory* 8 (1): 43–61. doi:10.1177/1368431005049327.

———. 2007. "Beyond national models: Civic integration policies for immigrants in Western Europe." *West European Politics* 30 (1): 1–22. doi:10.1080/01402380601019613.

Joppke, Christian, and Ewa Morawska. 2003. "Integrating Immigrants in Liberal Nation-States: Policies and Practices." In *Toward assimilation and citizenship: immigrants in liberal nation-states*, edited by Christian Joppke and Ewa Morawska. Migration, minorities and citizenship. Houndmills: Palgrave Macmillan.

Kaas, Leo, and Christian Manger. 2012. "Ethnic Discrimination in Germany's Labour Market: A Field Experiment." *German Economic Review* 13 (1): 1–20.

Kadirbeyoğlu, Zeynep. 2007. "Changing Conceptions of Citizenship in Turkey." In *Citizenship policies in the New Europe*, edited by Rainer Bauböck, Bernhard Perchinig, and Wiebke Sievers. Amsterdam: Amsterdam University Press.

Kahanec, Martin, and Mehmet S. Tosun. 2009. "Political Economy of Immigration in Germany: Attitudes and Citizenship Aspirations." *International Migration Review* 43 (2): 263–91. doi:10.1111/j.1747-7379.2009.00765.x.

Kalter, Frank. 2006. "Auf der Suche nach einer Erklärung für die spezifischen Arbeitsmarktnachteile von Jugendlichen türkischer Herkunft." *Zeitschrift für Soziologie* 35 (2): 144–60.

Kalter, Frank, and Nadia Granato. 2002. "Demographic Change, Educational Expansion, and Structural Assimilation of Immigrants: The Case of Germany." *European Sociological Review* 18 (2): 199–216. doi:10.1093/esr/18.2.199.

Kalter, Frank, Nadia Granato, and Cornelia Kristen. 2011. "Die strukturelle Assimilation der zweiten Migrantengeneration in Deutschland: Eine Zerlegung gegenwärtiger Trends." In *Integration durch Bildung*, edited by Rolf Becker, 257–88: VS Verlag für Sozialwissenschaften.

Kalter, Frank, and Clemens Kroneberg. 2014. "Between Mechanism Talk and Mechanism Cult: New Emphases in Explanatory Sociology and Empirical Research." *Köln Z Soziol* 66 (1): 91–115. doi:10.1007/s11577-014-0272-7.

Kanstroom, Daniel. 1993. "Wer Sind Wir Wieder? Laws of Asylum, Immigration, and Citizenship in the Struggle for the Soul of the New Germany." *Yale Journal of Int. Law* 18.1: 155–211.

Kaya, Ayhan. 2012. "Transnational citizenship: German-Turks and liberalizing citizenship regimes." *Citizenship Studies* 16 (2): 153–72. doi:10.1080/13621025.2012.667608.
Kelle, Udo. 2006. "Computer-assisted qualitative data analysis." In *Qualitative Research Practice*, edited by Clive Seale, Giampetro Gobo, Jaber F. Gubrium, and David Silverman. London: Sage.
———. 2008. "Strukturen begrenzter Reichweite und empirisch begründete Theoriebildung. Überlegungen zum Theoriebezug qualitativer Methodologie." In *Theoretische Empirie. Zur Relevanz qualitativer Forschung*, edited by Stefan Kalthoff, Stefan Hirschauer, and Gesa Lindemann. Frankfurt/Main: Suhrkamp.
Kelle, Udo, and Susann Kluge. 2010. *Vom Einzelfall zum Typus. Fallvergleich und Fallkontrastierung in der qualitativen Sozialforschung (2nd Ed.)*. Opladen: Leske+Budrich.
Klink, Andreas, and Ulrich Wagner. 1999. "Discrimination Against Ethnic Minorities in Germany: Going Back to the Field." *Journal of Applied Social Psychology* 29 (2): 402–23.
Kluge, Susann. 2000. "Empirically Grounded Construction of Types and Typologies in Qualitative Social Research." *Forum Qualitative Social Research* 1 (1).
Kristen, Cornelia, and Nadia Granato. 2007. "The educational attainment of the second generation in Germany." *Ethnicities* 7 (3): 343–66. doi:10.1177/1468796807080233.
Kroneberg, Clemens. 2005. "The Definition of the Situation and the Variable Rationality of Actors. A General Model of Action." *Zeitschrift für Soziologie* 34 (5): 344–63.
———. 2012. "Die Rettung von Juden im Zweiten Weltkrieg." *Köln Z Soziol* 64 (1): 37–65. doi:10.1007/s11577-012-0156-7.
Kroneberg, Clemens, and Frank Kalter. 2012. "Rational Choice Theory and Empirical Research: Methodological and Theoretical Contributions in Europe." *Annual Review of Sociology* 38 (1): 73–92. doi:10.1146/annurev-soc-071811-145441.
Kroneberg, Clemens, Meir Yaish, and Volker Stocké. 2010. "Norms and Rationality in Electoral Participation and in the Rescue of Jews in WWII: An Application of the Model of Frame Selection." *Rationality and Society* 22 (1): 3–36. doi:10.1177/1043463109355494.
Kross, Ethan, Marc G. Berman, Walter Mischel, Edward E. Smith, and Tor D. Wager. 2011. "Social rejection shares somatosensory representations with physical pain." *Proceedings of the National Academy of Sciences* 108 (15): 6270–75. doi:10.1073/pnas.1102693108.
Kühnel, Steffen, and Jürgen Leibold. 2003. "The Others and We: Relationships Between Germans and Non-Germans from the Point of View of Foreigners Living in Germany." In Alba, Schmidt, and Wasmer 2003.
Laitin, David D. 1998. *Identity in formation: The Russian-speaking populations in the near abroad*. Ithaca: Cornell University Press.
Lamont, Michèle. 1992. *Money, morals, and manners: The Culture of the French and American Upper-Middle Class*. London: University of Chicago Press.
———. 2000. *The Dignity of Working Men: Morality and the Boundaries of Race, Class, and Immigration*. New York: Russel Sage.
———. 2009. "Responses to Racism, Health, and Social Inclusion as a Dimension of Successful Societies." In *Successful Societies. How Institutions and Culture Affect Health*, edited by Peter A. Hall and Michèle Lamont. New York: Cambridge University Press.
———. 2014. "Reflections inspired by Ethnic Boundary Making: Institutions, Power, Networks by Andreas Wimmer." *Ethnic and Racial Studies* 37 (5): 814–19. doi:10.1080/01419870.2013.871312.
Lamont, Michèle, and Christopher A. Bail. 2005. "Sur les frontières de la reconnaissance. Les catégories internes et externes de l'identité collective." *Revue européenne des migrations internationales* 21 (2): 61–90.
Lamont, Michèle, Stefan Beljean, and Matthew Clair. 2014. "What is missing? Cultural processes and causal pathways to inequality." *Socio-Economic Review*. doi:10.1093/ser/mwu011.

References

Lamont, Michèle, and Nissim Mizrachi. 2012. "Ordinary people doing extraordinary things: responses to stigmatization in comparative perspective." *Ethn. Racial Stud.* 35 (3): 365–81. doi:10.1080/01419870.2011.589528.

Lamont, Michèle, and Virág Molnár. 2002. "The Study of Boundaries in the Social Sciences." *Annual Review of Sociology* 28: 167–95.

Lamont, Michèle, Ann Morning, and Margarita Mooney. 2002. "Particular universalisms: North African immigrants respond to French racism." *Ethn. Racial Stud.* 25 (3): 390–414. doi:10.1080/01419870020036701e.

Lamont, Michèle, Graziella M. Silva, Jessica Welburn, Joshua Guetzkow, Nissim Mizrachi, Hanna Herzog, and Elisa Reis. 2016. *Getting Respect: Responding to Stigma and Discrimination in the United States, Brazil, and Israel:* Princeton University Press.

Lamont, Michèle, Jessica S. Welburn, and Crystal Fleming. 2013. "Responses to Discrimination and Social Resilience Under Neo-Liberalism: The United States Compared." In Hall and Lamont 2013.

Leeuw, Edith D. de, Don A. Dillman, and Joop Hox, eds. 2008. *International handbook of survey methodology.* New York, NY: Erlbaum.

Leeuw, Edith D. de, and W. de Heer. 2002. "Trends in household survey non-response: A longitudinal and international comparison." In *Survey non-response*, edited by Robert M. Groves, Don A. Dillman, J. L. Etlinge, and Roderick J. A. Little. New York: John Wiley.

Leeuw, Edith D. de, Joop Hox, and Don A. Dillman. 2008. "Mixed-mode Surveys: When and Why." In *International handbook of survey methodology*, edited by Edith D. de Leeuw, Don A. Dillman, and Joop Hox. New York, NY: Erlbaum.

Levin, Ines. 2013. "Political Inclusion of Latino Immigrants: Becoming a Citizen and Political Participation." *American Politics Research* 41 (4): 535–68. doi:10.1177/1532673x12461438.

Lewicki, Aleksandra. 2014. *Social Justice Through Citizenship? The Politics of Muslim Integration in Germany and Great Britain:* Palgrave Macmillan.

Liang, Zai. 1994. "Social Contact, Social Capital, and the Naturalization Process: Evidence From Six Immigrant Groups." *Social Science Research* 23 (4): 407–37. doi:10.1006/ssre.1994.1016.

Long, J. S., and Jeremy Freese. 2014. *Regression Models for Categorical Dependent Variables Using Stata [3rd ed.].* College Station: Stata Press.

Lucassen, Leo. 2005. *The immigrant threat: The integration of old and new migrants in Western Europe since 1850.* Urbana, Ill. University of Illinois Press.

Lucassen, Leo, and Charlotte Laarman. 2009. "Immigration, intermarriage and the changing face of Europe in the post war period." *The History of the Family* 14 (1): 52–68.

Maehler, Débora B. 2012. *Akkulturation und Identifikation bei eingebürgerten Migranten in Deutschland.* Münster: Waxmann.

Mandel, Ruth. 2008. *Cosmopolitan Anxieties. Turkish Challenges to Citizenship and Belonging in Germany.* Durham: Duke University Press.

Marshall, T. H. 1992. "Citizenship and Social Class." In *Citizenship and Social Class, Part I*, edited by T. H. Marshall and Tom Bottomore, 3–51. London and Concord, MA: Pluto Press.

Mäs, Michael, Kurt Mühler, and Karl-Dieter Opp. 2005. "When are individuals called "German"? Empirical results of a factorial survey." *Koln. Z. Soziol. Sozialpsych.* 57 (1): 112–34. doi:10.1007/s11577-005-0113-9.

Mau, Steffen, Fabian Gülzau, Lena Laube, and Natascha Zaun. 2015. "The Global Mobility Divide: How Visa Policies Have Evolved over Time." *Journal of Ethnic and Migration Studies*, 1–22. doi:10.1080/1369183x.2015.1005007.

McCook, Brian. 2007. "Polnische industrielle Arbeitswanderer im Ruhrgebiet (>Ruhrpolen<) seit Ende des 19. Jahrhunderts." In *Enzyklopädie Migration in Europa. Vom 17. Jahrhundert bis zur Gegenwart*, edited by Klaus J. Bade, Pieter C. Emmer, Leo Lucassen, and Jochen Oltmer. Paderborn: Ferdinand Schöningh.

Merton, Robert K. 1968. *Social Theory and Social Structure*. New York: The Free Press.
Miller-Idriss, Cynthia. 2006. "Everyday Understandings of Citizenship in Germany." *Citizenship Studies* 10 (5): 541–70. doi:10.1080/13621020600954978.
Mizrachi, Nissim, and Hanna Herzog. 2012. "Participatory destigmatization strategies among Palestinian citizens, Ethiopian Jews and Mizrahi Jews in Israel." *Ethn. Racial Stud.* 35 (3): 418–35. doi:10.1080/01419870.2011.589530.
Mollenkopf, J., and J. Hochschild. 2010. "Immigrant Political Incorporation: Comparing Success in the United States and Western Europe." *Ethn. Racial Stud.* 33 (1): 19–38. doi:10.1080/01419870903197373.
Mood, Carina. 2010. "Logistic Regression: Why We Cannot Do What We Think We Can Do, and What We Can Do About It." *European Sociological Review* 26 (1): 67–82.
Nagel, Joane. 1994. "Constructing Ethnicity: Creating and Recreating Ethnic Identity and Culture." *Social Problems* 41 (1): 152–76.
Neuman, Gerald L. 1991. "We are the people: Alien suffrage in German and American perspective." *Michigan Journal of Int. Law* 13: 259–335.
Ong, Aihwa. 1996. "Cultural Citizenship as Subject-Making: Immigrants Negotiate Racial and Cultural Boundaries in the United States." *Current Anthropology* 37 (5): 737–62.
Owen, David. 2010. "Resident Aliens, Non-resident Citizens and Voting Rights: Towards a Pluralist Theory of Transnational Political Equality and Modes of Political Belonging." In *Citizenship acquisition and national belonging: migration, membership and the liberal democratic state*, edited by Gideon Calder, Phillip Cole, and Jonathan Seglow. Basingstoke: Palgrave Macmillan.
Pan, Yuling, and Manuel de La Puente. 2005. *Census Bureau Guideline for the Translation of Data: Collection Instruments and Supporting Materials: Documentations on how the Guideline Was Developed*. Washington DC: US Bureau of the Census.
Pedroza, Luicy. 2013. "Access to Electoral Rights. Germany." *EUDO Citizenship Observatory*, 1–16.
Porst, Rolf. 2001. "Wie man die Rücklaufquote bei postalischen Befragungen erhöht." *ZUMA How-to-Reihe* Nr.9: 1–12.
Portes, Alejandro, and John W. Curtis. 1987. "Changing Flags: Naturalization and Its Determinants among Mexican Immigrants." *International Migration Review* 21 (2): 352–71.
Portes, Alejandro, and Rubén G. Rumbaut. 2001. *Legacies. The Story of the Immigrant Second Generation*. London: University of California Press.
Portes, Alejandro, and Min Zhou. 1993. "The New Second Generation: Segmented Assimilation and Its Variants." *Annals of the American Academy of Political and Social Science* 530:74–96. doi:10.2307/1047678.
Prümm, Kathrin. 2004. *Einbürgerung als Option: die Bedeutung des Wechsels der Staatsangehörigkeit für Menschen türkischer Herkunft in Deutschland*. Münster: Lit.
Putnam, Robert D. 2007. "E pluribus unum: Diversity and community in the twenty-first century the 2006 Johan Skytte Prize Lecture." *Scandinavian political studies* 30 (2): 137–74.
Reichel, David, and Bernhard Perchinig. 2015. "Reflections on the value of citizenship – explaining naturalisation practices." *Austrian Journal of Political Science* 44 (1): 32–45.
Robbins, Derek. 2007. "Sociology as Reflexive Science On Bourdieu's Project." *Theory, Culture & Society* 24 (5): 77–98.
Rodríguez, Cristina M. 2010. "Noncitizen voting and the extraconstitutional construction of the polity." *International Journal of Constitutional Law* 8 (1): 30–49.
Rotter, Julian B. 1966. "Generalized expectancies for internal versus external control of reinforcement." *Psychological monographs: General and applied* 80 (1): 1–28.
Royston, Patrick, and Ian R. White. 2011. "Multiple imputation by chained equations (MICE): implementation in Stata." *J Stat Softw* 45 (4): 1–20.

Sabini, John, Michael Siepmann, and Julia Stein. 2001. "The Really Fundamental Attribution Error in Social Psychological Research." *Psychological Inquiry* 12 (1): 1–15. doi:10.2307/1449294.

Sachweh, Patrick. 2013. "Symbolische Grenzziehungen und subjektorientierte Sozialstrukturanalyse. Eine empirische Untersuchung aus einer Mixed-Methods-Perspektive." *Zeitschrift für Soziologie* 42 (1): 7–27.

Saldaña, Johnny. 2013. *The coding manual for qualitative researchers (2nd. ed.)* 14. Los Angeles: Sage.

Salentin, Kurt. 2007. "Determinants of experience of discrimination in minorities in Germany." *International Journal of Conflict and Violence* 1 (1): 32–50.

Salentin, Kurt, and Frank Wilkening. 2003. "Ausländer, Eingebürgerte und das Problem einer realistischen Zuwanderer-Integrationsbilanz." *Köln Z Soziol* 55 (2): 278–98. doi:10.1007/s11577-003-0051-3.

Salikutluk, Zerrin. 2016. "Why Do Immigrant Students Aim High? Explaining the Aspiration–Achievement Paradox of Immigrants in Germany." *European Sociological Review* 32 (5): 581–92. doi:10.1093/esr/jcw004.

Sauer, Martina. 2013. *Einbürgerungsverhalten türkeistämmiger Migrantinnen und Migranten in Nordrhein-Westfalen. Ergebnisse der dreizehnten Mehrthemenbefragung 2012*. Essen: ZfTI.

Schacht, Diana, Cornelia Kristen, and Ingrid Tucci. 2014. "Interethnische Freundschaften in Deutschland." *Köln Z Soziol* 66 (3): 445–58. doi:10.1007/s11577-014-0280-7.

Schneider, Jan, Ruta Yemane, and Martin Weinmann. 2014. *Diskriminierung am Ausbildungsmarkt. Ausmaß, Ursachen und Handlungsperspektiven*. Berlin: SVR GmbH.

Schneider, Jens. 2001. *Deutsch sein: das Eigene, das Fremde und die Vergangenheit im Selbstbildnis des vereinten Deutschland*. Frankfurt/Main: Campus.

———. 2002. "Discourses of Exclusion: Dominant Self-Definitions and" The Other" In German Society." *Journal of the Society for the Anthropology of Europe* 2 (1): 13–21.

Schnell, Rainer. 2012. *Survey-Interviews: Methoden standardisierter Befragungen*. Wiesbaden: VS.

Semyonov, Moshe, Rebeca Raijman, Anat Y. Tov, and Peter Schmidt. 2004. "Population size, perceived threat, and exclusion: a multiple-indicators analysis of attitudes toward foreigners in Germany." *Social Science Research* 33 (4): 681–701. doi:10.1016/j.ssresearch.2003.11.003.

Shachar, Ayelet. 2007. "Against birthright privilege: redefining citizenship as property." In *Identities, affiliations, and allegiances*, edited by Seyla Benhabib, Ian Shapiro, and Danilo Petranović. New York: Cambridge Univ Press.

Small, Mario L. 2011. "How to Conduct a Mixed Methods Study: Recent Trends in a Rapidly Growing Literature." *Annual Review of Sociology* 37 (1): 57–86. doi:10.1146/annurev.soc.012809.102657.

Söhn, Janina. 2008. *Die Entscheidung zur Einbürgerung: die Bedeutung von Staatsbürgerschaft für AusländerInnen in der Bundesrepublik Deutschland-Analysen zu den 1990er-Jahren*: VDM Verlag Dr. Müller.

Son Hing, Leanne S. 2013. "Stigmatization, Neoliberlalism, and Resilience." In Hall and Lamont 2013.

Souleimanov, Emil A., and Jasper Schwampe. 2017. "Devout Muslims or tough highlanders? Exploring attitudes toward ethnic nationalism and racism in Europe's ethnic-Chechen Salafi communities." *Journal of Ethnic and Migration Studies*, 1–18. doi:10.1080/1369183X.2017.1287560.

Soysal, Yasemin N. 1994. *Limits of Citizenship: Migrants and Postnational Membership in Europe*. [2. Dr.]. Chicago: University of Chicago Press.

Spielhaus, Riem. 2013. "Vom Migranten zum Muslim und wieder zurück - Die Vermengung von Integrations- und Islamthemen in Medien, Politik und Forschung." In *Islam und die deutsche Gesellschaft*, edited by Dirk Halm and Hendrik Meyer. Wiesbaden: Springer.

Spiro, Peter J. 2010. "Dual citizenship as human right." *International Journal of Constitutional Law* 8 (1): 111–30.

Steinbach, Anja. 2004. *Soziale Distanz. Ethnische Grenzziehung und die Eingliederung von Zuwanderern in Deutschland.* Wiesbaden: VS.

Stichs, Anja. 2016. "Wie viele Muslime leben in Deutschland? Eine Hochrechnung über die Anzahl der Muslime in Deutschland zum Stand 31. Dezember 2015." Im Auftrag der Deutschen Islam Konferenz. *BAMF Working Paper* (71): 1–44.

Street, Alexander. 2013. "Naturalization Dynamics in Immigrant Families." *Comparative Migration Studies* 1 (1): 23–44.

———. 2014. "My Child will be a Citizen: Intergenerational Motives for Naturalization." *World Politics* 66 (2): 264–92.

———. 2017. "The Political Effects of Immigrant Naturalization." *International Migration Review* 51 (2): 323–43. doi:10.1111/imre.12229.

Surak, Kristin. 2012. "Nation-Work: A Praxeology of Making and Maintaining Nations." *European Journal of Sociology / Archives Européennes de Sociologie* 53 (02): 171–204. doi:10.1017/S0003975612000094.

Swedberg, Richard. 2012. "Theorizing in Sociology and Social Science: Turning to the Context of Discovery." *Theor Soc* 41 (1): 1–40. doi:10.1007/s11186-011-9161-5.

Taylor, Donald M., Stephen C. Wright, Fathali M. Moghaddam, and Richard N. Lalonde. 1990. "The Personal/Group Discrimination Discrepancy: Perceiving My Group, but not Myself, to be a Target for Discrimination." *Personality and social Psychology Bulletin* 16 (2): 254–62. doi:10.1177/0146167290162006.

Teddlie, Charles, and Abbas Tashakkori. 2009. *Foundations of Mixed Methods Research: Integrating Quantitative and Qualitative Approaches in the Social and Behavioral Sciences.* London: Sage.

Teney, Céline, and Marc Helbling. 2014. "How Denationalization Divides Elites and Citizens." *Zeitschrift für Soziologie* 43 (4): 258–71.

Tilly, Charles, ed. 1975. *The formation of national states in Western Europe.* Princeton: Princeton University.

Tiryakioğlu, Bilgin. 2006. "Multiple Citizenship and its Consequences in Turkish Law." *Ankara Law Review* 3 (1): 1–16.

Topçu, Canan. 2007. *EinBÜRGERung: Lesebuch über das Deutsch-Werden. Portraits, Interviews, Fakten.* 1. Aufl. Frankfurt am Main: Brandes&Apsel.

Topçu, Özlem, Khuê Pham, and Alice Bota. 2012. *Wir neuen Deutschen. Wer wir sind, was wir wollen.* Reinbek: Rowohlt.

Torpey, John. 1998. "Coming and going: On the state monopolization of the legitimate "means of movement"." *Sociol. Theor.* 16 (3): 239–59.

Tversky, Amos, and Daniel Kahneman. 1986. "The Framing of Decisions and the Psychology of Choice." In *Rational Choice. Readings in Social and Political Theory*, edited by Jon Elster. Oxford: Blackwell.

van Hook, Jennifer, Susan K. Brown, and Frank D. Bean. 2006. "For Love or Money? Welfare Reform and Immigrant Naturalization." *Social Forces* 85 (2): 643–66. doi:10.1353/sof.2007.0029.

Vink, Maarten P., and Rainer Bauböck. 2013. "Citizenship configurations: Analysing the multiple purposes of citizenship regimes in Europe." *Comparative European Politics* 11 (5): 621–48.

Vink, Maarten P., Tijana Prokic-Breuer, and Jaap Dronkers. 2013. "Immigrant Naturalization in the Context of Institutional Diversity: Policy Matters, but to Whom?" *International Migration* 51 (5): 1–20. doi:10.1111/imig.12106.

Walzer, Michael. 1983. *Spheres of Justice. A Defense of Pluralism and Equality:* Basic Books.

Wasmer, Martina, and Achim Koch. 2003. "Foreigners as Second-Class Citizens? Attitudes Towards Equal Civil Rights for Non-Germans." In Alba, Schmidt, and Wasmer 2003.

Weber, Max. 1947. *Gesammelte Aufsätze zur Religionssoziologie.* Tübingen: Mohr.

Weingartner, Sebastian. 2013. "Hochkulturelle Praxis und Frame-Selektion." *Köln Z Soziol* 65 (1): 3–30.
Weinmann, Martin, Inna Becher, and Christian Babka von Gostomski. 2012. *Einbürgerungsverhalten von Ausländerinnen und Ausländern in Deutschland sowie Erkenntnisse zu Optionspflichtigen. Ergebnisse der BAMF-Einbürgerungsstudie 2011.* Ergebnisse der BAMF-Einbürgerungsstudie. Nürnberg: BAMF.
Williams, Richard. 2006. "Generalized ordered logit/partial proportional odds models for ordinal dependent variables." *The Stata Journal* 6 (1): 58–82.
Wimmer, Andreas. 2002. *Nationalist exclusion and ethnic conflict: shadows of modernity:* Cambridge University Press.
———. 2008a. "Elementary strategies of ethnic boundary making." *Ethn. Racial Stud.* 31 (6): 1025–55.
———. 2008b. "The making and unmaking of ethnic boundaries: A multilevel process theory." *American Journal of Sociology* 113 (4): 970–1022.
———. 2009. "Herder's Heritage and the Boundary-Making Approach: Studying Ethnicity in Immigrant Societies." *Sociol. Theor.* 27 (3): 244–70.
———. 2013. *Ethnic boundary making. Institutions, Power, Networks.* New York: Oxford University Press.
———. 2014. "Ethnic boundary making as strategic action: Reply to my critics." *Ethnic and Racial Studies* 37 (5): 834–42. doi:10.1080/01419870.2014.887212.
Windzio, Michael. 2012. "Integration of Immigrants' Children into Inter-ethnic Friendship Networks: The Role of 'Intergenerational Openness'." *Sociology* 46 (2): 258–71. doi:10.1177/0038038511419182.
Witzel, Andreas, and Herwig Reiter. 2012. *The Problem-Centred Interview.* London: Sage.
Worbs, Susanne. 2003. "The Second Generation in Germany: Between School and Labor Market." *International Migration Review* 37 (4): 1011–38. doi:10.1111/j.1747-7379.2003.tb00168.x.
Wunderlich, Tanja. 2005. *Die neuen Deutschen. Subjektive Dimensionen des Einbürgerungsprozesses.* Stuttgart: Lucius&Lucius.
Wüst, Andreas M. 2004. "Naturalised citizens as voters: behaviour and impact." *German Politics* 13 (2): 341–59. doi:10.1080/0964400042000229972.
Yang, Philip Q. 1994. "Explaining Immigrant Naturalization." *International Migration Review,* 449–77.
Zolberg, Aristide R., and Long L. Woon. 1999. "Why Islam is like Spanish: Cultural Incorporation in Europe and the United States." *Politics & Society* 27 (1): 5–38. doi:10.1177/0032329299027001002.

Laws

AufenthG	Aufenthaltsgesetz (Residence Law)
GG	Grundgesetz (Basic Law)
StAG	Staatsangehörigkeitsgesetz (Citizenship Law)
StGB	Strafgesetzbuch (Penal Code)
WehrRÄndG	Wehrrechtsänderungsgesetz (Law amending Military Law)

Official Statistics

Statistisches Bundesamt (2015): Bevölkerung und Erwerbstätigkeit. Einbürgerungen. 2014.
Statistisches Bundesamt (2013): Bevölkerung und Erwerbstätigkeit. Einbürgerungen. 2012.
Statistisches Bundesamt (2013): Bevölkerung und Erwerbstätigkeit. Ausländische Bevölkerung Ergebnisse des Ausländerzentralregisters. 2012.
Statistisches Bundesamt (2012): Bildungsstand der Bevölkerung. 2012.

Appendix A. Tables and Figures

Table A1 Scoring Coefficients for Independent Variables (Factor Analysis)

Item	Job	Pol. GER	Travel	ID Turk pass	Rights TUR
Job: Improve income	0.250	-0.105	0.011	-0.018	0.063
Job: Find a job easier	0.261	-0.090	-0.018	0.072	0.057
Job: Less discrimination on job	0.234	-0.033	-0.018	-0.094	-0.090
Job: Citizenship required	0.175	0.105	-0.058	-0.013	-0.119
Political rights GER: Federal	0.279	-0.060	-0.108	0.129	0.030
Political rights GER: Local	0.258	-0.059	0.001	-0.056	0.006
Political rights GER: EU	-0.092	0.346	-0.015	-0.096	0.000
Travel: Inside EU	-0.080	0.340	0.025	-0.047	-0.094
Travel: Between GER and TUR	-0.108	0.338	-0.007	-0.030	0.005
Travel: Outside EU and TUR	-0.016	0.232	-0.026	0.051	0.025
Identity and passp.: Being a Turk	-0.089	-0.003	0.414	-0.006	-0.013
Identity and passp.: Turk. identity	-0.059	-0.039	0.397	0.000	0.005
Genuine rights TUR: Vote	-0.043	0.020	0.333	0.001	-0.025
Genuine rights TUR: Property, heritage	0.020	-0.068	0.022	0.522	-0.004

Regression based on varimax rotated factors.

Table A2 Response Statistics

	Male	Female	Gender unknown	Total
Pool	19,924	16,693		36,617
Original Sample	1,000	1,000		2,000
Wrong address / person moved house (UO)	-40	-31		-71
Thereof contacted again under new address	4	3		7
Reception rejected / Mailbox full (UO)	-2	0		-2
Gross Sample	962	972		1934
Nonresponse	-837	-852		-1689
Online Response	24	11	4	39
Mail Response	105	114	2	221
Break-Offs (more than 50% missing values)	-4	-5	-2	-11
Total Response I (I+P)	125	120	4	249
Response Rate (base: Original sample; RR2)	12.5%	12.0%		12.5%
Response Rate (base: Gross sample)	13.0%	12.3%		12.9%

UO, I, P, and RR2 refer to AAPOR (2011) standard definitions. Sources: Public Register Hamburg, 2012; ACN 2012.

Table A3 Intention to Naturalise According to Different Studies (in %)

Study	Authors own calc.	Diehl and Blohm (2011, 2008)			Diehl and Blohm (2003)		Diehl (2002)		Kahanec and Tosun (2009)		This study
Data	IAB-SOEP-M 2013	SOEP 2001-2003			SOEP 1998		Integrationssurvey des BiB		ZfES (2002), "Ausländer in Deutschland – Marplan Studies"		ACN 2012
Nationality	Turk.	Turk.	Former Yug.	EU-15	Former Yug.	Turk.	Turk. young adults	Italian young adults	ESP, IT, TUR, GRE, Former Yug.	Turk.	Turk.
Spatial reference	GER	GER	GER	GER	GER	GER	GER	GER	Hamburg	West. GER	Hamburg
Interest ++	22.9				8.8	15.2	23.6	2.2	18.8	25.6	14.1
Interest +	19.6				10.8	20.8	16.9	9.9	32.8	23.5	37.4
Interest -	20.2				36.2	34.7	17.9	35.4			24.9
Interest --	36.3				31.8	40.4	11.8	39.8	48.4	41.9	20.1
Naturalized	32.6	17.1	14.6	6.8	5.4	6.5	28.9	13.0	26.3	24.3	
Intention to nat. in the next 6 month									14.1	21.4	
Intention to nat. in the next 2 years		33.6	22.3	5.8							
N	674	NR	NR	NR	297	558	1,104	820	NR	NR	249

All statistics as reported in the respective publications. NR: not reported. Compilation by author.

Table A4 Linear Regression (OLS) on Intention to Naturalise

	M1	M2	M3
Aspects of symbolic membership			
Feel at home in Germany[i]	0.426***	0.338***	
	(5.54)	(4.22)	
Perceived group discrimination[i]	-0.276***	-0.309***	
	(3.39)	(3.89)	
Turkish passport identity-relevant[i]	-0.048	-0.058	
	(0.76)	(0.95)	
German passport identity-relevant	0.070	0.074	
	(1.16)	(1.27)	
Share of German family members	-0.124*	-0.108	
	(1.80)	(1.60)	
Share of close friends that naturalised	-0.018	0.006	
	(0.25)	(0.08)	
Aspects of legal membership			
Interest in political rights Germany[i]			0.188***
			(3.13)
Expected job-related benefits[i]			0.142**
			(2.38)
Expected travel-related benefits[i]			0.158**
			(2.60)
Interest in cit. specific rights Turk.[i]			-0.375***
			(6.34)
Socio-demographics			
Gender female		-0.181	
		(1.54)	
Age		-0.070*	
		(1.79)	
Age squared		0.001	
		(1.29)	
Log. Personal income[i]		0.012	
		(0.30)	
Education in years		-0.003	
		(0.23)	
Generation 1.5 (ref.: 1st gen.)		0.187	
		(1.32)	
Generation 2 (ref.: 1st gen.)		0.361*	
		(1.91)	
Constant	2.020***	3.856***	2.519***
	(4.92)	(4.62)	(42.83)
N	218	218	218
Adj. R^2	0.18	0.26	0.22

(Table continues on next page)

Table A4 Linear Regression (OLS) on Intention to Naturalise (cont'd)

	M4	M5
Aspects of symbolic membership		
Feel at home in Germany[i]		0.241***
		(3.22)
Perceived group discrimination[i]		-0.245***
		(3.26)
Turkish passport identity-relevant[i]		-0.039
		(0.69)
German passport identity-relevant		0.017
		(0.32)
Share of German family members		-0.143**
		(2.28)
Share of close friends that naturalised		-0.021
		(0.30)
Aspects of legal membership		
Interest in political rights Germany[i]	0.248***	0.240***
	(4.29)	(4.14)
Expected job-related benefits[i]	0.134**	0.136**
	(2.28)	(2.40)
Expected travel-related benefits[i]	0.121**	0.095*
	(2.09)	(1.70)
Interest in cit. specific rights Turk.[i]	-0.332***	-0.247***
	(5.72)	(4.21)
Socio-demographics		
Gender female	0.051	-0.032
	(0.45)	(0.29)
Age	-0.108***	-0.080**
	(2.88)	(2.18)
Age squared	0.001**	0.001*
	(2.57)	(1.79)
Log. Personal income[i]	0.007	0.028
	(0.17)	(0.73)
Education in years	0.002	0.002
	(0.15)	(0.14)
Generation 1.5 (ref.: 1st gen.)	0.180	0.180
	(1.36)	(1.35)
Generation 2 (ref.: 1st gen.)	0.501***	0.427**
	(3.00)	(2.40)
Constant	4.471***	4.119***
	(5.92)	(5.09)
N	218	218
Adj. R^2	0.32	0.38

|t|-statistics in parentheses, [i] variables that have imputed values; * $p < 0.10$, ** $p < 0.05$, *** $p < 0.01$; Source: ACN 2012, own calculations.

Table A5 Non-Proportional Odds Regression (gologit) on Intention to Naturalise

	M5a	
Beta		
Aspects of symbolic membership		
Feel at home in Germany[i]	0.723***	(3.47)
Perceived group discrimination[i]	-0.742***	(3.47)
Turkish passport identity-relevant[i]	-0.181	(0.75)
German passport identity-relevant	0.041	(0.29)
Share of German family members	-0.338**	(2.02)
Share of close friends that naturalised	-0.714**	(2.31)
Aspects of legal membership		
Interest in political rights Germany[i]	0.772***	(4.60)
Expected job-related benefits[i]	0.393**	(2.49)
Expected travel-related benefits[i]	-0.234	(1.05)
Interest in cit. specific rights Turkey[i]	-0.702***	(4.10)
Socio-demographics		
Gender female	0.979*	(1.93)
Age	-0.249**	(2.41)
Age squared	0.003**	(2.04)
Log. Personal income[i]	0.125	(1.17)
Education in years	0.097*	(1.81)
Generation 1 (omitted)		
Generation 1.5	0.463	(1.29)
Generation 2	1.035**	(2.15)
Gamma 2		
Turkish passport identity-relevant[i]	-0.189	(0.27)
Share of close friends that naturalised	0.798	(0.34)
Expected travel-related benefits[i]	0.785	(0.27)
Gender female	-1.006	(0.54)
Education in years	-0.151	(0.06)
Gamma 3		
Turkish passport identity-relevant[i]	0.419	(0.30)
Share of close friends that naturalised	1.268	(0.38)
Expected travel-related benefits[i]	0.720	(0.31)
Female	-1.706	(0.63)
Education in years	-0.088	(0.07)
Constant		
cons1	7.471***	(3.03)
cons2	4.506*	(1.92)
cons3	1.279	(0.56)
N	218	
Mc Fadden's Pseudo R^2 / Wald chi2 (27)	0.28 / 96.48	

|z|-statistics in parentheses, [i]variables that have imputed values; * $p < 0.10$, ** $p < 0.05$, *** $p < 0.01$; Gammas are deviations from proportionality. Source: ACN 2012, own calculations.

Table A6 Ordered Logistic Regression on Intention to Naturalise

	M5b		M5c	
Aspects of symbolic membership				
Feel at home in Germany[i]	0.724***	(3.61)	0.744***	(3.73)
Perceived group discrimination[i]	-0.641***	(3.18)	-0.619***	(3.04)
Turkish passport identity-relevant[i]	-0.057	(0.39)	-0.060	(0.41)
German passport identity-relevant	0.018	(0.13)	-0.004	(0.03)
Share of German family members	-0.328**	(2.03)	-0.308*	(1.92)
Share of close friends that naturalised	1.369**	(2.04)	-0.022	(0.12)
Aspects of legal membership				
Interest in political rights Germany[i]	0.678***	(4.39)	0.661***	(4.28)
Expected job-related benefits[i]	0.418***	(2.75)	0.361**	(2.43)
Expected travel-related benefits[i]	0.225	(1.58)	0.229	(1.61)
Interest in genuine rights Turkey[i]	-0.693***	(4.28)	-0.665***	(4.15)
Controls				
Female	-0.080	(0.28)	-2.753**	(2.41)
Age	-0.153	(1.56)	-0.254**	(2.52)
Age squared	0.003**	(2.09)	0.002*	(1.84)
Log. Personal income[i]	0.086	(0.89)	0.093	(0.94)
Education – Secondary[a]	0.431	(1.11)	0.269	(0.70)
Education – Abitur / University[a]	0.091	(0.27)	-0.009	(0.03)
Generation 1.5b	0.303	(0.86)	0.420	(1.20)
Generation 2b	0.786*	(1.72)	0.896*	(1.93)
Interaction Effects				
Age * Share of friends that naturalised	-0.038**	(2.17)		
Age * Female			0.072**	(2.49)
Age * Feel at home in Germany				
Generation 1.5 * Feel at home in Ger.				
Generation 2 * Feel at home in Ger.				
Cutpoints				
cut1	-3.764	(1.53)	-7.780***	(3.37)
cut2	-0.846	(0.34)	-4.890**	(2.14)
cut3	0.902	(0.37)	-3.117	(1.38)
N / Pseudo R^2	218	0.22	218	0.22

(Table continues on next page)

Table A6 Ordered Logistic Regression on Intention to Naturalise (cont'd)

	M5d		M5e	
Aspects of symbolic membership				
Feel at home in Germany[i]	-2.120**	(2.51)	0.826***	(3.01)
Perceived group discrimination[i]	-0.628***	(3.04)	-0.648***	(3.18)
Turkish passport identity-relevant[i]	-0.073	(0.50)	-0.034	(0.23)
German passport identity-relevant	-0.010	(0.07)	0.009	(0.06)
Share of German family members	-0.321**	(1.99)	-0.347**	(2.13)
Share of close friends that naturalised	-0.100	(0.57)	-0.050	(0.29)
Aspects of legal membership				
Interest in political rights Germany[i]	0.657***	(4.25)	0.650***	(4.21)
Expected job-related benefits[i]	0.316**	(2.11)	0.327**	(2.16)
Expected travel-related benefits[i]	0.214	(1.48)	0.228	(1.58)
Interest in genuine rights Turkey[i]	-0.669***	(4.12)	-0.669***	(4.16)
Controls				
Female	0.071	(0.25)	0.003	(0.01)
Age	-0.481***	(3.72)	-0.201**	(2.08)
Age squared	0.002*	(1.94)	0.002*	(1.69)
Log. Personal income[i]	0.054	(0.57)	0.064	(0.67)
Education – Secondary[a]	0.128	(0.33)	0.208	(0.54)
Education – Abitur / University[a]	-0.126	(0.38)	-0.043	(0.13)
Generation 1.5b	0.235	(0.66)	0.087	(0.06)
Generation 2b	1.057**	(2.29)	4.457**	(2.15)
Interaction Effects				
Age * Share of friends that naturalised				
Age * Female				
Age * Feel at home in Germany	0.075***	(3.38)		
Generation 1.5 * Feel at home in Ger.			0.058	(0.14)
Generation 2 * Feel at home in Ger.			-1.018*	(1.77)
Cutpoints				
cut1	-16.87***	(4.42)	-6.277***	(2.84)
cut2	-13.88***	(3.68)	-3.368	(1.53)
cut3	-12.10***	(3.24)	-1.635	(0.75)
N / Pseudo R^2	218	0.23	218	0.22

(Table continues on next page)

Table A6 Ordered Logistic Regression on Intention to Naturalise (cont'd)

	M5f	
Aspects of symbolic membership		
Feel at home in Germany[i]	-1.779*	(1.82)
Perceived group discrimination[i]	-0.617***	(2.96)
Turkish passport identity-relevant[i]	-0.115	(0.78)
German passport identity-relevant	-0.016	(0.11)
Share of German family members	-0.318*	(1.93)
Share of close friends that naturalised	1.143*	(1.67)
Aspects of legal membership		
Interest in political rights Germany[i]	0.686***	(4.36)
Expected job-related benefits[i]	0.349**	(2.25)
Expected travel-related benefits[i]	0.233	(1.61)
Interest in genuine rights Turkey[i]	-0.674***	(4.11)
Controls		
Female	-2.334**	(2.05)
Age	-0.473***	(3.35)
Age squared	0.003**	(2.42)
Log. Personal income[i]	0.096	(0.97)
Education – Secondary[a]	0.160	(0.40)
Education – Abitur / University[a]	-0.064	(0.19)
Generation 1.5b	0.281	(0.19)
Generation 2b	1.738	(0.80)
Interaction Effects		
Age * Share of friends that naturalised	-0.033*	(1.83)
Age * Female	0.062**	(2.11)
Age * Feel at home in Germany	0.069***	(2.78)
Generation 1.5 * Feel at home in Ger.	-0.003	(0.01)
Generation 2 * Feel at home in Ger.	-0.208	(0.34)
Cutpoints		
cut1	-15.02***	(3.40)
cut2	-11.94***	(2.72)
cut3	-10.11**	(2.32)
N / Pseudo R^2	218	0.25

$|z|$-statistics in parentheses; [i]Variables that have imputed values; [a,b]Ref.cat.: Prim. educ.; 1st gen.;* $p < 0.10$, ** $p < 0.05$, *** $p < 0.01$. Source: ACN 2012, own calculations.

Table A7 Descriptive Statistics of Language Skills

	ACN 2012	ZiD 2001		ACN 2012	ZiD 2001
Turkish, oral skills			German, oral skills		
Very poor	0.8			3.2	
Poor	5.2			19.7	
Fair	47.8	89.7		45.0	50.8
Very good	46.2			32.1	

Sources: ACN 2012; ZiD 2001 are self-gathered data from Salentin and Wilkening (2003) for non-naturalised Turks on national level. They summarized 'fair' and 'very good'.

Table A8 Descriptive Statistics of Political Interest

	ACN 2012		ACN 2012		GSOE P 1996
Franchise, federal level Germany		Franchise, national Turkey		Political interest	
Not important at all	4.4		11.4	no	84.6
Rather unimportant	11.4		25.3		
Rather important	31.7		26.1		
Very important	44.9		33.3	yes	15.4

Sources: ACN 2012; GSOEP 1996 as reported in Diehl and Blohm (2001) for Turkish persons on national level; Missing up to 100%: Missing values.

Table A9 Descriptive Statistics of Education

Highest educational degree		Highest educational degree*			Highest educational or professional degree**	
	ACN 2012		ZiD	GSOEP		
None	5.2	None	14.6	24.1	None	34.0
Primary (5th grade)	12.1					
Secondary (8th/9th grd.)	20.9				Second. (8th/9th)	36.6
Secondary (10th grd.)	23.3	Secondary	76.4	70.3	Second. (10th)	13.5
Gymnasium (12th/13th grd.)	20.1	Gym.	9.0	14.7	Gymnasium	9.2
Tertiary	17.7				Tertiary	(2.1)
					Still in system	6.1

*Salentin and Wilkening (2003) for non-naturlized Turks on national level based on self-gathered data (ZiD 2001) and GSOEP 2000.

**All Turkish nationals living in Germany above the age of 15. Statistics are not strictly comparable for several reasons: Official statistics refer to the national level in 2012, not to Hamburg, they refer to all persons above the age of 15, and shares for educational degrees and professional degrees were calculated separately, where 'Tertiary' counts as a professional degree (Statistisches Bundesamt, Bildungsstand der Bevölkerung, 2012).

Other Sources: ACN 2012; Missing up to 100%: Missing values.

Appendix A. Tables and Figures

Table A10 Typology Coping Strategies: Five Dimensions

bright boundary applies	locus of control	hope for recognition	perceived bright boundary	perceived blurred boundary	
			alienation	accommodation	
yes	external	yes	**frustrated** "They will never accept us"	-	-
yes	external	no	-	**light-hearted** "I will always be a foreigner" "I feel good"	-
yes	internal	no	**resigned** "I am a foreigner" "Citizenship doesn't matter"	-	-
no	internal	yes	-	**bullish** "I do my work" "I never had any problems"	**confident** "I cannot sit and wait" "I never had any problems"

Table by author.

Table A11 Coping Strategies: Two Dimensions

Relation with host society	Arranging with bright boundary	Struggling to blur boundary
Alienation	**resigned** "I am a foreigner" "Citizenship doesn't matter"	**frustrated** "'We' worked hard for Germany" "They will never accept us"
Accommodation	**light-hearted** "I will always be a foreigner" "I feel good"	**confident / bullish** "I do my work" "I never had any problems"

Table by author.

Table A12 Operationalization of Symbolic Exclusion

Concept	Item (response scales)
Ethnic otherness	How often did you have the impression that you were treated differently? How often did you have the impression that this happened because ... [include option: doesn't apply]
	I look as if I wasn't from here
	I have a name that doesn't sound [national]
	I don't speak [national language] properly
	I don't drink alcohol
	I go out (shopping, restaurant ...) with my family
Religious otherness	If you consider yourself Muslim please indicate how often you had the impression that this happened because ... [include option: doesn't apply]
	I don't eat meat unless its halal
	I (want to) take breaks for prayer at work
	I go to the mosque regularly

Table by author.

Figure A1 QQ Plot of Age in Sample and Realised Sample

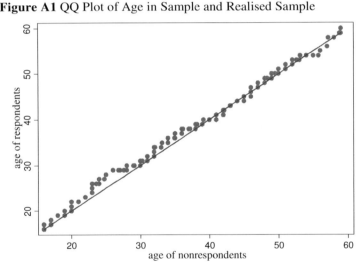

Sources: Public Register Hamburg, 2012; ACN 2012.

Appendix B. Survey Material

A. Cover Letter (Frontside)

Bremen International Graduate School of Social Sciences

Universität Bremen · BIGSSS · Postfach 33 04 40 · D 28334 Bremen

Herr

Dipl.-Soz. Nils Witte
FVG, Raum M1060
Wiener Straße/Ecke Celsiusstraße
Postfach 330 440
28334 Bremen/Germany
Telefon: 0421 - 218 66378
Fax: 0421 - 218 66353
E-Mail: nwitte@bigsss.uni-bremen.de
Internet: www.bigsss-bremen.de

Lütfen Türkçe mektup için arka tarafı çeviriniz.

Einladung zu einer Befragung

Bremen, den 23.11.2012

Sehr geehrter Herr XXX,

Ich bin Diplom-Sozialwissenschaftler von der Universität Bremen und arbeite derzeit an einem Forschungsprojekt zum Thema „Einbürgerung" in Hamburg. Ich möchte Sie freundlich bitten, mich dabei zu unterstützen.

In dem beiliegenden Fragebogen geht es um *Ihre Meinung* zur deutschen und türkischen Staatsangehörigkeit. Ich möchte mir gerne ein Bild *aller* Meinungen machen. Es ist deshalb besonders wichtig, dass auch Sie den Fragebogen ausfüllen. Das gilt auch dann, wenn Sie sich nicht für die deutsche Staatsangehörigkeit interessieren sollten. Ich wäre Ihnen daher äußerst dankbar für Ihre Teilnahme. Ein frankierter Briefumschlag für den ausgefüllten Fragebogen liegt diesem Brief bei. Ihnen entstehen also keine Kosten.

Sie möchten den Fragebogen lieber **online** ausfüllen? Dann nutzen Sie bitte die folgende Internetadresse und das folgende Passwort. Es stehen dort die deutsche und die türkische Sprache zur Auswahl:

www.soscisurvey.de/ese2012/   Passwort: XXX

Freiwilligkeit & Anonymität

Sie wurden per Zufall unter allen in Hamburg lebenden Personen mit türkischer Staatsangehörigkeit ausgewählt, um an meiner Umfrage teilzunehmen. Die Teilnahme ist freiwillig und Ihnen entstehen keine Kosten. Den beiliegenden Schlüsselanhänger können Sie in jedem Fall behalten. Die Umfrage ist rein wissenschaftlicher Art und wird nicht im Auftrag der Stadt Hamburg durchgeführt. Ihre Antworten werden nicht mit ihren persönlichen Daten in Verbindung gebracht. Für eventuelle statistische Auswertungen werden ausschließlich anonymisierte Daten verwendet. Auf die Anonymität Ihrer Angaben lege ich größten Wert. Nach dem Ende der Befragung werden Ihre Adressdaten gelöscht. Sie werden danach nicht zur Teilnahme an weiteren Befragungen aufgefordert.

Ihre Fragen an mich

Sollten Sie Nachfragen zu der Umfrage haben, können Sie mich telefonisch (Mo-Fr 9-12 und 13-17 Uhr), postalisch oder per E-Mail über die oben genannten Kontaktinformationen erreichen. Nähere Informationen zum Forschungsprojekt finden Sie auch auf meiner Homepage: www.bigsss-bremen.de/user/nwitte/ese-2012

Für Ihre Teilnahme bedanke ich mich vielmals! Çok teşekkür ederim! Sie leisten damit einen wichtigen Beitrag zur sozialwissenschaftlichen Forschung.

Mit freundlichen Grüßen / Saygılarımla,

Nils Witte, Diplom-Sozialwissenschaftler

B. Cover Letter (Backside)

Bremen International Graduate School of Social Sciences

Universität Bremen · BIGSSS · Postfach 33 04 40 · D 28334 Bremen

Bay

Dipl.-Soz. Nils Witte
FVG, Raum M1060
Wiener Straße/Ecke Celsiusstraße
Postfach 330 440
28334 Bremen/Germany

Telefon: 0421 - 218 66378
Fax: 0421 - 218 66353
E-Mail: nwitte@bigsss.uni-bremen.de
Internet: www.bigsss-bremen.de

Bitte wenden für deutschen Brief
Anket davetiyesi
Bremen, 23.11.2012

Sayın Bay XXX,

Bremen Üniversitesi'nde sosyal bilimci olarak çalışmaktayım ve Hamburg şehrinde „Alman vatandaşlığına geçiş" konulu bir araştırma projesinde yer almaktayım. Sizden bu konuda bana yardımcı olmanızı rica ediyorum.

Ekte bulunan anket sizin Alman ve Türk vatandaşlığı hakkındaki görüşlerinizi ele almaktadır. Bu anket sonucunda bütün fikirlerin yardımıyla genel bir bakış açısı oluşturmayı amaçlıyorum. Bu nedenle sizin de anketi doldurmanız ayrı bir önem taşımaktadır. Anketimize katıldığınız için teşekkür ederim. Doldurmuş olduğunuz anketi göndermeniz için posta ücreti bize ait olacak şekilde bir zarf ekte bulunmaktadır. Yani anketi göndermek için herhangi bir ücret ödemeniz gerekmemektedir.

Eğer anketi internet üzerinden doldurmak isterseniz lütfen aşağıdaki internet adresini ve parolayı kullanınız. İnternet adresinde Türkçe ve Almanca dil seçeneklerini bulabilirsiniz:

www.soscisurvey.de/ese2012/   Parola: XXX

Gönüllülük ve Gizlilik

Anketime katılmanız için Hamburg'da yaşayan ve Türk vatandaşlığına sahip kişiler arasından rastgele seçildiniz. Ankete katılım gönüllüdür ve her hangi bir ücrete tabii değilsiniz. Yolladığınız anahtarlıkları küçük bir hediye olarak saklayabilirsiniz. Bu anket tamamen bilimsel yöntemlerle hazırlanmıştır ve Hamburg şehrine bağlı değildir. Vermiş olduğunuz cevaplar kişisel bilgileriniz ile ilişkilendirilmeyecektir. Yapılacak olası istatistiksel değerlendirmeler için yalnızca anonim (gizli) veriler kullanılacaktır. Bilgilerinizin gizliliği benim için çok önemlidir. Anket çalışması sonuçlandıktan sonra adres bilgileriniz silinecektir. Bu anketten sonra başka herhangi bir ankete katılmanız istenmeyecektir.

Sorularınız

Eğer anket hakkında sorularınız olursa, yukarıda belirtilen telefon numarası (Pzt.-Cum. 9.00-12.00 ve 13.00-17.00 saatleri arasında), posta adresi ya da e-mail adresi aracılığıyla bana ulaşabilirsiniz. Bu araştırma projesi hakkında daha detaylı bilgileri internet sayfasında bulabilirsiniz: www.bigsss-bremen.de/user/nwitte/ese-2012

Ankete katıldığınız için çok teşekkür ederim! Ankete katılmanız ile sosyal bilim araştırmalarına önemli bir katkıda bulunmaktasınız.

Saygılarımla / Mit freundlichen Grüßen,

Nils Witte, Sosyal Bilimci

C. Questionnaire (German version)

Appendix B. Survey Material

Vielen Dank, dass Sie sich die Zeit nehmen, den Fragebogen auszufüllen! Es gibt keine richtigen und keine falschen Antworten. Wo nach Ihrer Meinung gefragt ist, antworten Sie einfach so, wie es Ihrer Meinung entspricht. Wo es um Ihre Lebensumstände geht, antworten Sie bitte so, wie es wirklich ist. Der ausgefüllte Fragebogen wird bei uns völlig anonym behandelt. Noch eine Bitte: Benutzen Sie einen gut sichtbaren Stift (z.B. Kugelschreiber, Füller, ...) und setzen Sie die Kreuze eindeutig; also nur ein Kreuz pro Frage. Auf Ausnahmen wird hingewiesen. Und jetzt: Viel Spaß beim Ausfüllen!

1. **Welche Staatsangehörigkeit(en) besitzen Sie derzeit?**
   Kreuzen Sie alles an, was auf Sie zutrifft (mehrere Antworten möglich).
   ☒ Türkische Staatsangehörigkeit
   ☐ Deutsche Staatsangehörigkeit (→ SPRINGEN ZU FRAGE 10)
   ☐ Andere Staatsangehörigkeit, und zwar _____ *(bitte eintragen)*

2. **Haben Sie schon einmal über eine mögliche Einbürgerung nachgedacht?**
   ☐ Ja
   ☐ Nein

3. **Wie gut sind Ihre Informationen über die Einbürgerung in Deutschland?**
   ☐ Sehr gut
   ☐ Eher gut
   ☐ Eher schlecht
   ☐ Sehr schlecht

4. **Kennen Sie die wesentlichen Voraussetzungen für eine Einbürgerung in Deutschland nach dem Staatsangehörigkeitsrecht?**
   ☐ Nein (→ SPRINGEN ZU FRAGE 5)
   ☐ Ja

   4a. **Erfüllen Sie diese Voraussetzungen?**
   ☐ Ja, alle
   ☐ Ja, teilweise
   ☐ Nein

5. **Haben Sie vor, die deutsche Staatsangehörigkeit zu beantragen?**
   ☐ Ja, ganz sicher ⎫
   ☐ Ja, wahrscheinlich ⎭ Und zwar im Alter von _____ Jahren *(bitte eintragen)*
   ☐ Eher unwahrscheinlich
   ☐ Ganz sicher nicht

6. **Haben Sie die deutsche Staatsangehörigkeit beantragt?**
   ☐ Nein, ich habe bisher keinen Antrag auf Einbürgerung gestellt
   ☐ Ja und das Verfahren läuft
   ☐ Ja und der Antrag wurde angenommen ⟶ SPRINGEN ZU FRAGE 8
   ☐ Ja und der Antrag wurde abgelehnt

7. **Warum haben Sie bisher keinen Antrag gestellt?**
   ☒ *Bitte kreuzen Sie für jeden Aspekt die Kategorie an, die Ihre Meinung am besten zum Ausdruck bringt.*

	trifft voll und ganz zu	trifft eher zu	trifft eher nicht zu	trifft überhaupt nicht zu
Ich möchte auf keinen Fall die deutsche Staatsangehörigkeit haben.	☐	☐	☐	☐
Ich habe zurzeit nicht ausreichend Geld für die Gebühren.	☐	☐	☐	☐
Ich verfüge noch nicht über ausreichend Sprachkenntnisse.	☐	☐	☐	☐
Ich bin zurzeit noch in einem Orientierungs- oder Einbürgerungskurs und will den Einbürgerungstest erst danach machen.	☐	☐	☐	☐
Ich hoffe, dass das Gesetz geändert wird und ich bei einer Einbürgerung meine bisherige(n) Staatsangehörigkeit(en) beibehalten kann.	☐	☐	☐	☐

1

8. Mit wem haben Sie sich bisher über die Möglichkeit der Einbürgerung beraten?

☒ *Kreuzen Sie alles an, was auf Sie zutrifft (mehrere Antworten möglich).*
☐ Familie
☐ Freunde
☐ Arbeitskollegen
☐ Internet-Forum
☐ Andere, und zwar _____ *(bitte eintragen)*
☐ Ich habe mich noch mit niemandem über die Möglichkeit der Einbürgerung beraten.

9. Wer die deutsche Staatsangehörigkeit annimmt, muss normalerweise die türkische Staatsangehörigkeit abgeben. Es gibt jedoch Ausnahmen. Wie ist das bei Ihnen?

☐ Ich darf die türkische Staatsangehörigkeit behalten, kann also beide Staatsangehörigkeiten gleichzeitig halten (→SPRINGEN ZU FRAGE 10)
☐ Ich muss die türkische Staatsangehörigkeit abgeben
☐ Weiß ich nicht

9a. Wenn es möglich wäre, außer Ihrer jetzigen Staatsangehörigkeit zusätzlich die deutsche Staatsangehörigkeit zu erlangen, würden Sie von dieser Möglichkeit Gebrauch machen?

☐ Ja, ganz sicher
☐ Ja, wahrscheinlich
☐ Eher unwahrscheinlich
☐ Ganz sicher nicht

10. Mit dem Erhalt der deutschen Staatsangehörigkeit gewinnt man bestimmte Rechte. Unabhängig davon, ob Sie die deutsche Staatsangehörigkeit beantragen wollen oder nicht: Wie wichtig sind für Sie persönlich die im folgenden genannten Rechte:

☒ *Bitte kreuzen Sie für jeden Aspekt die Kategorie an, die Ihre Meinung am besten zum Ausdruck bringt.*

	sehr wichtig	eher wichtig	eher unwichtig	überhaupt nicht wichtig
Das Recht, den Bundestag (der Bundestag wählt den Kanzler / die Kanzlerin) zu wählen, ist mir	☐	☐	☐	☐
Das Recht, die Hamburger Bürgerschaft und meinen Bezirksrat zu wählen, ist mir	☐	☐	☐	☐
Das Recht, das Europa-Parlament zu wählen, ist mir	☐	☐	☐	☐
Das Recht, in Deutschland bei Wahlen als Kandidat anzutreten, ist mir	☐	☐	☐	☐
Das Recht auf diplomatischen Schutz im Ausland durch deutsche und europäische Botschaften, ist mir	☐	☐	☐	☐
Der Schutz vor Ausweisung (z.B. bei derzeit unsicherem Aufenthaltstitel) ist mir	☐	☐	☐	☐

11. Mit der Einbürgerung in Deutschland geht normalerweise der Verlust der türkischen Staatsangehörigkeit einher. Damit verlieren Sie bestimmte Rechte in der Türkei. Wie wichtig sind Ihnen persönlich die im folgenden genannten Rechte:

	sehr wichtig	eher wichtig	eher unwichtig	überhaupt nicht wichtig
Das Recht, die Große Nationalversammlung der Türkei zu wählen, ist mir	☐	☐	☐	☐
Das Recht auf Erbschaft und auf Grundbesitz in der Türkei ist mir	☐	☐	☐	☐

12. Haben Sie die Absicht, in die Türkei zurückzukehren bzw. Ihren Wohnsitz in die Türkei zu verlegen?

☐ Auf jeden Fall
☐ Wahrscheinlich ja
☐ Wahrscheinlich nicht
☐ Auf keinen Fall

Appendix B. Survey Material 213

13. Ist Ihr Aufenthaltsstatus befristet oder unbefristet? Der Status ist unbefristet, wenn er nicht regelmäßig verlängert werden muss.
- ☐ Unbefristeter Status
- ☐ Befristeter Status
- ☐ Weiß ich nicht

14. Im folgenden soll es kurz um Ihre Familie und Ihren Freundeskreis gehen.
☒ Bitte kreuzen Sie für jeden Aspekt die Kategorie an, die am besten auf Sie passt.

	alle	mehr als die Hälfte	weniger als die Hälfte	niemand
Wie viele Ihrer in Deutschland lebenden unmittelbaren Familienmitglieder (Eltern, Geschwister, Kinder) haben die deutsche Staatsangehörigkeit?	☐	☐	☐	☐
Wenn Sie an Ihren engeren Freundeskreis denken: Wie viele dieser Freunde haben die deutsche Staatsangehörigkeit?	☐	☐	☐	☐
Wie viele Ihrer engeren Freunde haben die deutsche Staatsangehörigkeit durch Einbürgerung erworben?	☐	☐	☐	☐

15. Haben Sie eigene Kinder? Wenn ja, wie viele?
- ☐ Nein
- ☐ Ja, und zwar ☐ (bitte Anzahl eintragen)

16. Die Einbürgerung hat auch Einfluss auf die Staatsangehörigkeit Ihrer Familie. Im Folgenden sind einige Aspekte aufgeführt, die dabei von Bedeutung sein können. Wenn Sie schon Kinder haben, denken Sie an diese Kinder. Wenn Sie noch keine haben, denken Sie an Ihre zukünftigen Kinder. Inwieweit treffen die im Folgenden genannten Aspekte auf Sie zu?

	trifft voll und ganz zu	trifft eher zu	trifft eher nicht zu	trifft überhaupt nicht zu
Ich möchte die türkische Staatsangehörigkeit behalten, damit auch meine zukünftigen Kinder die türkische Staatsangehörigkeit bekommen.	☐	☐	☐	☐
Ich möchte mich in Deutschland einbürgern lassen, damit ich die gleiche Staatsangehörigkeit wie meine Kinder habe.	☐	☐	☐	☐
Ich möchte mich in Deutschland einbürgern lassen, damit ich die gleiche Staatsangehörigkeit wie mein Partner habe.	☐	☐	☐	☐
Mein Partner behält die türkische Staatsangehörigkeit, damit auch unsere Kinder die türkische Staatsangehörigkeit bekommen.	☐	☐	☐	☐

17. Unabhängig davon, ob Sie bereits den deutschen Pass besitzen oder nicht: Inwieweit stimmen Sie folgenden Aussagen bezüglich der Vorteile der deutschen Staatsangehörigkeit beim Verreisen zu?

	trifft voll und ganz zu	trifft eher zu	trifft eher nicht zu	trifft überhaupt nicht zu
Die deutsche Staatsangehörigkeit bringt mir viele Vorteile bei Reisen innerhalb der Europäischen Union.	☐	☐	☐	☐
Die deutsche Staatsangehörigkeit bringt mir viele Vorteile bei Reisen zwischen der Türkei und Deutschland.	☐	☐	☐	☐
Die deutsche Staatsangehörigkeit bringt mir viele Vorteile bei Reisen außerhalb der EU und der Türkei, z.B. nach Amerika, Asien, Australien usw.	☐	☐	☐	☐
Die deutsche Staatsangehörigkeit bringt mir viele Vorteile für Reisen in Zusammenhang mit meiner beruflichen Tätigkeit.	☐	☐	☐	☐
Die deutsche Staatsangehörigkeit bringt mir viele Vorteile für Familienbesuche.	☐	☐	☐	☐
Die deutsche Staatsangehörigkeit bringt mir viele Vorteile für andere private Reisen.	☐	☐	☐	☐

18. Unabhängig davon, ob Sie bereits den deutschen Pass besitzen oder nicht: Inwieweit stimmen Sie folgenden Aussagen bezüglich der deutschen Staatsangehörigkeit und Beruf zu?

	stimme voll und ganz zu	stimme eher zu	stimme eher nicht zu	stimme überhaupt nicht zu
Durch die Einbürgerung würde sich mein Einkommen verbessern.	☐	☐	☐	☐
Durch die Einbürgerung würden sich meine Chancen verbessern, einen Job zu finden.	☐	☐	☐	☐
Durch die Einbürgerung würde ich seltener von Kollegen und Vorgesetzten ungerecht behandelt.	☐	☐	☐	☐

19. Im Hinblick auf Ihren derzeitigen Beruf oder zukünftige Berufe: Inwiefern trifft folgendes auf Sie zu?

	trifft voll und ganz zu	trifft eher zu	trifft eher nicht zu	trifft überhaupt nicht zu
Ich möchte eine Arbeit ausführen, für die ich die deutsche Staatsangehörigkeit benötige (z.B. bestimmte Tätigkeiten im öffentlichen Dienst oder Berufe, die mit Reisen verbunden sind).	☐	☐	☐	☐

20. Eine Einbürgerung verursacht einigen finanziellen und bürokratischen Aufwand. Sie müssen einen Antrag auf dem deutschen Amt stellen und für die Entlassung möglicherweise mit türkischen Ämtern in Kontakt treten. Inwieweit stimmen Sie folgenden Aussagen zu?

	stimme voll und ganz zu	stimme eher zu	stimme eher nicht zu	stimme überhaupt nicht zu
Die Einbürgerung in Deutschland ist mir zu teuer.	☐	☐	☐	☐
Die Ausbürgerung in der Türkei ist mir zu teuer.	☐	☐	☐	☐
Ich möchte den Kontakt mit deutschen Behörden vermeiden.	☐	☐	☐	☐
Ich möchte den Kontakt mit türkischen Behörden vermeiden.	☐	☐	☐	☐
Ich muss noch Militärdienst in der Türkei leisten.	☐	☐	☐	☐

21. Der Verlust der türkischen Staatsangehörigkeit ist der Normalfall bei Einbürgerung. Einmal unabhängig davon, ob Sie die deutsche Staatsangehörigkeit beantragen wollen, und unabhängig davon, ob Sie persönlich den türkischen Pass abgeben müssten: Inwieweit stimmen Sie folgenden Aussagen zu?

	stimme voll und ganz zu	stimme eher zu	stimme eher nicht zu	stimme überhaupt nicht zu
Wenn ich die türkische Staatsangehörigkeit abgebe, bin ich kein Türke mehr.	☐	☐	☐	☐
Mit Abgabe der türkischen Staatsangehörigkeit ginge auch meine türkische Identität verloren.	☐	☐	☐	☐
Mit der Annahme der deutschen Staatsangehörigkeit erwirbt man ein Stück deutsche Identität.	☐	☐	☐	☐

22. Bei den folgenden Fragen geht es um Ihre persönliche Wahrnehmung der beiden Länder Deutschland und der Türkei.
Es gibt unterschiedliche Möglichkeiten, sich zu beschreiben: Als Hamburger, als Sportlerin, als Mensch usw. Im Folgenden soll es jedoch einmal nur um die ethnische Zugehörigkeit gehen. Manche Menschen sehen sich als Deutsche, aber werden als Türken wahrgenommen. Andere sehen sich als Türken, werden aber als Deutsche wahrgenommen. Wie ist das normalerweise bei Ihnen?

	türkisch	deutsch	deutsch-türkisch	andere Ethnie, und zwar (z.B. kurdisch, griechisch, etc.)
Ich sehe mich am ehesten als	☐	☐	☐	
Meine Freunde in Deutschland sehen mich am ehesten als	☐	☐	☐	
Meine Freunde in der Türkei sehen mich am ehesten als	☐	☐	☐	
Fremde in Deutschland sehen mich am ehesten als (beim Einkaufen, im Restaurant, auf der Straße ...)	☐	☐	☐	
Fremde in der Türkei sehen mich am ehesten als (beim Einkaufen, im Restaurant, auf der Straße ...)	☐	☐	☐	
Wenn ich es mir aussuchen könnte, würde ich mir wünschen, dass andere Personen mich wahrnehmen als	☐	☐	☐	

Appendix B. Survey Material

23. Wenn Sie an die beiden Länder Deutschland und die Türkei denken: Wo fühlen Sie sich zu Hause?

	stimme voll und ganz zu	stimme eher zu	stimme eher nicht zu	stimme überhaupt nicht zu
Ich fühle mich in der Türkei zu Hause.	☐	☐	☐	☐
Ich fühle mich in Deutschland zu Hause.	☐	☐	☐	☐
Ich fühle mich in beiden Ländern zu Hause.	☐	☐	☐	☐

24. Wenn Sie an Ihre Gefühle zur Türkei und zu Deutschland denken: Wie würden Sie ihre Gefühle für die beiden Länder auf einem Thermometer beschreiben? Heiß oder kalt? Zuneigung oder Fremdheit?

☒ *Bitte setzen Sie für jedes Land ein Kreuz auf dem Thermometer, so wie es ihrem Empfinden entspricht.*

Deutschland — heiß — Türkei
mittel
kalt

25. Bitte nehmen Sie Stellung zu folgenden Aussagen:

☒ *Bitte kreuzen Sie für jeden Aspekt die Kategorie an, die Ihre Meinung am besten zum Ausdruck bringt.*

	stimme voll und ganz zu	stimme eher zu	stimme eher nicht zu	stimme überhaupt nicht zu
Die nach Deutschland gekommenen Türken haben das Land verändert.	☐	☐	☐	☐
Als Mensch türkischer Herkunft kann man in Deutschland leicht dazugehören.	☐	☐	☐	☐
In Deutschland kann man nur richtig dazugehören, wenn man hier geboren ist.	☐	☐	☐	☐
Die in Deutschland lebenden Türken haben Grund, stolz auf Deutschland zu sein.	☐	☐	☐	☐
In Deutschland gehöre ich voll dazu.	☐	☐	☐	☐
Der Islam sollte zu Deutschland gehören.	☐	☐	☐	☐
Der Islam gehört bereits zu Deutschland.	☐	☐	☐	☐
Die Deutschen sind stolz auf ihr Land.	☐	☐	☐	☐
Die Deutschen haben Grund, stolz auf ihr Land zu sein.	☐	☐	☐	☐

26. Als nächstes geht es darum, inwieweit Migranten die deutsche Kultur annehmen sollten. Wie sehr stimmen Sie folgenden Aussagen zu? Wie sehr lehnen Sie die Aussagen ab?

	stimme voll und ganz zu	stimme eher zu	stimme eher nicht zu	stimme überhaupt nicht zu
Einwanderer sollten die Kultur ihres Herkunftslandes beibehalten und gleichzeitig die deutsche Kultur annehmen.	☐	☐	☐	☐
Einwanderer sollten die Kultur ihres Herkunftslandes beibehalten und sie nicht mit der deutschen Kultur vermischen.	☐	☐	☐	☐
Einwanderer sollten die Kultur ihres Herkunftslandes aufgeben, um die deutsche Kultur anzunehmen.	☐	☐	☐	☐
Es spielt keine Rolle, ob Einwanderer ihre Kultur beibehalten oder die deutsche Kultur annehmen, denn jeder Mensch ist frei, sich seine eigene Kultur zu schaffen.	☐	☐	☐	☐

27. Die folgenden Fragen beziehen sich auf Ihre Kenntnisse der türkischen und der deutschen Sprache. Bitte schätzen Sie Ihre Sprachkenntnisse einmal selbst ein.

Wie gut sprechen und schreiben Sie türkisch?

	sehr gut	ziemlich gut	eher schlecht	sehr schlecht
sprechen	☐	☐	☐	☐
schreiben	☐	☐	☐	☐

Wie gut sprechen und schreiben Sie deutsch?

	sehr gut	ziemlich gut	eher schlecht	sehr schlecht
sprechen	☐	☐	☐	☐
schreiben	☐	☐	☐	☐

28. Es kommt vor, dass man von anderen Menschen ungerecht behandelt wird. Wie ist das für Menschen türkischer Herkunft im Allgemeinen? Und wie ist das für Sie persönlich?

	nie	selten	häufig	sehr häufig
Wie oft hatten Sie das Gefühl, dass Menschen türkischer Herkunft in Deutschland <u>nur aufgrund ihrer Herkunft</u> ungerecht behandelt werden?	☐	☐	☐	☐
Wie oft hatten Sie das Gefühl, dass Sie persönlich in Deutschland <u>nur aufgrund Ihrer Herkunft</u> ungerecht behandelt werden?	☐	☐	☐	☐

(SPRINGEN ZU FRAGE 30)

29. In welchen der unten genannten Umfeldern und Situationen fühlten Sie sich aufgrund Ihrer Herkunft schon einmal ungerecht behandelt?

☒ *Kreuzen Sie alles an, was auf Sie zutrifft (mehrere Antworten möglich).*
- ☐ Arbeit
- ☐ Schule
- ☐ Hochschule / Universität
- ☐ Amt / Behörde
- ☐ Andere

30. Wir kommen nun zu einigen Fragen, die die Stadt Hamburg betreffen. Der Hamburger Bürgermeister verschickt derzeit ein Schreiben an in Hamburg lebende Personen ohne deutsche Staatsangehörigkeit. Es informiert über die Möglichkeit einer Einbürgerung. Haben Sie dieses Schreiben erhalten?

- ☐ Ja
- ☐ Nein, nicht ich, aber eine andere Person in meinem Haushalt.
- ☐ Nein (→SPRINGEN ZU FRAGE 31)

30a. Falls Sie das Schreiben erhalten oder gesehen haben, wie bewerten Sie es?

sehr positiv	eher positiv	eher negativ	sehr negativ
☐	☐	☐	☐

→31. Im Stadtgebiet sind seit längerem Plakate zu sehen, die das Thema Einbürgerung ansprechen („Hamburg. Mein Hafen – Deutschland. Mein Zuhause"). Wie häufig sind Ihnen diese Plakate aufgefallen?

- ☐ Sehr häufig
- ☐ Weniger häufig
- ☐ Fast nicht
- ☐ Überhaupt nicht (→SPRINGEN ZU FRAGE 32)

31a. Falls Sie die Plakate gesehen haben, wie bewerten Sie sie?

sehr positiv	eher positiv	eher negativ	sehr negativ
☐	☐	☐	☐

→32. Seit eineinhalb Jahren gibt es in Hamburg zusätzliche Beratungsangebote in Bezug auf die Einbürgerung. Welche der folgenden Angebote kennen Sie? Welche haben Sie bereits genutzt?

☒ *Kreuzen Sie alles an, was auf Sie zutrifft (mehrere Antworten möglich).*

	kenne ich	habe ich bereits genutzt
Einbürgerungslotsen	☐	☐
Andere Angebote der Türkischen Gemeinde Hamburg (z.B. Integrationskurs)	☐	☐
Telefonische Beratung mit der Behörde	☐	☐
Persönliche Beratung in der Behörde	☐	☐

Appendix B. Survey Material

Ich möchte Sie nun noch um einige Angaben zu Ihrer Person bitten. Alle Angaben werden wie gesagt streng vertraulich und in anonymisierter Form behandelt.

33. Ihr Geschlecht und Geburtsjahr
    ☐ Männlich ☐ Weiblich Geburtsjahr: 19___ (bitte eintragen)

34. In welchem Land sind Sie geboren?
    ☐ Deutschland ☐ Türkei ☐ Anderes Land
    (→SPRINGEN ZU FRAGE 35)

    34a. In welchem Jahr sind Sie in Deutschland angekommen?
    19___ (bitte eintragen)

35. In welchem Land sind Ihre Eltern geboren?
    Vater: ☐ Deutschland ☐ Türkei ☐ Anderes Land
    Mutter: ☐ Deutschland ☐ Türkei ☐ Anderes Land

36. Zu welcher der folgenden Religionen, Glaubensrichtungen oder Weltanschauungen bekennen Sie sich?
    ☐ Keine Religion, Glaubensrichtung
    ☐ Islam
    ☐ Christentum
    ☐ Judentum
    ☐ Andere Religion, Glaubensrichtung oder Weltanschauung

37. Welches ist Ihr bisher höchster Bildungsabschluss
    ☐ Kein Schulabschluss (→SPRINGEN ZU FRAGE 38)
    ☐ Grundschule (bis 5. Klasse)
    ☐ Grundschule / Volksschule / Hauptschule oder vergleichbarer Abschluss (bis 8./9. Klasse)
    ☐ Realschule oder vergleichbarer Abschluss (bis 10. Klasse)
    ☐ Gymnasium oder vergleichbarer Abschluss (bis 12./13. Klasse)
    ☐ Universität / Fachhochschule / Hochschule

    37a. In welchem Land haben Sie diesen Abschluss erworben?
    ☐ Deutschland ☐ Türkei ☐ Anderes Land

38. Sind Sie zur Zeit
    ☒ *Kreuzen Sie alles an, was auf Sie zutrifft (mehrere Antworten möglich).*
    ☐ Berufstätig
    ☐ Arbeitssuchend oder arbeitslos
    ☐ Hausmann / Hausfrau
    ☐ Schüler / Schülerin
    ☐ Auszubildender / Auszubildende
    ☐ Student / Studentin
    ☐ Freiwilliger Wehrdienst, Freiwilliges Soziales Jahr o.ä.

39. Bitte nennen Sie Ihr persönliches durchschnittliches monatliches Einkommen, und zwar nach Abzug aller Steuern und Sozialabgaben (Netto): _____ Euro

40. Bitte nennen Sie das durchschnittliche monatliche Einkommen für Ihren Haushalt insgesamt nach Abzug aller Steuern und Sozialabgaben (Netto): _____ Euro

41. Wer lebt außer Ihnen in Ihrem Haushalt?
    ☒ *Kreuzen Sie alles an, was auf Sie zutrifft (mehrere Antworten möglich).*
    ☐ Niemand
    ☐ Partner
    ☐ Eigene Kinder ──────────► ____ (bitte Anzahl eintragen)
    ☐ Eltern
    ☐ Geschwister ──────────► ____ (bitte Anzahl eintragen)
    ☐ Großeltern
    ☐ Andere (z.B. Wohngemeinschaft) ──► ____ (bitte Anzahl eintragen)

42. Sind Sie zur Zeit
☐ Verheiratet   ☐ Geschieden   ☐ Unverheiratet   ☐ Verwitwet

43. Welche Staatsangehörigkeit(en) hat Ihr derzeitiger Partner / Ihre derzeitige Partnerin?
☐ Trifft nicht zu (→ SPRINGEN ZU FRAGE 44)
Er / sie hat folgende Staatsangehörigkeit(en) *(mehrere Antworten möglich)*
  ☐ Deutsche
  ☐ Türkische
  ☐ Andere Staatsangehörigkeit(en)

43a. In welchem Land ist Ihr Partner / Ihre Partnerin geboren?
☐ Deutschland   ☐ Türkei   ☐ Anderes Land

➤44. Dürfen wir Sie nochmals kontaktieren, wenn es um ein persönliches Gespräch mit Ihnen geht?
☐ Nein
☐ Ja ⟶ Dann hätten wir zum Abschluss noch eine Bitte. Ein Fragebogen wie dieser muss in mancher Hinsicht relativ oberflächlich bleiben. Im Anschluss an diese Befragung würde ich daher gerne persönliche Gespräche mit einigen Teilnehmern und Teilnehmerinnen führen. Sie sind in meinen Augen die Experten beim Thema Einbürgerung. Durch die persönlichen Gespräche könnte ich Ihre Antworten besser verstehen und die Gründe für Ihre Antworten besser nachvollziehen. Wären Sie grundsätzlich zu solch einem Gespräch bereit? Dann würde ich Sie bitten, im Folgenden einige oder mehrere Ihrer Kontaktinformationen zu hinterlassen. In dem Fall würde ich Sie möglicherweise in etwa einem halben Jahr kontaktieren, damit wir uns zu einem Gespräch verabreden können. Ihre Daten werden selbstverständlich streng vertraulich behandelt und nicht an Dritte weitergegeben.

Telefon	
E-Mail	@
Name	
Adresse	

(Straße, Hausnummer, Postleitzahl)

➤Ich danke Ihnen vielmals für die Teilnahme; çok teşekkür ederim! Bitte stecken Sie den Fragebogen in den beigelegten Briefumschlag und geben Sie den Umschlag so in die Post. Der Umschlag muss nicht frankiert werden. Das Porto zahlen wir.

Falls Sie noch Anmerkungen zum Fragebogen haben, nutzen Sie dafür bitte dieses Feld.

Studien zur Migrations- und Integrationspolitik

Herausgegeben von Uwe Hunger, Roswitha Pioch und Stefan Rother

Bisher in dieser Reihe erschienen:

D. Softic
Migranten in der Politik
Eine empirische Studie zu Bundestagsabgeordneten
mit Migrationshintergrund
2016. XV, 380 S., Br. € 49,99
ISBN 978-3-658-11159-5

B. Nieswand · H. Drotbohm (Hrsg.)
Kultur, Gesellschaft, Migration.
Die reflexive Wende in der Migrationsforschung
2014. XIII, 346 S. Br. € 39,99
ISBN 978-3-658-03625-6

C. Ghaderi
Politische Identität-Ethnizität-Geschlecht
Selbstverortungen politisch aktiver MigrantInnen
2014. XX, 411 S., Geb. € 49,99
ISBN 978-3-658-05296-6

Der nächste Band der Reihe:

L. Block
Policy Frames on Spousal Migration in Germany
Regulating Membership, Regulating the Family

Stand: November 2015. Änderungen vorbehalten.
Erhältlich im Buchhandel oder beim Verlag.

Einfach portofrei bestellen:
leserservice@springer.com
tel +49 (0)6221 345-4301
springer.com

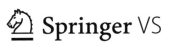

Druck:
Canon Deutschland Business Services GmbH
im Auftrag der KNV-Gruppe
Ferdinand-Jühlke-Str. 7
99095 Erfurt